Praise

'While reading *The Change Engineer* I was hit by how
many things I've been involved in, both consciously
and subconsciously, while competing at the highest
level in elite sport. At British Cycling we must
constantly adjust to stay ahead of the ever evolving
and improving opposition. The only way to do that
is through creating a high-performance collaborative
environment. Garry has summed it up perfectly in
this book, as well as highlighting a few areas where
I think we could improve further. A must read for
any team leaders.'
   — **Neil Fachie OBE**, Paralympic Champion Cyclist

'In *The Change Engineer*, Garry shares effective
principles and tools for communicating strategy
and leading change. The approach he presents
has supported successful change and improved
performance in my global teams.'
   —**Pia Aaltonen-Forsell**, former CFO, Outokumpu,
      and Board Member, UPM, Finland

'Garry's book, *The Change Engineer*, really resonated
with me, given my own career evolution from engineer
to senior leader of an engineering organisation. It is a
valuable read and practical guide for any senior leader
of technical and knowledge-based organisations who
seek to create environments that empower their people
to be their best.'
   — **Chris Young**, President and CEO, Plummer,
      Texas, USA

'*The Change Engineer* is a much-needed leadership guide to navigating the complexities of our current world, in which digital transformation and driving ever better performance with dispersed teams, is our daily reality. In water infrastructure, people will remain at the heart of all we do, despite the advances in AI. Motivating people through storytelling, empathy and inclusion are important themes that underpin this book. Garry brings his vast experience and behavioural science, together with resonating examples, into practical guidance for leaders seeking to engage their people to deliver better outcomes.'
— **Tania Flasck**, Director of Water Operations, Southern Water, former Chair, Waterwise, and former Board Member, British Water

'Garry's *The Change Engineer* is the essential guide to navigating today's infrastructure transitions, addressing challenges like energy security and achieving net zero. It underscores the necessity for enhanced collaboration, offering innovative strategies to foster more effective teamwork. This is the blueprint for transformative leadership.'
— **John Davies CEng**, Founder and CEO, 2DegreesKelvin

'In his book, which is an easy read and an appropriate length, Garry sets out with clarity the critical human factors which either enable, or all too often derail, vital organisational evolution and more significant change initiatives, most of which frankly

do not deliver. Armed with Garry's insights, I defy
you not to improve your and your organisation's
performance in both aspects.'
— **Mark Ashton**, Founder and CEO, Resolve

'The perspectives on leading strategic change that
Garry presents in *The Change Engineer* resonate
and have fundamental benefits for my current
challenges. Our purpose at Vaisala is to take every
measure for the planet. Fulfilling this relies not
just on innovative technology but on successfully
navigating the complex interdependencies between
people and organisations. The behavioural approach
put forward in this book has given me an additional
set of tools to drive the required collaboration and
transformation.'
— **Anne Jalkala**, Chief Sustainability &
Strategy Officer, Vaisala, Finland

'This is an excellent book. Garry has combined
his deep knowledge of human behaviour with an
engineer's practical orientation to create a clear
roadmap for a high performing collaborative
environment. He argues convincingly that this
is essential to deliver transformational change at
the speed needed today. While Garry draws from
all his knowledge in infrastructure industries the
lessons are equally applicable to all organisations
and certainly the food and manufacturing industries
where I've spent my working life.'
— **Neil Campbell**, former Leader of Walkers,
Tropicana North America and Warburtons

'*The Change Engineer* presents a concept for understanding and improving the behavioural aspects of strategic collaborations which are increasingly critical to addressing complex challenges in business, infrastructure and wider society. Conventional, "management process" based approaches struggle with the complexity and interdependence of the human, industrial, social, and political systems that need to connect and collaborate effectively across boundaries to meet these challenges. Garry offers a leadership model for influencing collaborative performance that I believe will help move us towards "Collaboration 2.0" which will be informed by cutting edge behavioural and digital innovation.'

　　— **Michael Taylor**, CEO and Co-founder, SchellingPoint, Pennsylvania, USA

'I have known Garry for over 15 years, and we share a passion for promoting and enabling collaboration. The water sector faces a demanding set of interdependent challenges and opportunities. In this complex landscape success depends on water professionals and wider stakeholders working even more closely together, combining their expertise and capabilities. *The Change Engineer* presents Garry's valuable insights that support the leadership and collaboration essential for our industry to tackle the challenges and pursue the opportunities.'

　　— **Professor Tony Conway**, Director, British Water, Chair, Water Industry Forum, and former water utility Executive Director

THE
CHANGE
ENGINEER

Create the environment for
revolutionary collaborative
performance in your
organisation

Garry Sanderson

R^ethink

First published in Great Britain in 2024
by Rethink Press (www.rethinkpress.com)

© Copyright Garry Sanderson

For
Sarah
Ann and Ian
Amalie and Arran
Mike

Contents

Foreword   1

Introduction   7

1   Collaborative Performance: An
    Evolutionary Imperative   17

    The relentless storm of change   18

    What is collaboration?   23

    What is behaviour?   29

    Collaborative performance   36

    A simple equation for collaborative
    performance   39

    The low-performing uncollaborative
    environment   43

    Chapter takeaways   44

2   Meaningful   47

    The power of purpose   48

    The power of leadership narrative   55

Focus your leadership narrative   65

Chapter takeaways   71

3   Functional   **73**

Responsive working relationships   74

Respect commitments   83

Pay attention to the right things   90

Chapter takeaways   100

4   Fearless   **103**

Psychological safety   104

Mind your language   116

Unlock discretionary effort   123

Chapter takeaways   130

5   Adaptive   **133**

Find out what's *really* going on   134

Cultivate learning and knowledge
sharing   142

Understand and address resistance to
change   152

Chapter takeaways   160

6   Revolutionary   **163**

Change the environment, not the people   164

The workplace environment   168

Influence powered by STEAM   176

Test and learn   190

Chapter takeaways   195

**7 Transformative Mindset Shifts For
Collaborative Leadership**   **197**

Chapter takeaways   217

Conclusion   **219**

Notes   **223**

Further Reading   **229**

Acknowledgements   **233**

The Author   **237**

Foreword

M any knowledge-based companies will fail in the fast evolving, digital world. They will not keep up and will gravitate to mediocrity and commoditisation. Until it is too late, they will not believe they are losing competitive advantage except for the symptom that their pricing is under pressure and their backlog is falling. They will rationalise the issue as a marketing department failure versus an offering that is not fit for the changing environment.

The larger firms will watch smaller firms use continuous innovation and technology to grow their business faster. They will question how smaller firms, with the obvious investment and talent deficit to them, could possibly be winning over their former clients with niche ideas and technological enhancements. These winning firms are forward focused on the evolving changing world, not their past legacy. They see these times as the most opportunistic time since the industrial revolution.

In a rapidly changing world, the past winners and current larger firms are at a decided disadvantage. Their stable internal power structure and hubris from past success hardly allows change, much less, the speed of adaption required. But, not to be discouraged, the larger firm can do with enlightened top leadership that is not distracted by daily activity.

In a world that emphasises revolutionary speed changes, competitive advantage comes from the '*how*', not the '*what*'. Knowledge-based organisations have access to the same talent pool, tools, systems etc. They compete in the same markets for the same clients. They often know what their competitors are selling. Most firms will have intuitive and smart leaders that generally know the direction of the clients' needs. It is not hard declaring a differentiating strategy. Many strategies could work, few will. They will fail because it is not just the 'what' but the 'how' that is the most difficult to master.

As the previous leader in MWH Global, a water infrastructure sector-dominant global consultant, we knew that change was happening, and we had to experiment outside of what we did every day. We experimented in software, intellectual property, technological tack-ons, geographical exchange, knowledge management and stealing the better ideas of other industrial sectors. We repetitiously launched several new internal initiatives each year. We did not expect many of them to fully succeed. We had to create a risk-free environment for the pioneer leaders. Many of our initiatives were 'before their time'. As one American CEO said, 'Being fifteen years early is the same as being wrong in strategy.' When, and if, they failed we had to have the timely nerve to admit it and capture the learning.

I never minded being too early in our failures but was always beside myself when internal antibodies killed any new endeavour because it was a threat to the status quo. Internally, it was the 'how' we nurtured in the budding businesses, not the 'what'. This is not all leadership or technology or packaging. It's psychology, it's behavioural science. We often had to separate and grow independent of the core business to allow it from being an internal target. The 'how' success requires what Garry introduces in this book – engineering the environment to influence revolutionary collaborative performance.

To focus on the 'how' of success, we had to share our vocabularies and create visual representations of our model to show the strategic phase we were in and our direction of travel. Garry reveals in Chapter 3 one form of this that became very important. It is the four levels of activity that frame the leaders' time and attention, from level 1 problem solving for operations to level 4 long term transformation of the enterprise.

In the book, Garry builds on our approach introducing the concept of 'behavioural gravity'. Leaders may talk the right language about strategic direction but are inevitably pulled down to the reactive behaviour of lower levels by the day-to-day details. The leader must divide their time and attention between them through self-disciplined time management. Each month they should review where their time has been spent against these levels.

At MWH Global, we did not have a Corporate Chief of Strategy or a Chief of Marketing. The Chief Strategy Officer was the CEO. We decentralised marketing and, instead, created a Corporate Office of Strategy Implementation. As leader of this office, Garry focused on the future success of our initiatives and their post-integration to the business, if successful. I picked Garry because he had excelled in driving change in Europe and had a curious mind about the human 'how' versus the 'what'. We knew the 'what' of our initiatives – how to make them successful was the challenge. Garry facilitated the company's planning process and our 'buy-in' sessions. He had a unique ability to cut through the static and see the larger challenge of change management. Leaving MWH Global, Garry went back to school to study foundational human behaviour to facilitate with strategy change.

Garry now works through his company, Visualyze, to support leaders and teams to drive collaborative performance in pursuit of their most important strategic objectives. This is his first book to document his findings. His unique capabilities of working with people in a non-threatening and constructive manner are extraordinary.

For me, I still participate on boards and still try to convince CEOs that digital world change is both threat and opportunity. Doing nothing is a formula for mediocrity. To be successful, they need to focus and prioritise how they spend their time on Levels 3 and 4 if the enterprise is to be sustainable. No one else will, if not them. Their companies are made up of smart, content-focused people. Leadership requires process and behavioural effectiveness in change management, regardless of the direction.

Robert B. Uhler, P.E., President and Founder, The Uhler Group, and former CEO and Chairman of the global water-sector firm of MWH Global

Introduction

'My job is 80% psychology.' This statement, made to me by my boss in 2008, got me thinking. Why would the CEO of a global technical organisation say this? The idea that the effective leadership of engineers and other professionals might rely on an understanding of psychology and human behaviour – something that is not studied in any technical degree course or for any related professional qualification – fascinated me. How do we get professional, technical people to do what we want them to do? I've been pondering and working with leaders to get answers ever since. The result is this book.

Engineers and technical professionals are at the forefront of efforts to solve the world's most significant problems, creating the infrastructure for better

futures for our families, communities and environment. The challenges faced are increasingly complex
and dynamic, exacerbated by major global trends.
The rapid pace of digital technology innovation;
the changing demographics and expectations of the
workforce; the responsibility to manage and mitigate climate change. To solve these problems, leaders
must get the best from their people and teams in an
environment of ever-increasing pressure on budgets,
resources and time.

Many leaders in knowledge-based organisations have
risen to their positions through personal success in
their core professional area. They now face the unfa-
miliar situation of relying on the collaborative efforts
of *other people* to achieve results. These leaders may
suspect that the working environment, which they are
now responsible for, may not be conducive to meeting the challenges they now face. They recognise the
importance of a highly collaborative environment to
achieving their vision. They believe that there must
be a better, more people-centric way of operating than
how things have always been done.

It was my own belief that 'there must be a better way'
that led me on a journey of exploration into the behavioural aspects of leadership and how to get big things
done through collaborative efforts. I am a chartered
civil engineer with frontline experience of the design
and delivery of major infrastructure projects and programmes. I have built and developed teams, global

knowledge communities and businesses. I have held technical, management and global executive leadership roles with knowledge-based organisations in the UK and the USA. I was the 1999 winner of the UK Young Consulting Engineer Award and in 2008 I completed the Harvard Business School Advanced Management Programme.

Through thirty years of engineering and leadership experience, I have learned the importance of the skills of influence and the ability to build collaborative environments to achieving results with diverse and often virtual groups of technical people. This sparked my interest in behavioural science, in which I gained a degree from the London School of Economics. I am passionate about the importance of the behavioural aspects of leadership, particularly a leader's responsibility to shape the environment to ensure the team's success.

Throughout my career, and from my interactions with numerous leaders, I have recognised a common struggle to answer questions like:

- Why don't they understand what we need to do and just get on with it?

- Why won't they collaborate and freely share their knowledge?

- Why won't they change?

The result of not addressing these questions is a leader who is unable to achieve their vision. They are most likely stressed and frustrated by the team's performance and missed opportunities. Unfortunately, all too many leaders feel this way.

The way we structure and organise the workplace often prevents us from establishing the conditions for success. Creating the required collaborative and innovative environment is an art form that technical professionals simply have not been trained in. I was driven to write this book by my personal frustration at working within sub-optimal environments, and watching others suffer in them.

Infrastructure leaders are facing increasingly complex challenges that require a high level of interaction, innovation and collaboration across enterprises comprising multiple organisations. Gone are the transactional days when one party could perfectly scope a solution to a problem and simply hand it to another party to deliver. The world's biggest and most pressing problems need us to draw on the experience, skills and creativity of multiple parties and combine these in new, innovative ways. The speed at which this must happen is rapidly increasing as business, and life in general, is accelerated by digital transformation and rising customer expectations.

In engineering and infrastructure, traditionally, a 'client' organisation would scope a set of clear outputs to meet their future requirements, these outputs would be developed into a detailed design by another party, then constructed by yet another party, before being handed back to the client to operate and maintain. Over the course of my career, we have collectively realised that this approach is not fit for purpose in meeting our current and future infrastructure needs. It cannot deliver the outcomes demanded in the environment of ever higher levels of complexity, speed and interdependence.

Increasingly, the solutions that achieve the required outcomes are delivered not by single organisations working in sequence but by enterprises that integrate the capabilities and inputs of multiple organisations. For such enterprises to deliver, effectively navigating the inherent complexities of multiple parties working together, *collaboration* that accelerates knowledge and idea flow must be the common behavioural currency.

The need for increased and wider collaboration is not new. Many process and contractual based approaches have made positive steps to reduce obstacles to collaboration. Yet the core need to change individual and organisational *behaviours* often remains unaddressed.

The most enlightening aspect of my learning journey from engineer to leader to behavioural scientist has been a specific realisation: we think we are logical creatures, making decisions and choices rationally based on relevant information, but we are actually much more driven by evolutionarily hardwired emotions that steer our behaviour, often below the level of conscious awareness.

The leadership lesson I have drawn from this realisation is that transmitting lots of information to try to influence behaviour and change people's minds is simply not effective. People must work it out for themselves. But as a leader, *you can engineer the environment in which people make their choices and act*. The environment you create drives the behaviour you get from your people. You can become a 'change engineer'.

What are the specific behaviours associated with collaboration, in the context of delivering infrastructure solutions for modern life? How do we ensure that these behaviours are present in complex interdependent enterprises?

In this book, I seek to address this, presenting five specific aspects of behaviour that are fundamental to collaboration and a model for how leaders can create and sustain a **high-performing collaborative environment**. This is based on my extensive experience of and learning about what works and what doesn't in professional, knowledge-based organisations. The model has five interconnected components that form the structure in which the required behaviours are encouraged and reinforced. With these components in place, the leader will have created the conditions for success. The team will understand and have the very best chance of delivering the leader's vision. The leader will have increased confidence in the team, feel less frustrated and have more time to lead. A chapter is dedicated to each of the five components.

The foundation is the leadership narrative that explains the purpose of the team and ensures that their collective efforts are **meaningful**. This narrative captures the vision and passion of the leader. Importantly, though, it can be shared by all key people in the team.

The basics of a **functional** collaborative environment unlock the potential for high performance. Responsive relationships ensure that ideas, information, knowledge and support flow unhindered. People make and meet clear commitments. With this, the key ingredients that drive intrinsic motivation are put in place.

Ensuring psychological safety allows team members to bring their entire selves to work. People offer ideas, challenges and critical contributions without fear of humiliation, criticism or being ignored. Leadership language and behaviour strengthens and reinforces this **fearless** environment, unlocking discretionary effort across the team.

Understanding and confronting what is actually going on is the precursor to the environment becoming **adaptive**. Increasing the frequency with which feedback is sought, shared and acted upon accelerates

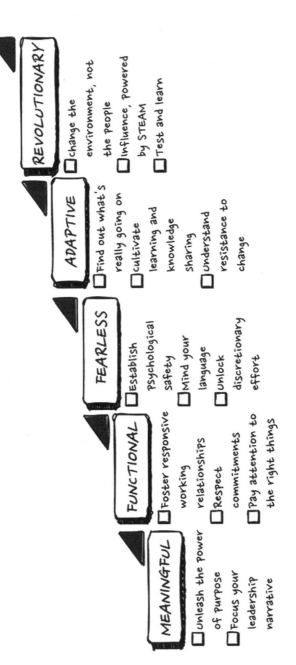

The high-performing collaborative environment

MEANINGFUL
- ☐ Unleash the power of purpose
- ☐ Focus your leadership narrative

FUNCTIONAL
- ☐ Foster responsive working relationships
- ☐ Respect commitments
- ☐ Pay attention to the right things

FEARLESS
- ☐ Establish psychological safety
- ☐ Mind your language
- ☐ Unlock discretionary effort

ADAPTIVE
- ☐ Find out what's really going on
- ☐ Cultivate learning and knowledge sharing
- ☐ Understand resistance to change

REVOLUTIONARY
- ☐ Change the environment, not the people
- ☐ Influence, powered by STEAM
- ☐ Test and learn

learning curves. Learning and knowledge sharing is cultivated across the entire enterprise.

Creating a high-performing collaborative environment involves changing the environment, not the people. The approach of testing and learning leverages behavioural innovation to set conditions that enable **revolutionary** performance levels.

I have written this book for professionals who, like me, evolved from working with technical subject matter to being responsible for creating the conditions in which many people must collaborate to achieve high-level performance. These leaders have the strong foundation and mindset that comes from their professional discipline yet may have had minimal education in the behavioural aspects of the complex challenges they now face. They are frustrated by working with low-performing teams in traditionally managed, overly bureaucratic organisations. They realise that they must reflect with humility on their own behaviours and shift their own mindset in parallel with creating the conditions for high levels of collaborative performance. They know there must be a better way. As this book will show you, there is.

ONE

Collaborative Performance: An Evolutionary Imperative

Imagine a world in constant flux, bombarded by rapid technological advancements, shifting demographics and constant environmental, economic and geopolitical threats. This is the reality we face. To thrive in this world, high-performance collaboration is no longer a 'nice to have', but an evolutionary imperative. Legacy structures and misaligned goals often hinder collaboration, creating an 'adaptation gap' between the speed of change and the organisational response.

Leaders must act as architects, designing and building high-performing collaborative environments. Imagine a space that's psychologically safe, transparent and goal-oriented – a breeding ground for innovation and knowledge sharing. By unlocking the power of collaboration, organisations can weather the storm of change and emerge stronger.

The relentless storm of change

In workshops with leaders I use a simple diagram to generate discussion about the nature of the change their organisations are facing. I draw a horizontal axis representing time and a vertical axis representing rate of change on a flipchart and ask them how they feel that the rate of change in their business environment has altered over recent years. Invariably they say 'exponentially', so I draw a curved line upwards from left to right. I then ask them to consider how their organisation has adapted to these external changes. Generally, the response leads me to draw a straight line, rising slightly from left to right. The space created by these two lines – what I call the 'opportunity gap' – resonates with every group I have worked with, in multiple contexts globally.

The common realisation is this: the perceived current pace of organisational adaptation is slower than the pace of change in the wider environment. The implication is that there was a point in recent history when the two lines crossed. At this moment, the rate of change in the external environment overtook the rate at which many organisations could learn and adapt.

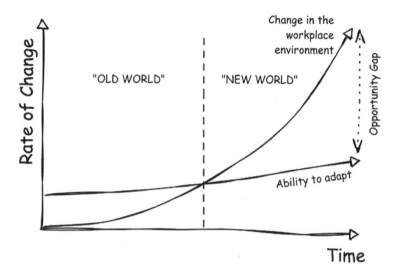

Change and adaptation over time

It is at that point, I explain to them, that the 'old world' ways of doing things – the ways that organisations have embedded into their culture – are no longer fit for purpose. Decision-making is too cumbersome, too slow. Processes are too complex.

There is an evolutionary consequence for natural organisms and systems that cannot adapt fast enough to a change in their environment: extinction. To survive in the 'new world', the gap between the rate of change in the environment and the adaptative response must be closed. I have been discussing this pattern with leaders for many years. Many still feel trapped in the old world. This suggests that closing the opportunity gap requires more than the usual management process-led change. The new world requires a *behavioural* response.

Our VUCA world

What drives the accelerating rate of change in our working environment and the world in general? This is a huge question, as modern life is subject to a bewildering range of transformations in all aspects. We use the term 'megatrends' to categorise a headline set of themes that we see impacting the business over the medium to long term. Some of the megatrends that are most impacting infrastructure leaders are:

- **Demographic shifts** including population growth, migration and change in consumption patterns, for example of water, food and energy.

- **Climate change** and the resulting extreme weather events, such as droughts and flooding.

- **Security threats** that require critical infrastructure to be strong. Assets must be resilient to extreme climatic events, as well as physical and cyber terrorist attacks.

- **Scarcity** and imbalance in supply of key resources such as water, energy and other natural resources result in a need for preservation and efficiency.

- **Globalisation and geopolitics** significantly impact public and private investment in our markets and how nations and organisations spend, procure and operate.

- **Technology** continually evolves, responding to new challenges. In particular, digital technology is accelerating communications and social connectivity among the global population. Companies that aren't capitalising on artificial intelligence and automation with be quickly overtaken by those that are.

- **Economic cycles** overlay a shorter-term set of issues influencing how markets and organisations respond to the longer-term trends.

- **Global health.** The COVID-19 pandemic of 2020 brought the dynamics of global health in a highly connected and interdependent world to the top of the list of megatrends.

Any one of these topics could be the subject of many books and in-depth strategic analysis. But the overlap and interaction of these trends creates a compounding effect that can be summed up with a strange term: we now live in a 'VUCA' world.

The concept of VUCA was first developed by the US Army War College in the 1980s, in response to the dynamics of change seen in the closing stages of the

Cold War. A VUCA environment is one with high levels of:

- Volatility: the nature, dynamics and speed of change

- Uncertainty: the lack of predictability and the prospects for surprise

- Complexity: the multiplicity and interactivity of issues causing change

- Ambiguity: the haziness of reality and confusion over cause-and-effect relationships[1]

Since its inception, VUCA has been used in strategic planning to represent the conditions faced by countries, markets and organisations. Many people will recognise the symptoms of VUCA both at work and in their day-to-day lives. In short, we face a world of relentless change. Some fast, some slow. Some predictable, some surprising.

In nature, evolutionary success is based on the ability of species to adapt to their dynamic environment and pass on their genes to future generations. In the modern world of work, arguably the most important characteristic that organisations need in order to survive and flourish is *adaptability*. In addition, successfully navigating and adapting to the relentless storm of change requires collective, rather than individual efforts. It requires *collaboration*.

What is collaboration?

It is now almost a cliché to say that the need for better collaboration to meet the challenges of our modern world has never been greater. We recognise that no one individual, leader or organisation can shape and deliver the solutions that we need. Collaboration falls into the category of things that are 'hard to describe, yet we know it when we see it'. We have no problem identifying behaviour that is non-collaborative. But do we understand what collaboration actually is? And can we recognise blockers and triggers for collaborative behaviour?

An Oxford Dictionary definition for the word 'collaboration' is 'the act of working with another person or group of people to create or produce something'.[2]

This definition gives us no more than a superficial glimpse of what collaboration is. What is the 'act' of collaboration? Two of the fundamental attributes that set humans apart from other species and underpin the development of civilisation are relevant. One is our ability to use the processing power of our pre-frontal cortex to imagine 'alternative realities'. This means that we can mentally construct our projects, our solutions and even our future lives. Second, we have unparalleled ability to work together in groups to realise these plans.

As explained by Yuval Noah Harari, Homo sapiens – ie, modern humans with similar cognitive abilities to you and I – have been around for several hundred thousand years.[3] For most of this time, we lived a tribal existence, hunting and gathering to meet our immediate needs. Typically, tribes comprised around 100 to 150 individuals. In groups of this size, it was possible to know, and therefore collaborate with, all fellow members of the tribe. This collaborative behaviour is a key source of our evolutionary competitive advantage. However, to collaborate in the larger group size of organisations, religions and nations, Harari argues required an additional dimension. The ability to develop and communicate a *shared narrative* allowed entities with no physical form to come into being – nations, religions, limited liability companies. These narratives shape the behaviours of groups in size from tens of people to tens of millions.

Collaboration blockers

Why then, if humans' collaborative behaviour is evolutionarily hardwired, do we need to consider it at all? The issue is that the modern organisational structures and typical patterns of corporate behaviour create a multitude of blockers that stifle and discourage collaboration.

Some examples of collaboration blockers include outdated organisational structures, office politics, distracting digital applications, over-complicated contracts, misaligned commercial models, meaning-less reporting procedures, multitudinous key performance indicators, time zones, cultural differences, unclear objectives and so on. The list is infinite. It is a leadership imperative to continually identify and remove such blockers.

Delusions of collaboration

It is also worth reassessing efforts that are often perceived as improving collaboration yet are perhaps less effective than assumed. Below are several initiatives that I have experienced many times and have even put in place myself.

Co-location

It makes sense that bringing all the members of a team into one location should increase their ability to work together, but co-location does not necessarily equal collaboration. I have worked in co-located offices in which representatives from each organisation sit quietly in their own area, emailing people sat literally twenty feet away. Equally, I have been part of highly effective teams that have had team members located in several locations around the world. The dynamics of working in the COVID-19 environment have challenged the default mindset held by many leaders that people must be in the same physical space to collaborate.

Common branding

Major projects and programmes that bring together multiple organisations often create a new, specific identity and branding for all the people involved. This can have a positive, morale-building impact, helping break down barriers between the participating organisations and connecting everyone. But this approach can also cause people to become distant from their 'home' organisation, losing out on the benefits of connecting back for support, training and knowledge sharing.

Offsite teambuilding days

Golf days, paintballing, escape rooms and ten pin bowling can all help accelerate relationships and give people well-deserved time away from the coal face. Teambuilding sessions can add value in these ways but often do little to foster real and sustained collaboration at the coal face.

Mission statements on the wall

We've all seen the signed team charters, vision statements and values posters hanging on the wall. We may even have been involved with creating them. There is often a big gap between what's stated on the wall and what's happening on the ground.

Each of the above examples are well-intentioned efforts and potentially positive contributory factors in improving the environment for collaboration. Yet the mistake leaders can make is assuming that these kinds of one-off initiatives are the primary elements of a collaborative environment.

Collaboration is not a business initiative for management to define and implement. Rather, our human ability to collaborate is innate and unlocks our evolutionary competitive advantage. The role of leadership is not to 'push' collaboration but to create the *environment* in which high levels of collaborative behaviours are likely to show up.

Contractual and commercial mechanisms

There have been great strides forward in collaborative and commercial arrangements that improve the effectiveness transactions between *organisations*. As such these can, and do, reduce obstacles to collaboration. In my experience, however, they don't do much to influence and reinforce *individual* collaborative behaviours. I have heard it said often that in the best projects, the contract has 'remained in the drawer'. Something else has happened in the working environment to create the conditions for success.

Digital transformation is not the whole answer

In my experience, digital transformation and behavioural transformation are two sides of the same coin. Our smartphones change our behaviour. If we want to change our behaviour, technology can be a catalyst. Adding, automating and accelerating processes using artificial intelligence can drive efficiency and must be done to maintain competitive positioning. However, I have noticed a concerning tendency to over-rely on process-based digital initiatives to change how knowledge-based organisations operate and behave. This risks stifling their core strategic asset – the network of informal human connections and relationships, through which knowledge, learning and ideas flow. I believe it is this precious people network that is *the* source of competitive advantage for knowledge-based organisations.

Using technology to nurture people and knowledge networks and shape strategic collaborations is a massive opportunity. We need to focus on this behavioural transformation as much as digital transformation. Michael Taylor, co-founder and CEO of the applied research company SchellingPoint, told me, 'We have over forty years of process thinking and in the process world we are extremely mature. In the collaboration world, we are really at the front end of it.'

What is behaviour?

Technical professionals (such as engineers like me) can be nervous when asked to consider and deal with challenging areas such as emotions, feelings and behaviours. This can be outside of our comfort zone. We want to retreat into our scientific world of clear cause and effect relating to forces, materials and quantities. We steer well clear of the 'soft stuff'. Thinking about behaviour implies addressing thoughts, feelings, attitudes and other aspects of the opaque inner workings of the mind as well as making subjective judgements about what may constitute 'good' or 'bad' behaviour.

In behavioural science and for the purposes of this book, 'behaviour' is simply defined as 'what people say and do'. It is objective, observable and measurable. If Roberta is late for three meetings in a row, that is a measurable behaviour. Judging this behaviour as 'good' or 'bad' is subjective and context-dependent, but the behaviour itself is specific and objective.

Two systems of thought

I have found it fascinating to scrape the surface of understanding the most complex system in the universe – the human brain. Over a relatively recent period, neuroscientists have discovered a huge amount about the functioning of different parts of the brain in different situations. But we still have much to learn about how the chemical and electrical interactions in the substance of our brains creates our consciousness, personality and behaviour.

A useful model for how we think and behave was used by the Nobel Laureate, Daniel Kahneman. Through his work over many years, in partnership with long-time collaborator Amos Tversky, Kahneman has explored how our decision-making often appears to be less logical and rational than we might like to believe. In his book, *Thinking Fast and Slow*, Kahneman describes two systems of thought:[4]

1. **System 1** thinking is automatic, fast, effortless and emotional. Consider your response to the question, 'What is 3 x 3?' No doubt the answer will come to you easily. Think about your reaction to the unexpected pop of a balloon. Your involuntary jump will have been an instant reaction.

2. **System 2** thinking is conscious, slow, effortful and deliberate. Your response to being asked to calculate 43 x 19 will most likely be a methodical, ordered and perhaps somewhat tiring thought process. As I write this paragraph at what feels like a painfully slow pace, my thinking is entirely System 2.

We may feel that most of our conscious behaviour is due to our cool, calm consideration and that System 2 is the dominant force in our lives. But Kahneman has

shown that, as our lives play out, System 1 is the leading actor and System 2 takes a supporting role. More
than we might like to admit.

In the words of Kahneman, our mind is 'a machine
for jumping to conclusions'. Our System 1 mode of
thinking is continuously seeking to make sense of the
environment, rapidly creating a narrative based on
information readily to hand so that we can take action
to ensure our survival. When faced by a threat like a
sabre-toothed tiger or an oncoming bus, slow, deliberate review of data from our senses and the alternative courses of action available to us would ensure we
were quickly removed from the gene pool. The mental
programmes that our brains run to keep us alive as we
face challenges in our environment haven't changed
much since Homo sapiens first evolved. The environment we inhabit has changed beyond all recognition.

Given that we are running a mental operating system that is evolutionarily out of kilter with our current world, we mostly manage to function remarkably
well. However, the mental programmes associated
with System 1 do make us susceptible to behavioural
biases that may inappropriately influence our choices,
decisions and actions.

Context matters

We may believe that we are fully in charge of our
choices and actions, yet our behaviour is highly

contingent upon the context within which we find ourselves. The importance of context cannot be over-stated. We behave differently in a boardroom to in a restaurant. We behave differently among a crowd of fans at a rock concert than we do with a group of strangers on public transport. We can find ourselves leaving a supermarket laden down with shopping when all we went in for was a pint of milk. At all times, cues in our environment, including the behaviour of others, are influencing our choices and behaviour. Often we are completely unaware of it.

'It's the environment, stupid,' says fellow engineer-turned-behavioural explorer, Howard Lees. 'We operate in our environment; that is our behaviour is contingent on whatever environment we find ourselves in.'

In the environment of the workplace, our behaviour is influenced by the space we are in (physical and/or virtual) and the behaviour of those around us, particularly the leaders. If the environment changes, behaviour changes.

In 2019 I visited the head office of a major global organisation. It was a modern building with great facilities for those who worked there. Many were hot-desking, meaning that they had no dedicated desk and instead based themselves at one of many possible locations on a day-to-day basis, when they were not working elsewhere or from home. My contact explained that this way of working was proving to be popular, yet it had initially been a challenge to change from the traditional way of all day every day at the same desk. The shift in working behaviour was precipitated by an unplanned change in the environment.

The previous year, a failure in the building heating system had caused a significant amount of water damage to several floors. So great was the impact that the entire staff was forced to vacate the building. They worked from home for several weeks whilst repairs and refurbishment were carried out. This unforeseen event required the staff to figure out how to work together flexibly and remotely. When the building was ready to be re-occupied, it became clear that working patterns had been more permanently changed. Instead of all staff simply reverting to how things had always been, they settled into a more flexible balance between home-based and office-based working, with positive results. I remember being struck by the significant and lasting impact on behaviour that the unexpected change in the environment had caused and I wondered how this could be replicated on a larger scale.

Just a few months later, people across the world experienced lockdowns due to the terrible impact of COVID-19. This affected all areas of our lives, with ongoing implications that may last for a generation. In the early stages of the crisis, I participated in a group of Harvard Business School alumnae to share perspectives on how to lead their organisations through this unprecedented event. In a dramatically short period of time, these leaders had seen a huge change in the working environment caused by lockdowns and travel restrictions. At the same time, the capability of organisations was affected as people were impacted directly or indirectly by the virus. Many organisations were not set up with the technology and working practices needed to function in a predominantly virtual environment. For most, the gap between the rate of change and their ability to adapt widened hugely, almost overnight.

For many organisations, the scale of the gap shocked them into a dramatic set of changes that would perhaps have taken years to be implemented otherwise. Trends in behaviour and technology that were already moving slowly were accelerated at this point, for example:

- Flexibility for employees to work remotely from home became an absolute necessity for many organisations.

- The use of technology to connect and collaborate online skyrocketed, transforming the working day into a series of back-to-back virtual meetings.

- Travel for business needs was massively reduced, being replaced almost entirely by online alternatives for meetings, conferences and seminars etc.

- The use of digital and contactless payments for purchases in all aspects of our lives became the norm, with cash transactions declining significantly.

From a behavioural perspective, we collectively responded to the circumstances the pandemic created that were both immediate and unambiguous. Lockdowns had been imposed, restrictions were in place, so innovation and change were accelerated by necessity. These dynamics on a global scale are, thankfully, highly unusual. Mostly, megatrends move more stealthily and unpredictably. Their significance and even their existence is often debated (even denied by some, as in the case of man-made climate change).

Another dimension that the pandemic brought to light is just how interconnected all of the societal and natural systems that we rely on and take for granted are. The inconvenience of a large proportion of the workforce suddenly being required to work from home resulted in less traffic, with corresponding reductions in pollution and carbon emissions. Our reliance on broadband and digital technologies increased as we learned to work virtually.

As lockdowns extended, we began to experience the implications of reduced social contact with our fellow team members. In dealing with the immediate issues associated with keeping business, and society in general, operating through the pandemic, we set in motion changes that we do not yet fully understand.

The implications for the environment, our health and wellbeing will play out and become clear only over a much longer period.

The office flood and COVID-19 lockdowns were unforeseen and unwelcome changes in the environment that influenced seismic shifts in workplace behaviour. The lesson here is that environment *shapes our behaviour*.

Leaders are responsible for and have a significant degree of control over the environment in their organisations: the design of the office facilities; the systems and work practices; the behaviours and norms exemplified and reinforced by the leadership team. These factors all either contribute to, or inhibit, the collaborative behaviour required to achieve high levels of performance.

Collaborative performance

Before stepping into the five components of the high-performing collaborative environment in subsequent chapters, let's establish what we mean by 'collaborative performance'.

In any organisation, there are myriad metrics for business activities. These tend to be dominated by financial metrics, but others track important things such as health and safety, product or service quality, environmental impact and retention of staff. Of course, managers would like all these metrics to be as positive as they can be, all the time.

From a leadership perspective, there are three critical attributes of high collaborative performance to exemplify, reinforce and measure, relevant for any team or enterprise:

1. People understand and are motivated to achieve clear, shared outcomes.

2. They interact, learn, share and innovate to deliver these outcomes in a physically and psychologically safe working environment.

3. The team achieves its outcomes and maintains the collaborative environment even when the prevailing conditions become pressurised, complex and stressful.

We often consider elite sport when seeking to understand peak performance. Whilst we can learn much from sporting environments, there is an important distinction between sports and business environments. Typically, sports teams prepare for specific events, with known times, durations and rules. They can plan all aspects of their training and preparation to ensure that they 'peak' at the required time. In business, as in life, we do not have the luxury of this certainty. We must perform the best that we can in the conditions that we find ourselves in – and we must *continue* to do so, even as these conditions change unpredictably and relentlessly.

I have found myself working with leaders driving to achieve outcomes with groups of people operating at one or more of these three levels.

1. At the **team** level, leaders are working with people drawn from one organisation. It could be a handful of people in one team, or hundreds collaborating virtually from many global locations. They have a clear objective, and how they achieve it is determined entirely within the boundary of the organisation. An example would be a project team delivering a design for a new water treatment system.

2. At the **enterprise** level, success relies on a set of interconnected organisations working together to achieve common outcomes – a 'team of teams'. These organisations must work to understand and influence each other in order for the enterprise to be successful. An example would be an enterprise made up of a utility company, engineering consultants and contractors delivering a five-year capital programme.

3. At the **system** level, collaboration is required across a diverse array of stakeholders who may or may not be directly connected contractually to achieve shared outcomes. An example would be collaboration between utility companies, regulators and interested parties such as farming

unions and rivers trusts, to enhance and protect the natural environment.

The basic behavioural foundation at all three levels is the same. However, as leaders move from **team** to **enterprise** to **system** levels, they experience an exponential increase in complexity and interdependence that cannot be addressed by processes alone. A *behavioural* approach is needed to achieve collaborative performance.

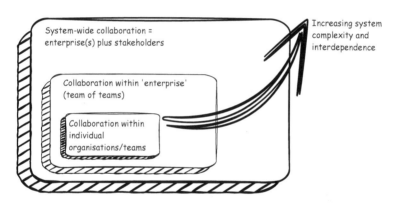

Hierarchy of collaborative environments

A simple equation for collaborative performance

Human behaviour is inherently complex, often completely unpredictable and utterly fascinating. At the time of writing, there are no unifying psychological models that can accurately and reliably predict how any one person will behave in any specific environment. Even so, as an engineer, I am attracted to the use of models, equations and other constructs that seek to make sense of cause and effect, and it can be enlightening to consider how rules that seem to hold true in certain environments could potentially shed light on aspects of human behaviour.

Infrastructure leaders deal with the creation and performance of physical infrastructure assets that enable the modern world to function effectively. Systems for water, transportation, energy, housing, communication and so on all rely on individual component assets functioning effectively and interdependently. Each of these individual assets needs to be fit for its specific purpose, with the right specification and correct installation. For example, in a water supply system an individual pump needs to have the correct capacity, be made of the right materials and be installed correctly within the wider system in order to function effectively. To maintain its performance over its anticipated lifespan, it must also be appropriately maintained, with regular inspections and servicing. It must also operate within an appropriate environment to ensure it is secure and protected from deterioration, which could be caused by, for example, exposure to rust-inducing sea water. The performance of the pump is, therefore, reliant on both its original specification and the environment within which it operates.

If you were to ask leaders what their greatest assets are, many would answer 'our people'. As an engineer-turned-behavioural scientist, I find it interesting to explore this analogy of 'people as assets'. It would follow that to get the desired performance from our 'people assets', we would require a combination of the right people (with the right capabilities) and the right environment.

Let me suggest a simple equation:[5]

$$\text{Collaborative Performance} = \text{Capability} + \text{Environment}$$

Here, *capability* is a function of people's skills, training and experience, and *environment* is a function of the workplace conditions and the behaviour of others in the same workplace, particularly the leaders.

It is a leadership responsibility not just to recruit and train the right people, but also to create the environment in which people can be successful. In my experience, too many leaders fail to recognise this responsibility. They may have the right people, but they fail to get the best out of their collective efforts by presiding over sub-optimal (and even toxic) environments.

I have had the great privilege of working closely with Neil Fachie, one of Great Britain's most successful Paralympians. Neil was born with a congenital eye condition, retinitis pigmentosa. He began his sporting career in athletics before transitioning to track cycling in 2009, where he rides tandem with an able-bodied 'pilot'. He has since dominated this discipline, winning multiple gold medals at the Paralympics, World Championships and Commonwealth Games. He is the current world record holder in the Kilo event, having broken his own previous record set when he won gold at the 2021 Tokyo Paralympics.

Neil and I have been exploring the critical factors for high performance, comparing elite sport with business leadership. When testing the performance equation with him, Neil recognised the relevance and importance of each term. For him, *capability* represents physical attributes such as stamina and strength, and mental attributes such as focus and relentless determination. He confirmed that capability alone is not enough to drive gold medal level performance. The environment that wraps around all aspects of athletes' lives is crucial. Coaching, training facilities, equipment, nutrition, physiotherapy and myriad other environmental factors are critical to athletes achieving their performance potential.

My intention in sharing this performance equation is to increase awareness of the *environmental* aspects of delivering any significant outcome through the collaborative efforts of people, in a dynamic and often uncertain situation. Leaders are responsible for both the terms in the equation. To use an analogy, they must sow the right seeds and ensure the soil is healthy. The most resilient seeds (and capable people) cannot grow and deliver in a toxic environment.

Having set out our goals, roadmaps and blueprints, do we understand what individuals must do differently? Indeed, *why* would they do things differently if nothing has changed in their environment? Without this clarity, we cannot expect to achieve active engagement and sustainable change at the coal face.

The low-performing uncollaborative environment

For the clients I work with, leadership is the art of getting big things done, through the collaborative efforts of people, in a changing, complex and unpredictable world. They often have the right people, with the right capabilities, but they aren't getting the results they want. The environment is not set up for their people to succeed. Symptoms include:

- Lack of a clear, meaningful and widely understood intent for the collaborative efforts. *If we don't know what the overall intent is, how can we collaborate?*

- People have their heads down, reacting to their own immediate needs and crises. *If we aren't lifting our heads to see the bigger picture and responding to the needs of others, how can we be collaborating?*

- People do the minimum to avoid reproach and only feel comfortable saying what they think the leaders want to hear. *If we don't feel safe to share our ideas and concerns, how can we work together to innovate and improve?*

- People are unwilling to give and receive feedback. They are keeping their knowledge to themselves and seem unwilling to change. *How can we be more than the sum of our parts if we don't share and build on our collective experience? If we don't learn and adapt together, how can we survive?*

- The workplace environment is not set up to influence the behaviours we need to be successful. *If the environment doesn't change and continues to reinforce our 'tried and tested' ways of working, why would we change?*

Great leaders realise that it is their responsibility to fix this. They must create and nurture high-performing collaborative environments. The following chapters explain how.

Chapter takeaways

- **Collaboration is an evolutionary advantage:** Collaboration isn't just beneficial, it's a survival imperative in the face of relentless change. The ability to work together and leverage collective strengths has been a distinct human advantage throughout history.

- **Megatrends influence change:** Anticipating and responding to megatrends, such as demographic shifts, climate change and technological advancements, is crucial for future-proofing organisations. These trends significantly impact how businesses operate and compete, making adaptability and collaboration more critical than ever.

- **Adapt quickly to change:** There's a stark contrast between the exponential rate of change in our environment and the much slower pace at which organisations adapt to that change. Closing this 'opportunity gap' is essential for survival and success, emphasising the need for agile and adaptive organisational cultures.

- **Identify obstacles to collaboration:** Many attributes of the modern workplace environment hinder rather than catalyse effective collaboration. For example, complex outdated organisational structures, cultural differences, misaligned objectives and convoluted processes.

- **Environment is key:** Leaders must accept ownership and intentionally design and cultivate environments that encourage and nurture collaborative efforts rather than obstruct them. They must create high-performing collaborative environments.

TWO
Meaningful

Collaborative performance is founded on clear, meaningful, shared intent. If your people don't know what their efforts are contributing to, and why, how can you expect them to collaborate effectively?

This chapter explores how leaders:

- Unleash the power of purpose by connecting their people to the purpose of their organisation

- Capitalise on the magic of intrinsic motivation

- Focus their leadership narrative to accelerate the execution of their strategic intent

The power of purpose

What gets you out of bed in the morning? What gives you the energy to achieve your goals and chase your dreams? Take a moment to think about this. Your thoughts may go to your family. Your friends. Your spiritual beliefs. Perhaps your home, your hobbies or even your car. You will likely think about your work. Ask yourself a few more questions. How *connected* do you feel to the purpose of the organisation that you work for? As a leader, how connected do you think your people feel? How would you know?

The much-repeated fable of Sir Christopher Wren and the bricklayers illustrates how we can have different perspectives on the same work. In 1671, so the story goes, Wren visited the construction of St Paul's Cathedral, which he had been commissioned to design. He observed three bricklayers and asked each what they were doing. The first replied, 'I'm a bricklayer, working hard to feed my family.' The second: 'I'm a builder. I'm building a wall.' The third, and the most productive, answered, 'I'm a cathedral builder. I'm building a great cathedral to Almighty God.' Three different perspectives on the same task, each with different levels of vision, pride and productivity. As a leader, you can help people see themselves as cathedral builders.

In many organisations, people feel little or no connection between their daily work and any meaningful purpose. They do what they need to do to get paid and provide for themselves and their families. Their organisations may be making a valuable contribution to the world, yet the people making this happen do not feel the connection to their individual efforts.

The magic of intrinsic motivation

Motivating people to act together in pursuit of a purpose or goal is a key leadership skill. But what is motivation? How is it created? We know the feeling of being motivated to achieve something. We have energy. We are focused and in control. We take action and avoid distractions. Each step we take moves us closer to our goal, building our confidence and sense of achievement.

In my experience, many of us do not feel highly motivated for most of the time. At times we feel stuck in a rut. We procrastinate. Time drags and we feel frustrated, bored and unfulfilled. Leaders step in to 'help' motivate us. They set targets and impose deadlines. They create bonus schemes, allude to promotions and threaten punishments for non-performance. This is what leaders should do, right? Perhaps. Such things are often useful and even necessary. But if dangling these carrots and wielding these sticks is all that leaders do, they are missing the magic ingredient that unlocks our inner drive to learn, grow and achieve: intrinsic motivation.

In the 1980s, psychologists Edward Deci and Richard Ryan developed Self Determination Theory (SDT). Their pioneering research differentiated between *extrinsic motivation*, coming from external sources, and *intrinsic motivation*, which is the drive to meet our innate psychological needs. Deci and Ryan identified three primary sources of intrinsic motivation: we want to be in control of our own lives (autonomy); we seek to control outcomes using our skills and learning (competence); and we want to connect with and care for others (relatedness).[6]

In his book *Drive*,[7] Daniel Pink framed SDT and intrinsic motivation as it relates to the work environment, as follows:

- **Mastery:** The desire to get better and better at something that matters

- **Autonomy:** Our urge to direct our lives and our work

- **Purpose:** The yearning to do what we do in the service of something larger than ourselves

Leaders seeking to motivate their people need to achieve an appropriate balance between extrinsic and intrinsic motivation. Our behaviour and performance at work is inevitably influenced by external factors such as salary, awards, recognition and promotion prospects. These areas need careful consideration and management. But a leader who unlocks the magic of intrinsic motivation creates an environment in which people feel that their work matters and makes a difference. They feel in control of their work and their career. They are learning, growing and fulfilling their potential as they are trusted to apply their skills in support of meaningful goals.

Leaders often disengage their people by seeking to control or micromanage them. They fail to give them growth opportunities. They fail to communicate how the work matters and makes an impact. This is a mistake.

EXTRINSIC MOTIVATION
Influenced by the outcomes
or consequences e.g.
money; awards;
recognition; promotion

INTRINSIC MOTIVATION
Influenced by the
meaning or enjoyment
we find in the task e.g.
purpose; curiosity;
self-expression; fun

Intrinsic and extrinsic motivation

Connect people to the purpose of the organisation

I like to begin my workshops with a philosophical question: *Why are we here?* I am, of course, seeking to clarify the intent of the session and why people are there. Yet it often elicits thoughtful expressions as people ask themselves a deeper version of the same question. 'Why am I here, now, spending the precious, limited moments of my life in this way?' For many, it's an uncomfortable thought process. They reflect on their time spent in endless back-to-back meetings, or buried under a mountain of emails. We quickly move on with the agenda.

The most impactful organisations have a clear purpose beyond increasing shareholder value. But what about individuals? In the context of our work, should we have a specific purpose? Beyond getting paid fairly for our efforts to support ourselves and our dependants, what is our goal? Why are we here? It is easy to be carried along for years by the forceful current of our career. Others make decisions for us about the work that we do, the roles that we take and even the locations that we work in. For some, this works out well. But others feel like a victim of the circumstances they find themselves in. Stuck in an endlessly demotivating loop of complaint and surrender to the status quo. There is no meaningful connection between the purpose of the organisation and that of the individuals within it. This is a leadership challenge.

Many organisations claim to be driven by their purpose and to live by their values. Intranet statements and posters on office walls claim to be 'best choice for our clients' or 'creating a better planet'. They put their 'people first' as their 'greatest assets'. Their products are 'best for quality' and they 'always put the customer first' (as well as their people). For most of the people these statements refer to, this is background noise. It does not relate to their day-to-day reality. The intranet statements gather digital dust. The posters slip off the walls.

How do leaders make a meaningful connection between the purpose and values of the organisation and the motivation of their people? This can't be fully achieved by issuing memos or transmitting webcasts. To make the connection real, there must be a conversation. A two-way dialogue. One through which people get a chance to understand the intent of the leader and the purpose of the organisation. More importantly, they feel the emotion and commitment of the leader. They begin to believe. Only then can they work out for themselves how their work contributes in a meaningful way. They are on the journey from bricklayers to cathedral builders.

CASE STUDY: From manipulating spreadsheets to improving lives

Through the delivery of a transformation programme for a major European manufacturing company, I had the opportunity to watch the chief financial officer explain the company's strategy to groups of frontline employees. The company produces a commodity material, which ends up being used in many ways. Operating in a highly competitive global market, they must continually improve their production efficiency, customer service and management of working capital to remain profitable. In her presentation, the CFO could have focused entirely on these important areas, but first she elevated everyone's perspective. Their product is a key ingredient in things that improve people's lives. It is used in medical equipment, automobiles and infrastructure. Common household appliances and even satellites rely on it. She then explained how their manufacturing process is the most sustainable, with a lower carbon footprint than all their competitors.

Rather than simply talking about the financial aspects of their strategy and performance, she first made it clear *why* the company existed: to improve people's lives with the most sustainable product. Through dialogue and patiently answering questions, she made the connection to the work that individuals were doing. This had the effect of shifting the employees' perspective, bringing a new layer of meaning to their day-to-day work with production systems and spreadsheets. Observing this, I could see people growing more energised and engaged. They could see how their individual efforts contributed to a meaningful purpose. They were proud. They were motivated.

The process of making the connection between the intent of an organisation and the needs of those it serves is a never-ending leadership task. This connection with clients, customers and the people in the organisation cannot be achieved by simply trans-mitting information. It requires dialogue. It requires active listening. It requires a clear and compelling *leadership narrative*.

The power of leadership narrative

Steve Jobs believed that 'the most powerful person in the world is the storyteller. The storyteller sets the vision, values and agenda of an entire generation to come.'[8] Great leaders are great storytellers. They share their vision. They demonstrate their passion. They energise and motivate. They sell. They do this through meaningful dialogue and clear, compelling narrative: they tell stories.

Addressing the challenges faced by modern society requires the collaborative efforts of people from many different groups and organisations. These organisa-tions may have complex contractual arrangements between them. They may not be connected at all beyond a high-level shared objective, for example protection of the natural environment or reduction of carbon emissions. Leaders cannot simply issue instructions and expect people in all these organisa-tions to carry them out. Instead, leaders must commu-nicate a compelling vision of the future that captures attention and motivates individuals to play their role in creating it. In business speak, this is the formulation and execution of strategy.

What is strategy?

Strategy is the topic about which there is perhaps more research material than any other in the world of leadership and management. Fundamentally, strategies must clearly answer a basic set of questions:

- **Why** are we doing this?
- **What** is it we are trying to achieve?
- **How** will we do it successfully?
- **Who** will do what and **when**?

Many organisations do not have good answers to simple questions such as: what are we selling? To whom? Why would they buy it from us? Some have great answers, but these are known only to a handful of people in the boardroom. A good question for a leader to consider is: if I were to ask ten people at different levels in my organisation what my strategy is, how many would be able to give the right answer? Better yet, actually go and ask those ten people.

As I mentioned earlier, strategic leadership is harnessing collaborative efforts to get big things done. The leader must both create the musical score and then conduct the orchestra. They do not play any of the instruments. They stand in front of their people and communicate their intent through their energy, passion and belief in where they are going together. Strategies are stories about the future, and the leader is the storyteller.

The magic of story

Before modern technology, how did we share knowledge? Before the printing press and widespread literacy, how did we chronicle and communicate history? We achieved much of this through the power of storytelling. We tell stories all the time – listen to conversations in any pub. Not many people are just transmitting data or receiving information – they are sharing anecdotes, re-living events, listening to others do the same. Storytelling is incredibly powerful. We respond to stories emotionally and physiologically, in ways that we don't to data sets or structured information. Stories have huge impact:

- Stories **bring us closer together**. We share them in groups sitting around the real or metaphorical campfire. We have a shared experience. We connect.

- Stories **engage our senses**. Stories transmit emotions from the storyteller to the audience. This happens whether we hear, read or see the story play out on screen. We feel embarrassment when someone recounts a mistake they have made. We jump when the shark appears.

- Stories **move us to act**. Seeing a picture of one sea turtle entangled in discarded plastic netting has a much greater impact on our behaviour than graphs plotting turtle deaths and tons of plastic in the ocean.

- Stories are how we **share knowledge**. Mentors don't just give lists of instructions and points to consider, they share their experience and what it means through stories.

- Stories are how leaders **bring strategies to life**.

Leadership narrative

We all have experience of being led. We remember when we were led well and when we were led badly. We feel the impact that leadership has on our motivation, actions and performance. Consider your own experience of being led. It is likely that, for most of the time, your leader was not standing over you, directing your specific actions and decisions. They may have been in another part of the building, another location or even another country. Yet their leadership still impacted your behaviour and performance as if they were standing right there beside you. You may not have been consciously considering the leader's perspective as you worked, yet you were still influenced by your understanding of their strategic intent. Their leadership narrative communicated their intent to you. Or failed to do so.

CASE STUDY: Building a leadership narrative

I had the experience of working with a visionary, energetic and highly intellectual leader of a global organisation. His passion and intensity came through incredibly strongly when he presented his strategy to people in the organisation in many different locations. The audience would invariably respond positively, becoming energised and motivated by their leader's charismatic performance. They would leave the room fired up and happy that they were part of an organisation with such visionary leadership. All good, you might think. The problem was that almost no one who heard the leader's speech could accurately articulate and share the key tenets of his strategy. They couldn't latch onto his intent in a way that connected to their specific area and influenced their behaviour. They left the room motivated yet went back to doing exactly what they had been doing beforehand. Understandably, the leader became exceptionally frustrated that his strategy was not gaining momentum. 'They just don't get it,' he would say. And he was right.

The leader was strong, his vision was sound. Yet the people in the organisation simply could not pick up and run with his strategy in a way that aligned with his vision. Worse still, certain individuals were almost certainly re-interpreting and misrepresenting the strategy in ways that benefited their own purposes, rather than the overall organisation.

I worked with this leader to focus the key components of his strategy into a straightforward, clear and compelling leadership narrative. This involved a process of dialogue and active listening to capture the essence of the story into bite-sized elements that were then presented in a clear and visually attractive framework. Importantly, as the framework developed, we engaged with the senior leadership team to test their understanding and gauge their perspectives. They could then see their fingerprints on the final version, which significantly increased their buy-in.

This framework became the foundation of how the strategy was communicated and translated across the entire organisation.

Through this process of crystallising a leadership narrative, the leader's strategic intent becomes something that can be shared with accuracy and confidence without the presence of the leader. Furthermore, the narrative can be translated and finessed into the specific circumstances of individual parts of the organisation without becoming disconnected from the overall intent. This results in the leader's vision being understood and acted upon across the organisation with a much greater level of speed and consistency than could have been achieved through the leader's efforts alone.

Crystal clarity on a shared leadership intent is something that many leaders fail to achieve. Some, driven by their ego, may feel that it is their job alone to articulate the strategy and issue all the primary directions to their people. It's clear in their mind: they are the leader; their people are followers. Others simply may not realise that what they are communicating to their people is not fully understood. It's complex, confusing and inconsistently presented. Leaders are seldom told that this is the case. In the absence of a clear leadership narrative, people will create their own, inevitably based on their personal assumptions, fears and ambitions.

Leadership narrative is the mechanism by which the vision, passion and energy of the leader is translated to the people in the team. It creates clarity of intent, giving the team the parameters within which they can bring their own skills, judgement and creativity to deliver their individual contribution to the overall success. Importantly, a strong, clear leadership narrative does all of this at a much faster pace than 'traditional' methods of cascading strategies through organisations.

A CEO once told me that any significant strategy took approximately one year to permeate down through each level of the structure of their organisation, and to achieve a substantial shift in the organisation's direction could take between five and seven years. This was a source of incredible frustration. In this leader's mind, what needed to be done was crystal clear. It had been explained to the entire organisation multiple times via meetings, presentations, memos and webinars. He was puzzled and even more frustrated at the realisation that bad news and gossip travelled through the entire organisation in no time at all.

Stories travel through the corridors of our minds with the swiftness of wildfire. Consider the phenomenon of gossip: a rapid process of dissemination of tales of intrigue and speculation. These narratives, particularly the negative ones, embed themselves in the fabric of our minds, resonating through the echo of emotions long after they're told. I can still recall the profound shock that reverberated through me upon hearing of the 9/11 attacks, a vivid testament to the power of an emotionally charged story to etch moments into our very essence.

Daniel Kahneman, in his exploration of cognitive function, encapsulates this notion succinctly: 'Our mind is a machine for jumping to conclusions.'[9] This evolutionary mechanism primes us for action with tales spun from the sparsest threads of information. A rustle in the bushes is not merely wind but a predator lurking; a car horn transforms from a friendly greeting to an imminent threat. This immediate, often negative storytelling is a primal response, a survival tactic ingrained within our very DNA.

Yet in our modern world of instant connectivity, this propensity can mislead. The silent pauses in digital conversation – seen as someone types a message that never comes – can spiral into narratives filled with apprehension and unease. But the reality often diverges significantly from the stories we create in our minds.

Effective leadership demands a profound understanding of this narrative-driven existence. The stories we tell, the actions we take and even the silences we hold shape the narratives within which others operate. Our words and deeds, observed through the prism of human perception, become the dots others connect to form their own understanding of the world. In this realm, the most potent tool at our disposal as leaders is the story we choose to weave, guiding those we lead towards a shared vision of the future.

CASE STUDY: The power of leadership narrative

I have experienced both the negative and the positive power of leadership narratives. My first experience of using the power of narrative to successfully drive organisational change came with a leadership challenge I took on in 2005. My task was to establish and lead a new centre of technical excellence operating across the UK, Europe, Middle East and India operations of a global engineering organisation. I had been given a unique opportunity to create something new, with a high-level set of (mostly financial) objectives, yet an unusually blank sheet of paper to start with. At the time, I was (relatively) young and didn't know what I didn't know. Perhaps more by luck than by judgement, I took an approach that helped me move the project forward at speed. Rather than spend hours locked in a room with a small group designing the new organisation in isolation, I started to present a high-level perspective of the intent of the new unit. I created a one-slide core 'picture' that presented a set of simple ideas about what we were doing and why we were doing it. I shared this multiple times, with many different groups of stakeholders. This created an opportunity for dialogue and influence around something that was at a formative stage. Looking back, I realise that I was simply telling, re-telling and refining a story. This story was taking shape in my mind and in the minds of the team. This shared leadership narrative dramatically helped the creation and subsequent success of the unit.

I have also made the mistake of failing to share a clear leadership narrative in an organisation undergoing change. Given the challenge to turn around a poorly performing operational unit, I formulated a sound strategy to re-shape the structure and re-focus priorities. As with so many similar challenges, this would involve several difficult issues involving key people potentially moving roles or even leaving the business. But for reasons of confidentiality (and perhaps more than a little paranoia) I was prevented from involving any of the critical people in the planning of the changes.

Unsurprisingly, people suspected that there was something going on. In the absence of clarity from me, they created their own stories regarding the imminent changes. A significant gap opened up between the 'unofficial' narrative in the organisation and what I was trying to communicate. This resulted in one of the most challenging and stressful periods of my career as I struggled to influence the perspectives of key people regarding the direction we were moving in. I had 'lost control of the narrative'. This had significant implications, both for myself as leader and for those I was attempting to lead through the change. I learned the painful lesson that the stories people tell themselves shape and define their reality, which may be far removed from the actual situation and even further from the leader's intent.

In my experience, stories move faster than strategies. They can also be much more powerful and influential. Effective leaders understand their own story, and they shape and communicate a clear and compelling leadership narrative. Stories bring their strategies to life.

Focus your leadership narrative

Developing an effective strategy is a logical management process that can be clearly defined, but composing a compelling leadership narrative is a creative process. It is iterative. It is frustrating. It is hard to pin down. What follows is my approach to translating strategy into a narrative that can be shared and acted upon across an entire organisation.

Get it all out

The first step to translating your strategic intent into leadership narrative is to speak it out loud. Describe where you are going, and why. Explain your rationale in as much detail as you feel necessary. The aim is simply to get everything out of your head.

Engagement with trusted advisers is important. They should actively listen and capture what you say, then summarise back to you what they've heard. You may be surprised to find that what they hear is not what you thought you said. It will take several sessions to get some words down that accurately capture the essence of what you feel to be important.

Break it down

At this stage, you are likely to have a messy, lengthy script. It's time to break it down, simplifying statements and categorising elements. You want to capture each key aspect of your intent in the fewest words. Typical elements, at an organisational level, include: purpose, core values, vision, strategic priorities, client outcomes and competitive differentiators. The list goes on. What you choose will be context-specific. What are the key themes for you and your team? The fewer the better.

Focus on outcomes

I have worked for and with many leaders over the years. Most, if not all, began as 'subject matter' professionals – engineers, scientists, lawyers, accountants, medics. Their rise through the ranks began with building and applying their professional expertise. This may be the case for you. At a point in their career, each of these leaders had to get over an invisible hurdle. On one side of the hurdle, their primary focus is applying their *own* skills; on the other side, as a leader, their focus must shift to influencing the collaborative activity of others. In other words, they are no longer *doing* the work that resulted in their leadership position. Others are doing this work. Now they, as the leader, are defining and communicating the *outcomes* of the work, then creating an environment in which people can best achieve these outcomes collaboratively.

I began my career as an engineer. I am still an engineer. I feel a need to solve problems and get things done using my core skills. With hindsight, I can see the point at which I was struggling to get over the hurdle described above. It was hard to let go and allow others to do the work. As I struggled, I may have thought I was giving useful guidance to my team. In fact, I was micro-managing them. Many leaders who have risen from technical and professional expertise backgrounds find it hard to step back, frame clear outcomes and trust their team to achieve these outcomes in their own way.

Make it easy to digest and share

The narrative is taking shape, but it must attract attention and be digestible to accelerate its spread through your organisation. If you need to be in the room to articulate the vision, then the pace of achieving it will be severely limited. The approach that I use with leaders is:

- Get it on one page – one slide that can be read from the back of the room.

- Structure the themes in an appropriate 'hierarchy'. Purpose, for example, might be at the top, followed by core values. Specific outcomes might be at the bottom.

- Involve a graphic designer. I'm an engineer; I've just about mastered bullet points. A creative expert will be able to provide visual impact. Attractiveness and accessibility will help others to get interested, understand it and then share the narrative.

Your goal is one page that accurately reflects the sentiment of your intent for your team, broken down into bite-sized, digestible and unambiguous elements and presented in a manner that is clear and grabs attention.

Focus your leadership narrative

Socialise it, test it and improve it

During the design of the one-pager, it is important to engage with key senior stakeholders. These are the people who are key to delivery. For a CEO, this might be the direct reports who lead different parts of the business. This is a dialogue, not a presentation. Tell the story, using the one-pager as the guide. What do they understand by it? What don't they get? What would they add? Get feedback and act on it. Seeing their fingerprints on it will increase their engagement and create a sense of shared ownership. They now understand where you are coming from and can share that with their people, confidently and accurately. They can then shape more specific goals for their teams that align with and deliver your key outcomes.

In my experience, this part of the process is the most impactful. Global organisations may operate several different business models, in multiple countries and across different sectors. This process facilitates the translation of high-level intent into meaningful goals at various coal faces.

Bring it to life with stories

Pithy, memorable statements that capture and communicate intent are important. The organisation's purpose can be crystallised in a few words. Use key words to capture values. Often, though, these statements languish in a dusty corner of the company intranet and sit unnoticed on the office notice board. They must be brought to life. Stories do this. A carefully chosen story, told well, will illustrate what it means to act in accordance with your leadership narrative, as the below case study shows.

CASE STUDY: A 'living our values' story

James Beazley is the managing director of 6-Group, a global executive search and leadership assessment organisation. He and his team live by two values: 'Partnering' and 'Go Beyond'. Nice words. But what do they mean? When new team members join, James demonstrates what they mean. He tells a story. Several years ago, his company supported a major Asian port authority to recruit a head of customs. This person had responsibility for all the cargo entering and leaving the country through one of the largest ports in the world. The successful candidate was well qualified, had impeccable references and started the role successfully. The client was happy. James's job was done.

Three months later, James checked in with the client to see if all was well. The client was happy enough with their new employee's performance, but there were a few concerning behaviours in his interactions with other team members. They didn't see it as a huge issue and were dealing with it, so James could have left it at that. He didn't. Instead, he went back to re-check each of the original candidate references. Alarmingly, they no longer existed. One call was answered by an old lady in Switzerland. Another company was fictitious. Alarm bells ringing, James called the client with the shocking and somewhat embarrassing news. They began to monitor the person's behaviour closely and noticed that he was letting certain containers through without security checks. The next time this happened, they were ready. They stopped and searched the container – it was half full of machine guns and ammunition, the other half was pornography. The man had been placed there by an organised crime syndicate.

James uses this story to illustrate two things. Doing the right thing can be the harder choice and place you in a vulnerable position. A trusted partnership is not founded on what is easy, or 'right' for just one of the partners. The client in this story was understandably very unhappy with the situation, but they appreciated that James did not have to follow up in the way that he did. He went beyond the necessary, and the relationship was ultimately strengthened.

Share it until you are sick of it

Your narrative has been captured, designed and refined. You have shaped the story, made it appealing and key people seem to be getting it. You are at the end of the beginning. Now you must share it – with multiple people, groups and teams. Again and again. And again. You must also encourage and support others to do the same. It's only at the point where you are sick to death of hearing it, that it just might be starting to sink in. Stories improve with the telling. (They also tend to 'grow' – beware of over-embellishment.) Your leadership narrative will improve, people will share and follow your story. They will follow *you*.

Chapter takeaways

- **Unleash the power of purpose:** Leaders must help their people connect deeply with the organisation's purpose by regularly communicating it and encouraging reflection on how individual work contributes to the larger goal. This sense of shared purpose fosters resilience, enhances productivity and imbues daily tasks with deeper meaning.

- **Harness intrinsic motivation:** SDT shows us that intrinsic motivation is more important than extrinsic. People are driven by a desire for autonomy, mastery and purpose, so create environments that foster intrinsic motivation by offering opportunities for personal growth.

- **Connect people to the organisation's purpose:** It's not enough for an organisation to have a noble purpose. Leaders must actively connect their people's daily work to this purpose, so facilitate open dialogue and share stories that link individual efforts to the organisation's impact to make it tangible and relatable.

- **Understand the power of leadership narrative:** Effective leaders are storytellers who can articulate a compelling vision of the future. This narrative should clarify the organisation's strategy and inspire action aligned with its goals, making sure it is understood and embraced at all levels.

- **Focus your leadership narrative for maximum impact:** The leadership narrative must be clear and concise, capturing the essence of the strategy. Create a one-page summary broken down into digestible parts and supported by visuals that highlight outcomes and facilitate easy sharing and understanding.

THREE
Functional

The lifeblood of collaborative performance is a set of basic, non-negotiable behaviours. To have any hope of achieving high performance, the environment must first be functional. Inconsistent demonstration of basic required behaviours is a fundamental obstacle to collaborative performance. This chapter explores how leaders of high-performing collaborative environments:

- Foster responsive working relationships

- Respect commitments

- Pay attention to the right things

Responsive working relationships

Why don't they reply to my messages? Why don't they turn up to meetings on time? Why don't they listen to me? As a leader, you will likely have felt these frustrations at times. Perhaps others feel this way about you. If we are not listening and responding to each other, we cannot be collaborating. We may be being 'productive'. We may be doing great individual work. But if we are not communicating, we are not collaborating.

Worse, we often assume that we have communicated with others and that they fully understand our intentions, expectations and requests. This questionable assumption (by both parties) is perhaps the biggest impediment to effective communication and by extension, successful collaboration.

I like to collect data. When I work with groups, I gather individual, confidential perspectives, asking two specific questions:

1. How well do you listen to people at work?

2. Do you feel you are actively listened to at work?

The pattern of the responses I collect across groups is consistent: the answers to the first question are more positive than for the second. My conclusion from this is that we consider ourselves to be better at listening to others than they are at listening to us. I discuss this with each group and people are generally quick to articulate their frustration at the lack of engagement from others. As the discussion progresses, some admit that they perhaps don't listen as well as they should.

I also ask leaders for their level of agreement with two statements:

1. I always respond to requests from others in a timely manner.

2. People who are critical of my work always respond to me quickly.

A similar pattern emerges but the skew is even more pronounced. We consider ourselves more responsive to others than they are to us. The problem is clear: it's other people. We justify our own behaviour and fail to recognise that, to others, *we* are the 'other people'.

Why don't we respond to each other? I have observed four blockers of collaborative performance in this regard:

1. Lack of time

2. Inability to manage distraction

3. Lack of awareness

4. Lack of empathy

Let's look at these in turn.

Lack of time

You ask, 'how are you today?' How often is the response 'busy'? Or, 'very busy'? Even, 'too busy'? Are we *all* too busy? Why is this?

During the 2020 COVID-19 lockdown, I carried out a project with a large utility company. All involved were working from home. Specifically, we were attending online meetings. Calendars were jammed. It wasn't possible to fit another meeting in edgeways. People were suffering 'back-to-back pain', running virtually between meetings that ended and started simultaneously. The waking nightmare of this relentless meeting culture was exacerbated by out-of-control email. One team member told me that to read all incoming email would take them the entire day.

Many wear busyness as a badge of pride. Others feel that they must be always visibly busy and fear the consequences of appearing idle. A former boss said that if he didn't see people 'running around with their hair on fire' then there was a problem, the team wasn't working hard enough. This misguided leadership behaviour infused negative energy through the team.

Some attempt to achieve a balance in how they spend their time, but they often meet resistance. A senior HR leader shared that she encourages her team to block out meeting-free chunks of time on their calendars to plan, think and focus. To get actual work done. When she shared her approach with her peers and boss, she was derided for being 'soft' on her team. One person said, 'That's what evenings and weekends are for.' This was in an organisation with a stated value of 'putting people first'.

In 2022 I surveyed seventy people on post-pandemic meeting behaviours: 40% of them were still working five days a week from home; 40% were in some form of hybrid arrangement, working from home two or three days a week; more than 60% still had calendars infected by relentless back-to-back online meetings, and 35% felt this was having a detrimental impact on their wellbeing. Somewhat confusingly, more than half said that they had a reasonable degree of control over their calendars. It seems that online meeting habits picked up in lockdown have persisted into the post-pandemic hybrid world, and we are letting this happen.

Inability to manage distraction

Digital technology is constantly hijacking our attention. Miniaturisation, wireless connectivity and psychologically informed design ensure that we can be hooked at any time. We complain about how busy we are, yet for an increasing proportion of our time, we are distracted and paying attention to the wrong things. LinkedIn updates. Instagram posts. Constant interruptions. Commercials. Special offers that end today. Relentless system notifications.

Through an anonymous survey of eighty senior leaders in a global organisation, I asked how much this statement resonated: 'I am constantly distracted and it's blocking me from flow.' Around half agreed or strongly agreed with the statement. If the *leaders* are this distracted, what does it mean for their people? For the performance of the organisation? We are living in the age of distraction. Even if we realise this, we seem ill-equipped to deal with it.

Lack of awareness

Many leaders are unaware of the negative impact of their over-booked schedules. On their own effectiveness. On others who need their input, support and leadership. Their unresponsiveness is detrimental to overall performance, but their calendars are 'protected' by personal assistants and so their lack of awareness persists. Of course, leaders must manage their time. But they must also be aware of others' needs that are not being met. Without this awareness, it will not be possible to achieve their desired leadership outcomes. I mentioned to a senior leadership client that many of their leadership team were quite unresponsive and hard to get hold of. The reaction was surprise and concern, particularly as they had been pushing an agenda of increasing responsiveness and engagement with their own clients.

Then there is the 'it's not my job' brigade. It is common to retreat behind role descriptions, which are often poorly defined and do not reflect the dynamic, interconnected nature of getting stuff done in a collaborative manner. This kind of siloed behaviour is rampant in large organisations, where individuals have next to no understanding of, or interest in, the functions and needs of people in other departments. In the worst cases, this can disintegrate into inter-silo competition. This could not be further from the environment required to execute the intent of the overall enterprise.

The American carrier Southwest Airlines famously has jobs that are 'flexible at the boundaries'. People are trained and accountable in their individual areas of expertise, yet each Southwest Airlines job description concludes with the requirement to do 'whatever you need to do to enhance the overall operation'.[10] This places a shared responsibility on everyone to be aware of the most significant operational challenges and to 'muck in' to help achieve them. For example, minimising the time taken to turn around each aircraft at the gate is critical. It is not uncommon to see pilots and flight crew helping load baggage to ensure an on-schedule departure. Elsewhere, this blatant crossing of boundaries would result in negative consequences, including union strife, but at Southwest Airlines behaviour that aligns with the organisational purpose is encouraged even if it blurs functional lines.

Lack of empathy

Imagine the scenario: a seven-year-old trying to get his dad's attention to show him the picture he painted at school. The father repeatedly tells the boy to stop bothering him because he is busy doing important work. Therapists' couches are often the venue where such stories are told, when complex issues related to childhood emotional neglect manifest in adulthood with significant and long-lasting implications. In many cases, the parent would be horrified by the impact of their unresponsiveness. It is the *empathy* practised by the therapist that is the first step to addressing such issues – empathy that was absent in childhood.

Empathy is defined in the Collins English Dictionary as 'the power of understanding and imaginatively entering into another person's feelings'. In a work environment, this extends to the ability to understand the perspectives, frames of reference and needs of another party. By contrast, narcissism is defined as having 'an exceptional interest in or admiration for oneself'. Unfortunately, too many working environments suffer from the centre of gravity being too close to narcissism and too far away from empathy. Examples of global leaders who demonstrate narcissistic behaviours easily come to mind. Those who have had a narcissist for a boss will have the scars to show for it. A lack of empathy in the work environment leads to various negative behaviours, including:

- **Only looking upwards in the hierarchy**, focusing attention on the boss and above to shape how one is perceived. A lack of awareness or interest in what is happening in the lower levels, or in how one is perceived from below.

- **Power plays**, making it painfully clear that 'I'm more important than you.'

- **Politics and jockeying for position**, requiring continual energy to spin one's personal reputation, manage alliances and keep safe from rivals.

- **Lack of responsive to those 'beneath'**, an inevitable consequence of the above.

Low-empathy work environments are created by *leaders*. They are *toxic*. A great leader I know is highly alert to those 'below' pandering to her and neglecting their own teams. She picks people up for responding instantly to her emails, making it clear that timely, considered responses are more appropriate and that in most circumstances she does not need an immediate response.

The productivity paradox

Conventional time-management philosophy encourages us to focus on those things that are important to us and to put those things first. Everything else can be relegated to the 'perhaps one day, but probably not' list and our productivity increases.

Here's the problem. How many items on your 'perhaps one day' list relate to things that are on someone else's 'important' list? Someone with whom you are supposedly collaborating. How would you even know? If you are not responsive to these people, you may be being productive, in your own narrowly defined sense, but you are not collaborating.

Active listening – the magic cure for unresponsiveness

How can leaders address a lack of responsiveness? By setting the tone. Seeking feedback on their own behaviour. Asking the right questions. Really listening to the answers. Acting on the feedback.

We learn how to listen as children. As adults, we often forget this skill. We aren't *listening*; we are *waiting to talk*. We aren't understanding what is actually being said, we are preparing our own anecdote, waiting to pounce on a gap in the conversation. Many interactions, and too many meetings, are dialogues of the deaf.

Active listening is a skill that requires conscious effort. To remain focused on the other party. To suppress the narrative running in your own brain. To arrive at deep shared understanding. I work with groups on a wide range of collaborative behaviours, and it is active listening that usually gets the most positive reaction. People commit to re-learning and practising the basic skills they learned as children, which are to:

- Stay focused on the other person – keep the connection; maintain eye contact; be patient; allow silence; be non-judgemental.

- Stop thinking about what you will say next – resist the urge to share your similar story. Instead, ask considered questions to learn more and build connection.

- Share back what you have heard – repeat, paraphrase and seek to understand the feelings behind the words.

Try it. It's simple (though not easy) and transformative.

Respect commitments

A foundational attribute of collaborative performance is making and following through on commitments. A leader who cannot rely on people to do what they say they will do, cannot achieve anything of significance. Likewise, people rely on their leaders to meet their commitments to them. It sounds basic, and it is, yet in many working environments there is an alarming lack of consistent follow-through on plans, identified actions and stated intent.

Have you experienced any of the following?

- When reviewing the minutes of a previous meeting, it becomes clear that many of the previously agreed actions have not been carried out.

- On the date a report is due, nothing arrives.

- A sales pitch for a piece of work promises 'of course we can meet the schedule' and 'we can absolutely solve those problems for you'. The performance fails to match the rhetoric.

- An individual intends to get more physically fit, commits to exercising three times a week, yet gives up after only a few weeks.

Consistently meeting commitments is a measure of integrity. At times we all fail to do this. Do we recognise this? Strive to improve? Or do we rationalise, explain and seek to justify?

Failing to meet commitments has implications. For you, for others, for the team. Credibility is damaged. Trust is eroded. Performance is compromised. Why do people and teams fail to meet their commitments? I have observed three collaborative performance blockers relating to this area:

- Lack of clarity on the commitment

- Overconfidence

- Absent or misaligned consequences

Let's explore each of these.

Lack of clarity

I am often held to task by my significant other. I haven't done something I had 'promised' to do. My recollection is fuzzy. I didn't think I had been quite so committal. My mistake. This kind of miscommunication is the root of many problems. Are the commitments we make crystal clear? Are actions points recorded in meetings unambiguous and mutually agreed? Have you ever got an action from a meeting that you didn't even attend?

In the work environment, we are 'given' actions all the time. It's easily done – our initials out against an item in the meeting minutes. An emailed instruction. An automated prompt to review a document. A list of obligations in a contract. Our time was already 100% accounted for, yet they continue to fall on us like snowflakes, gradually burying us.

To get any one of these actions done, we must first decide to do it and commit an appropriate amount of our limited resources. Only *we* can determine how we spend our time, where we focus our attention, what we do and in what order. No commitment, no action. It's only the actions we commit to doing that have a chance of getting done, whether that's writing a book or a one-line email.

Look at your 'to-do' list. Be honest with yourself. Which actions are you fully committed to taking?

Which actions may others think you have committed to? What actions are you relying on others to take? How committed are they to those actions? How would you know? Reaching unambiguous agreement on actions and shared commitments is time well spent. It requires two-way connection and active listening.

Overconfidence

It's far easier to make a commitment than to keep it. At New Year, many of us make commitments to improve our lives, but do we consider the implications? Typical resolutions require extended periods of discipline, abstinence and focus. New habits must be developed. Many don't last past January.

We also make work commitments without considering the implications, often in meetings. We have the best of intentions. We are optimistic, and find ourselves overcommitted and compromised. We exhibit overconfidence regarding our personal resources, capabilities and what we think we can achieve.

As a facilitator of countless strategy sessions, I've observed that there seem to be two parallel worlds. In 'workshop world', we elevate our thinking and commit to ambitious goals. Our energy and motivation to achieve them high. As we step back into the 'real' world, commitment evaporates as we get pulled back to floor level. Often absolutely nothing happens.

Overconfidence contributes to project delays and embarrassing failures. Kahneman and Tversky called this the 'planning fallacy', which in their words, is 'the tendency to underestimate the amount of time needed to complete a future task, due in part to the reliance on overly optimistic performance scenarios'.[11]

Anyone who has completed a home improvement project, such as the re-modelling of a kitchen, is likely to be uncomfortably familiar with the planning fallacy. We plan the layout. We estimate the cost and time to complete the project. We add what we consider to be an appropriate level of contingency. Inevitably, the project costs more. It runs later than planned. Almost every episode of TV home improvement shows such as *Grand Designs* seems to follow this pattern.

On a bigger scale, budget and programme overruns on iconic projects generate negative headlines. At its inception in 1997, the cost of the Scottish Parliament building was estimated at £40 million. As the project progressed, there was confidence in each updated estimate. This confidence was unfounded. By completion in 2004, the cost had risen to £431 million. We see this happen time and again: the Panama Canal (1900%), Sydney Opera House (1400%), California High Speed Rail (300%), HS2 (who knows). Bent Flyvbjerg has studied the impact of this bias to be optimistic on many mega project failures, observing that 'you want the flight attendant, not the pilot, to be an optimist.'[12]

Overconfidence also contributes to systemic failures. In May 2018, the UK rail network suffered a prolonged period of significant disruption, causing pain for millions of commuters.[13] The media hunted for a single guilty party, but the situation arose from an aggregation of issues in several interconnected areas: the electrification programme fell behind; catch-up work planned over the Christmas holiday hit unexpected problems, just as the new Thameslink service was to come online and the timetables were changing. Problems in just one of these areas would not have had the same impact on the system.

Overconfidence in our capacity, capability and knowledge is hard to self-diagnose. (For example, most of us consider our driving skills to be above average.) Perhaps we should consider making fewer, 'high quality' commitments that we can be sure we can follow through on. At the point of commitment, consider the zero-sum game of your resources: your time, energy and attention is finite. Ask yourself, 'If I commit to this, what am I *not* going to do?'

Absent or misaligned consequences

Have you ever noticed a lack of appropriate consequences for individuals who fail to meet work commitments? Notes of the last meeting are reviewed and people have not completed their actions so these actions are added to the notes of this meeting. No action. No consequence. And repeat.

Our every action (or inaction) generates a consequence for us. Or a set of consequences: things that happen (or don't happen) as a result. These consequences influence our future behaviour. We eat a cookie (action), we enjoy the taste (consequence), so we reach for another. We ignore or skip a health and safety procedure. Nothing untoward happens (fortunately). We do it again.

Aubrey Daniels[14] characterises consequences using three parameters, explaining that they can be either:

- Positive or negative
- Certain or uncertain
- Felt immediately or at some point in the future

Consequences that are *positive, certain* and *immediate* have the most influence on our behaviour.

When we reach for another cookie, we *know* that we will enjoy the experience of eating it. The salience of this positive, certain and immediate outcome is greater than that of the potential long-term health implications. The risk of contributing to obesity or diabetes is certainly a negative consequence, but it is uncertain and in the future. The cookie wins, again.

Consequences of our behaviour can be unintended. For example, an organisation sets a target to have zero accidents; accident-free days are measured and posted on the wall. Who wants to be the one to break the streak by reporting a minor incident? The imagined negative consequences keep people quiet, *increasing* safety risk. Such misalignment between actions and consequences is common.

In every moment, we *choose* how to spend our time, where to focus our precious attention, who to respond to. What action to take, or not take. What to commit to. Our choice may be deliberate and thoughtful, or unconscious and purely reactive. Leaders must spend their time on what matters most, paying attention to the right things.

Pay attention to the right things

As a leader, do you know where your time goes? Are you deliberate in directing your precious energy and attention towards what matters most? Or are your working (and waking) hours hijacked by the demands of others? By events? By distractions?

CASE STUDY: Level up your focus

It was 2010. Bob Uhler, CEO and chairman of MWH Global, and my boss, was concerned. He shared his frustration that senior leaders in the organisation were too focused on day-to-day matters. He was worried they were not spending enough time on preparing each part of the business for the future. How *should* leaders be spending their time? We kicked around some ideas and what emerged was a simple model: four time horizons that leadership should keep focused on. For each of these, we identified a relevant set of critical processes and activities, similar to the below:

- **Level 1:** Day-to-day focus on operational activities, eg staff recruiting, project deadlines and client engagement
- **Level 2:** Quarterly/yearly focus on delivering budgeted targets, eg operational budgets for sales and revenue
- **Level 3:** A two- to three-year focus on strategic planning and priorities, eg acquisitions, new product development and winning major programmes
- **Level 4:** A three- to ten-year focus on the direction and sustainability of the enterprise, eg executive succession plan and ownership transition

We used the model to stimulate discussion, to encourage each leader to consider where their time went and then to make conscious choices about how to distribute their time and attention appropriately across the four levels. Different roles required a different blend of each of the levels. The CEO and board spent most of their time at Levels 3 and 4. The operational leaders were mostly at Levels 1 and 2. This encouraged leaders to address any gap between how they should be spending their time and where their time was really going. Bob shared a rule of thumb that he had learned from one of his mentors – 'as CEO, delegate all issues that arise except the ones that threaten 10% or more of profit.'

I have since evolved the model referenced in the above case study, through discussion with leaders in many organisations. The result is presented in the figure below. Many of these leaders expressed frustration that 'gravity' continuously pulled them down to lower levels. It requires deliberate, conscious effort to resist this downwards force. Without focused effort, a leader becomes reactive. Dealing with events and contributing to others' agendas. 'Firefighting' rather than leading. Leaders must find ways to resist this behavioural gravity.

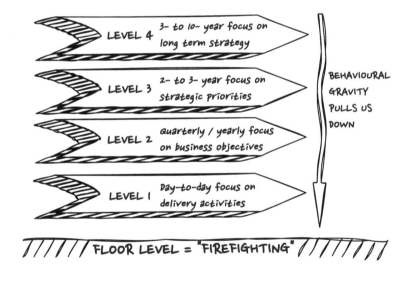

Behavioural gravity pulls leaders down

It was only after becoming immersed in behavioural science that I returned to this model and gave consideration to *why* leaders' time tends to be pulled down to the lowest levels.

Behavioural gravity is strengthened by our innate tendency to focus on the here and now. There is a clear evolutionary reason for this bias towards the present, as we could be injured or killed if we don't address immediate threats in our environment. The future is much less salient, unclear, uncertain, so we focus our attention on the current moment.

I have surveyed many leaders, asking them to estimate the percentage of their time that they spend at each level. I also ask how much time they think they *should* be spending at each level. There is invariably a gap. Most admit to spending more time at the lower levels than they feel they should. Many are frustrated at how much time they spend firefighting at ground level. The usual reasons are cited: too busy; too many distractions; unforeseen events. One expressed exasperation that 'I don't even have time to be reactive.'

It requires conscious, deliberate and focused effort to resist behavioural gravity. A few collaborative performance triggers can help:

- Intentional direction of time and attention

- Vertical goal alignment

- Strategic conversation rhythm

Let's look at how we can implement these.

Intentional direction of time and attention

When it comes to how we spend our time, it's easy to be a victim of external dynamics and distractions, and harder to intentionally direct our attention towards what matters most. Harder still to influence where other people focus theirs. In a busy corporate environment, it is easy for our day to simply happen to us. We get ourselves to the office, or to our first virtual meeting. We leave, or shut down, at the end of the working day. How much of what happened in between was determined by a deliberate choice to focus on what we considered to be the most important activities? How much was shaped by external distractions, events and the pressing needs of others? The appropriate balance is context-dependent; the important point is that we *notice*.

Below are some of the behaviours that help leaders, and their people, to better direct their attention:

- Awareness is fundamental. Leaders need to understand how they actually spend their time across the levels and compare this to how they *should* spend their time, making corrections to rebalance if necessary. Then encourage and support their people do the same.

- Leaders are intentional regarding how they and their team categorise their actions and spend their time. Are meetings or decisions at Level 1,

Level 2, Level 3 or Level 4? Are the attendees, venues and agendas set up to reflect this?

- The leader determines the nature of every interaction with their team, their peers and their customers. Will they gravitate down into weeds? Or elevate, enabling others to see the wood from the trees?

- If necessary, leaders make structural changes in the environment to ensure that due attention is given to critical strategic activities, particularly at Levels 3 and 4. For example, this could be by allocating time for people to spend on innovation. An example is the famous 3M '15% rule', according to which 3M expect their scientists and engineers to spend 15% of their time following their own ideas and shaping their own innovation projects.[15]

- Encourage the habit of pausing discussion to ask, 'What level are we at just now?' and 'What level should we be at?'

CASE STUDY: Global strategic taskforce

One way to ensure focus on a strategic priority in a large organisation is through the establishment of a dedicated team, a 'taskforce' with the full support of senior leadership to shape and influence the required changes. I led such a team in a global engineering company. The Level 3 mission was to improve project delivery by knowledge workers collaborating between operating units. A core team of senior representatives from Europe, North America, Asia-Pacific and India designed and drove the change. The team was connected directly into the leadership of each of the geographic units, as well as being directly accountable (through me) into the COO.

This approach countered the inertia and behavioural gravity that we knew could inevitably pull each of the individual units back to Level 1 problems and priorities. Instead, we were able to execute a Level 3 strategic priority for the global company.

Vertical goal alignment

We discussed the motivational power of compelling purpose and clear intent in Chapter 2. But this is not enough to ensure focus on the right activities, at the right levels. The high-level intent must be translated into component outcomes and goals at the lower levels. A five-year strategic goal cannot be achieved if we don't *begin,* and then consistently focus on activities that align with the goal – for five years. Purpose alone will not drive this discipline. How often is there disparity between the activities that fill our days and those that would help us achieve our goals?

We are wired to pursue and achieve goals. Our evolutionary drive to survive ensures that we seek out things that meet our basic needs: food, shelter and security. Each small achievement triggers a physiological response: a hit of dopamine, the reward chemical. It's addictive. It enhances focus. Stimulates us to strive more, achieve more. For most of us, though, our basic needs are met, so our attention is hijacked by our smartphones and our dopamine hits come from likes and shares. We are further distracted by small tasks and interruptions, attending as many back-to-back meetings as we can.

How do we direct our goal-striving mechanism to focus on the right activities? The ones that align with our high-level intent? We must break it down and track our intention backwards in time from the big future goal to today's 'to-do' list.

Many organisations have stated their intention to achieve carbon neutrality over the coming decade or so, a purposeful and motivating goal. It'll be great when we get there, but what are we doing differently today? Without a deliberate vertical goal alignment process, we will likely be doing nothing.

Strategic conversation rhythm

Leaders must maintain consistent focus on strategic imperatives to intentionally elevate their own attention, and that of key people, above the relentless storms of lower levels. Calendar discipline is key. That means non-negotiable events and time for the right people to dedicate attention to Level 3 and Level 4 processes and priorities. You need an appropriate rhythm for the review of progress and for course correction in response to new information and changes in the environment. This is collaboration at Level 2, 3 or 4, away from the muck and bullets of the lowest levels.

The nature and rhythm of these higher-level events and conversations are context-specific. For example, in my role leading strategic planning for a global engineering company, I facilitated quarterly reviews with each of the operating units. This was the right frequency to allow meaningful progress to be made between reviews, whilst also allowing for changes in the competitive landscape to be identified, understood and addressed in a timely manner.

Establishing the right environment for these events is important; to set the right tone, you must:

- **Create a 'safe space' to achieve the best outcomes.** This can be challenging, particularly with senior people in the room. When senior peers are together the underlying competitive dynamic is often stifling, or worse. We will explore the 'safety' aspect further in Chapter 4.

- **Clarify the intent.** This is the opportunity for the team to hear the leader's narrative again (and again), giving them the chance to discuss and internalise the leader's intent and consider how to translate their part of it into specific results. This dialogue also gives the leader valuable feedback on the internal and external dynamics, which must continue to inform and shape the narrative.

- **Beware of being hijacked by Level 1 distractions.** All must be on their guard from being dragged down into the comfort zone of short-term firefighting and operational issues. In my experience, this has been one of the most significant challenges in facilitating such meetings. Pulling the conversation away from immediate matters such as project delivery issues, specific bid opportunities or the latest set of financial results is a relentless activity; you've got to remind people that yes, these issues are important and must be addressed, but this is not the right place or time to do so.

- **Remember that what you are *not* doing is as important as what you are doing.** Strategy requires decisions about how to deploy limited resources. These resources then cannot and should not be deployed in other areas. Being explicit about and making understood what you are *not* going to do is critical to maintaining focus.

- **Facilitate dialogue between formal meetings.** A key part of my strategic planning role was fostering informal dialogue in between the formal sessions. This fulfilled multiple purposes: to clarify aspects that perhaps people did not feel safe to discuss in an open forum; test ideas; highlight risks; make connections; keep a live perspective on the external competitive environment; and, most importantly, to elevate at least some of the thinking above the tyranny of Level 1.

A functional working environment is the key that will unlock higher levels of collaborative performance. Like a garden, this environment needs regular attention, care and maintenance to keep the weeds at bay.

Chapter takeaways

- **Foster responsive working relationships:** Understanding and addressing the gap between perception and reality in listening and responding is crucial, so conduct self-assessment and feedback sessions within your team. Commit to improving communication by ensuring that messages are not only sent but received, understood and acted upon. Emphasise the importance of two-way communication, active listening and responsiveness as foundational behaviours for effective collaboration.

- **Overcome collaborative performance blockers:** Identify the major blockers to collaborative performance, such as lack of time, inability to manage distraction, lack of awareness and lack of empathy. Then implement strategies to address these issues within your team, for example through designated quiet times, technology etiquette, cross-functional awareness programmes and empathy-building exercises.

- **Respect commitments:** The integrity of collaborative efforts is determined by the reliability of commitments made. Clarify and formalise commitments to ensure they are understood and agreed upon by all parties. Develop an environment that values and rewards the fulfilment of commitments, and where there are consequences for unmet obligations. Encourage a mindset of thoughtful commitment, where each person considers their capacity and resources before making promises they can't keep.

- **Pay attention to the right things:** Leaders must deliberately allocate their time and focus to activities that align with the strategic goals of the organisation. Use the four-level model of time horizons to assess and realign where attention is given, ensuring that immediate operational demands do not overshadow longer-term strategic objectives. Schedule regular strategic review sessions and create mechanisms to resist the pull of 'behavioural gravity' towards immediate operational issues.

FOUR
Fearless

There is a gateway to higher levels of collaborative performance. It lies beyond establishing a meaningful purpose, and beyond implementing foundational collaborative behaviours. To many, this gateway is invisible. Some never get to the other side; they never experience a 'fearless' environment.

This chapter explores how leaders can capitalise on three collaborative performance triggers:

- Establish psychological safety

- Mind your language

- Unlock discretionary effort

Psychological safety

In 1992, I started my first job in a large engineering firm. It was a traditional partnership, with a stiff, hierarchical culture. Walking the corridors as a lowly graduate engineer, the partners wouldn't catch my eye. If I had had a cap, it would have been doffed in deference. I felt I had no standing, no real voice. I knew my place. I fitted in. I gained great experience and training and achieved my chartered professional status in 1998.

I moved to a different company in 1999 and stepped into a dramatically different environment. I was working in the same area of engineering, doing similar work for the same clients. But it could not have been more different. I immediately felt at home, part of a more dynamic and ambitious team.

Both were good companies, doing similar things, but my experience was completely different. In one, I felt my voice was heard and that my opinions mattered. I had a greater stake in the business that we were building together. I felt I could be much more myself.

Google's quest to understand the perfect team

The dramatic pace of change in digital technology in a highly competitive global market demands the highest levels of collaboration from those developing new products. In 2012, Google set out to determine the 'secret sauce' of high team performance as reported on in depth by Charles Duhigg in 2016.[16] Why did some teams soar, achieving remarkable results, whilst others failed to meet expectations? What was it about the make-up of teams – their personalities, habits and behaviours – that determined the likelihood of high performance? Their study was extensive. They examined the dynamics of multiple Google teams and reviewed fifty years of academic research on team performance.

The initial hypothesis was that the team composition and structure are the key determinants of performance. Getting the right blend of skills, educational background and personalities was assumed to be the critical factor. But Google's researchers failed to validate this hypothesis. But they did notice certain aspects of behaviour showing up repeatedly in successful teams, common ways in which leaders and team members treated each other. Based on their observations, they identified five behavioural ingredients of high-performing teams:

1. **Psychological safety:** Team members feel safe to take risks and be vulnerable.

2. **Dependability:** Team members do what they say they will do.

3. **Structure and clarity:** Team members have clear roles, plans and goals.

4. **Meaning:** The work is important to each team member.

5. **Impact:** Team members believe their work matters and influences change.

Ultimately, Google concluded that psychological safety was the most important of these factors – indeed, it was identified as the pre-requisite for high performance.

What is psychological safety?

Psychological safety is the belief that we can share our ideas, questions and concerns without risk of punishment, humiliation or being ignored. In an environment of high psychological safety, we feel comfortable expressing ourselves and taking risks. We bring our entire selves to work. As with other precious commodities such as trust or reputation, it takes conscious leadership effort over a prolonged period to create psychological safety. It is the work of moments to damage or destroy it.

Psychologically *unsafe* environments are characterised by blame. By a lack of constructive challenge. People keep their heads below the parapet. It's not a great place to be and many people spend too much of their careers in such environments, never knowing any alternative.

When I attended Harvard Business School in 2008, I was inspired by the teaching of Professor Amy Edmondson. Amy presented case studies regarding senior team decision-making and organisational learning. We discussed the Cuban Missile Crisis, the disastrous expeditions on Mount Everest in 1996, the Columbia Space Shuttle tragedy. We discussed learning from medical mistakes in children's hospitals and knowledge sharing in global corporates. Psychological safety – more specifically, the lack of it – was a contributing factor in each. Amy has continued to pioneer research in this area and creating psychological safety is now widely recognised as a leadership priority. According to Edmondson, psychological safety refers to an environment where individuals feel confident that they can voice their thoughts, take risks and make mistakes without fear of being punished or humiliated. It's about creating a culture where open communication and mutual respect are the norms, enabling team members to learn and grow together.[17]

I ask teams I work with if they have heard of psychological safety. Some people have. Many haven't, yet quickly embrace the concept. When I ask them to list things in their organisation that reduce or increase psychological safety, they can come up with lots of examples, some of which are presented below.

Examples of things that reduce and increase psychological safety

Reduces psychological safety	Increases psychological safety
Micromanagement	Volunteering to help
Assigning tasks without discussion and agreement	Trusting people to do their work
Lack of face-to-face communication	Interacting in smaller groups
Gossip and office 'politics'	Active listening and really understanding what people say
Meetings called by the boss with no clear objective and/or no agenda	A little humour
Dismissing feedback, alternative views or opinions	Seeking feedback, recognising effort and saying 'thank you'
Leaders fail to address poor or non-collaborative behaviour	Collaborative behaviour is reinforced and problematic behaviour is promptly addressed

Whether they know the term or not, people know what gets in their way – and what they should be doing.

CASE STUDY: A tale of two teams

According to Professor Amy Edmondson, the level of psychological safety in a team or workplace can be gauged with a specific set of questions, asked in a way that allows people to feel safe enough to give their honest opinions.[18] Anonymity, confidentiality and independence are critical. I have used this approach with many teams. In one example, I was tasked with improving the performance of two teams working together closely in a utility company. The process revealed shockingly different levels of psychological safety. In one team, people felt supported and listened to, by their peers as well as the team leader. In the other, there was mistrust and confusion, along with fear of 'stepping out of line'. Through a set of facilitated discussions, we confronted the issues that the data revealed, which enabled appropriate changes to be implemented.

Psychological safety, or the lack of it, is often 'local', related to individual teams and working relationships, rather than consistent across an organisation.

The catastrophic implications of low psychological safety

There are many examples in which low psychological safety has contributed to disaster. As well as space mission failures there have been plane crashes and oil rig explosions. For an extreme example of a psychologically unsafe environment, watch the first episode of the 2019 dramatisation of the Chernobyl nuclear disaster.[19] The atmosphere and behaviours in the plant control room portray an extreme culture of control and fear. As they initiate a planned system pressure test, the operatives immediately know that something is not right. But they simply cannot find a way to communicate this to the plant leadership: the hierarchy is concrete and absolute, allowing no challenge from the lower ranks. The plant culture reflects the culture of the Soviet state at that time: unquestioning of authority, with zero flexibility to deal with a rapidly deteriorating situation. Even when it becomes clear that the reactor has suffered a cataclysmic explosion, the hierarchical environment remains rigid and inflexible. Decisions are escalated to Moscow, rather than being made by the people on the ground with access to the facts. The system fights to protect the reputations of individual leaders, delaying rather than expediating critical decisions, such as that to evacuate the surrounding area.

Thankfully, such disastrous outcomes are rare. Even when workplaces are not overtly toxic and causing emotional harm, there are critical moments when people have the potential to contribute things of real value, yet may choose not to, feeling uncomfortable and exposed. Performance can suffer as much from missed opportunities as from mistakes or poor decisions. Below are some examples of potential contributions that could be made and the negative implications if they are not.

The implications of withheld contributions

Potential contribution	Implication of not making the contribution
Asking a question in a meeting	Knowledge that could benefit the entire group is not shared
Pointing out a minor safety related issue	The issue remains unaddressed and contributes to a major safety incident

Potential contribution	Implication of not making the contribution
Highlighting a problem	Risk of an incident or project failure
Admitting to a mistake	The issue is not rectified and there is no shared learning
Saying 'I don't know'	Creates unrealistic expectations and future problems
Offering an idea or alternative solution	Missed opportunity for innovation or a better way forward
Challenging a decision	Either strengthens the understanding of the decision or creates potential for a better approach
Sharing something personal	Others don't understand the context within which you are working
Requesting assistance	Risk of overwork or of making mistakes
Saying 'no' to a request	Risk of taking on too much work and potential for burn out

As you can see, the implications of these withheld contributions are potentially significant. It requires a degree of courage to make these contributions as, in the moment, the contributor is at risk. The reaction of others, particularly the leaders, if and when they do so, will determine whether this behaviour is repeated. If they are shot down, that is the last time they will bring anything up. If they are actively listened to and thanked for their contribution, they will make more. Others will observe the positive consequences of these actions and will follow suit.

I love how the cartoon below shows that risk and fear are *subjective*. Dependent on context and mindset. What you consider to be playful fun seems like an unacceptable, life-threatening risk to another.

As the   As the   As the
father sees   child sees   mother sees

Consider the airborne baby as representing the decision to speak up to make a critical contribution. The leader sees the situation as the father sees the baby's

trajectory: low risk. Others share the mother's perception: 'high risk, I'll keep my mouth shut.'

CASE STUDY: Low psychological safety – 'The vanishing manager'

During a client engagement, I was working closely with
a mid-level manager. Peter (not his real name) was well
known. He was proficient in a critical IT system, having
been intimately involved with its implementation.
One day, I tried to contact Peter and was not able to
get hold of him. Later, another team member told me,
'Peter's gone.' She had found out, quite by chance, that
Peter had 'left' the organisation, effective immediately.
We needed to carry on without him. There was no
announcement; no formal communication of any kind.
I never did find out what actually happened. There
was some whispered speculation. The crack in the ice
that Peter had fallen through closed quickly, leaving no
trace, and Peter was never mentioned again. Everyone
kept their heads down, seeking to avoid the same fate.

CASE STUDY: High psychological safety – multi-organisational working group

A former colleague shared an experience of participating
in an industry working group, the success of which was
helped by a high level of psychological safety. The group
comprised leaders from public utilities, regulators and
private companies and was charged with developing
a common approach to the planning of investment in
a specific area. The industry dynamic was challenging,
as the organisations were effectively in competition

with each other. The working group could easily have mirrored these dynamics, but the chairperson did several things to address this, including:

- Creating a sense of the urgency for the change
- Building a shared vision and making it clear how this aligned with widely shared goals relating to improving customer service and caring for the environment
- Setting out how this could only be achieved through wide collaboration of group members
- Ensuring that all working group members had a chance to share and discuss their opinions and perspective on key matters
- Allowing time for informal discussions before and after the group meetings, to encourage group members to get to know each other
- Seeking and exploring dissenting opinions rather than rushing to move forward with their own view or that of the majority

The result was an active and engaged group that co-created a new industry approach that has been widely praised as innovative and forward-thinking. Key members even delayed their retirement to participate, citing the experience as a career highlight.

Belonging versus fitting in – Charlie's story

Are your people able to be themselves at work? Do they feel they belong? Or are they doing what they need to do to 'fit in'? A story from Charlie (not their real name), a senior executive leader, unfortunately encapsulates how many people are made to feel in large organisations.

> 'I have often been in environments in which the senior leaders are all saying the right things regarding equality, diversity and inclusion. By definition, what they are saying implies that being 'different' (or thinking differently) should be encouraged, celebrated and cultivated. Yet, on several occasions in my career as a senior manager and director I have had other senior people tell me, "You're very different." Somewhat naively at first, I thought this was a good thing, but on each subsequent occasion with each new role, the same words would make my heart sink. I knew that what they were really telling me was, "We don't know what to do with you, how to manage you or how to incorporate your ideas." I have come to recognise this one-sided conversation as the precursor to the inevitable end of my time with that team or organisation. I have often felt like a fish swimming upstream against a tidal wave of conformity – being on my own is exhausting.'

I have known Charlie for many years and greatly respect their determination to 'swim upstream' and refusal to simply mould behaviour to what was expected. In reflective conversation with Charlie,

I recognised that for many years of corporate life I too had been unconsciously adapting my behaviour and repressing aspects of my nature in order to fit in.

Great leaders recognise that psychological safety starts and ends with them. A psychologically safe environment cannot exist without the leader consciously and visibly speaking and acting in a way that frames, models and reinforces what is expected. Discrepancies between a leader's statements and their actual behaviour are glaringly visible. Psychological safety is hard won, requiring consistent effort over time, but can be lost quickly with one wrong move.

Psychological safety is fundamentally driven by leaders actively listening to their people. This may not come naturally. At times of challenge, it is all too easy to slip back into default behaviours. A leader who recognises and then apologises for their own transgressions provides a powerful reinforcement of what is expected.

Mind your language

In 1992, my move from Northern Ireland to Glasgow revealed the profound impact of the Troubles on my early life. I was raised in relative safety, yet the culture of fear and silence had shaped me at a deep level. Adhering to the unspoken rule of 'Whatever you say,

say nothing,' I avoided discussions on religion or politics. It was only with distance that I understood this culture's influence on me. This experience underscores the subtle, yet powerful ways environments shape our behaviours and beliefs, highlighting the importance of awareness and dialogue in overcoming ingrained cultural norms.

I have been in work environments with similar dynamics, where silence is protective. Words are weapons. Certain topics are off-limits. This story typifies. A team meeting is held online and the leader speaks for two thirds of the meeting, simply transmitting information and issuing instructions. They ask, 'Who doesn't get it?' Silence. 'Any questions?' Silence. 'Great meeting, everyone.' And that's that. No discussion, let alone dissent or constructive challenge. Perhaps you have been in similar meetings?

Look who's talking

Everyone will have had experience of negative feelings associated with an ineffective meeting or group interaction. Frustration at not been listened to. Exasperation at one person, often the most senior, dominating the airtime. Lack of meaningful progress, despite lots being said. Conversely, some meetings feel incredibly balanced, engaging and effective. Carrying out a simple analysis of who says what in meetings can be revealing of the dynamics causing these feelings.

Meetings can swing between frustration with one-sided dominance to the constructive harmony of balanced engagement based on who speaks and how much. Analysing meeting dynamics offers insightful revelations into the root causes of our most profound meeting experiences, both negative and positive. To gain these insights for yourself, invite an observer to one of your meetings and ask them to record:

- Who is speaking? For how long?

- What is the nature of what is being said? Are people proposing new ideas? Are they building on what had been said? Are they disagreeing with a position? Are they simply broadcasting information that could have been shared beforehand?

The results will be revealing, as for this leadership team meeting that I observed where:

- The share of voice was dominated by the leader, who spoke for 40% of the time. There were eight people in the meeting.

- There were four people who each spoke for less than 5% of the meeting. One person said absolutely nothing.

- Over 80% of the 'discussion' was simply transmitting information, despite the purpose of the meeting being to shape the future team direction. Only 10% of the discussion related to proposing and building on new ideas and concepts.

This simple analysis helped explain why team members were feeling frustrated with a lack of progress. They were using their precious time together to exchange information that could easily have been shared offline. The leader was able to see objective data regarding just how much he was dominating the airtime and the negative consequences this was having.

Perhaps not surprisingly, I've found share of voice to be a strong predictor of hierarchy: the most senior person often says the most. Those at the lowest levels of the organisational structure say little or nothing at all. This poses a challenge for teams seeking to collaborate and innovate, as performance depends on the collective wisdom of all involved. Ensuring that everyone's voice is heard is also key to avoiding disastrous mistakes.

If you are a leader who genuinely wants to hear from everyone in a group (many don't), you can try this exercise. First, ask everyone to consider the matter at hand individually, without talking, and write down their perspective, viewpoint, position, questions etc. Then ask them to share what they have written with the group. Ask the most junior and least 'dominant' people to go first, and share your perspective as leader last.

Collaborative language

'We tried that before.' Have you ever been stopped in your tracks by such a statement? Your motivation killed with just four words. Seemingly neutral comments can be loaded with passive aggressive, negative intent. Steep power gradients heighten the impact of such statements. Other examples include:

- 'That sounds like a good idea, if you can get some budget.'

- 'That's very interesting, but I'm not sure talking about this now is the best use of our time.'

- 'Could we have a quick show of hands to see who is siding with Garry on this suggestion?'

- 'You've not worked here very long, have you?'

- 'Good luck with that.'

No doubt you will have examples of your own. Listen out for these statements. Recognise the feelings of frustration and deflation they trigger. Step away from the motivation killer, re-engage with your idea and don't let the spark go out. Try another way. It's not easy, but it's important. It could make all the difference.

The greater challenge is to mind your *own* language. To remove these weapons of mass demotivation from your vocabulary. Are your words adding energy and building motivation? Or killing it? How would you know? We must actively listen to ourselves as well as to others.

Here are some examples of unhelpful language patterns:

- **Dismissive responses:** Saying something like, 'We've already tried that, and it didn't work' immediately shuts down new ideas. It discourages innovation and signals that past failures are more significant than future possibilities.

- **Undermining questions:** Asking, 'Do you really think that's a good idea?' can sow doubt and undermine confidence. It may imply that the idea or the person proposing it is not competent.

- **Sarcastic remarks:** Comments like 'Great, another groundbreaking idea' can belittle and embarrass, creating a hostile environment where people are afraid to speak up.

By contrast, here are some helpful language patterns:

- **Encouraging exploration:** Instead of shutting down ideas, saying something like, 'That's an interesting perspective; how can we build on that?' encourages further thinking and values contribution.

- **Affirming contributions:** Simple acknowledgements like, 'I appreciate you bringing this up, it's a valuable point' validate someone's input, fostering a culture where contributions are recognised and valued.

- **Open-ended questions:** Asking, 'What led you to this conclusion?' instead of making assumptions invites explanation and discussion, promoting a deeper understanding and respect for different viewpoints.

Further collaborative language strategies include:

- **Active listening:** Demonstrate through your responses that you have genuinely listened to the speaker's ideas or concerns. This can be as simple as summarising their points before providing feedback, showing that you recognise their input.

- **Use 'Yes, and…':** This improvisational comedy technique is a powerful tool. Instead of saying 'but', which negates what was said before, 'yes, and' acknowledges the previous point and adds to it, fostering a collaborative atmosphere.

- **Focus on solutions:** When discussing challenges or issues, steer the conversation towards solutions rather than dwelling on problems. Questions such as, 'What would it take to address this?' encourage positive, forward-thinking dialogue.

- **Personalise acknowledgement:** Tailor your acknowledgement to the individual's contribution, showing that you recognise their unique input. For example, 'The way you analysed that data provided us with insights we hadn't considered before' is more impactful than a generic 'thank you'.

Unlock discretionary effort

Have you ever been in a workplace where almost everyone has left for home within a few minutes of the earliest time they are allowed to? Alternatively, have you experienced a workplace in which people put in extra effort, not because they *must*, but because they *want* to? The difference between the worker behaviour in these two workplaces is 'discretionary effort'. Aubrey Daniels defines discretionary effort as 'that level of effort that people could give if they wanted to, but which is beyond what is required'.[20] It is given willingly and, by definition, there are no negative consequences for not giving it.

It is entirely up to each individual whether they want to contribute discretionary effort, or simply do what is required or expected. This is not to be confused with people putting in extra effort due to specific circumstances, for example to meet a deadline or so as not to leave the workplace before the boss does.

Great leaders will recognise the significant opportunity associated with creating an environment in which people give more effort than they are required to. As people are choosing to make additional effort, they must find it meaningful, enjoyable or positively reinforcing in some way, resulting in increased motivation and better performance.

Managers are often satisfied to simply get what is expected from their people. They put in place policies and procedures to ensure that the minimum that needs to be done is done. They miss the opportunity to shape the work environment in a way that influences people's choice as to whether to offer or withhold discretionary effort. They fail to recognise the power of positive reinforcement.

The power of positive reinforcement

The concept of 'positive reinforcement' can conjure up images of pats on the back, high fives and other cringeworthy management efforts. This narrow perspective undervalues the massive power of positive reinforcement for influencing any desired behaviour.

Positive reinforcement is any consequence that follows a behaviour and increases its frequency in the future. In other words, it occurs when an individual does something or exhibits a certain behaviour and gains a favourable outcome, event or reward. This contrasts with negative reinforcement, whereby people behave in ways that ensure that they avoid a consequence that they don't want. Below are some examples of positive and negative reinforcement.

Positive and negative reinforcement

Positive reinforcement	Negative reinforcement
A treat given to a dog as a reward for walking to heel	Dog owner stops holding leash tightly when the dog walks to heel
Taking a child to the playground after they have tidied their room	Child puts toys away in the right place to avoid being told off
Receiving a standing ovation following a concert performance	Travelling slower than a police car on the motorway to avoid being pulled over
Being promoted for successfully completing a major project	Working late on a task to avoid being reprimanded for missing a deadline
Being thanked for doing a task well	Ticking the boxes in the quality procedures to avoid issues in an audit

The difference in impact between positive and negative reinforcement is stark and significant. In an environment characterised by positive reinforcement, people *choose* to do more of certain behaviours. This leads to discretionary effort and an associated increase in motivation and performance. In environments characterised by negative reinforcement, people tend to do the minimum required – they do just enough of the behaviour to avoid the negative consequence of not doing it.

I spent several months on a consulting project with a large corporate organisation and experienced the negative reinforcement ingrained in their organisational culture first-hand. On arrival, I asked people for their perspective on the workplace environment. Many spoke in glowing terms about how friendly everyone was, how the terms and conditions of employment were both generous and supportive in areas such as parental leave, pension contributions and so on. Indeed, one of the organisation's stated values related specifically to putting 'people first'. But after a period immersed in the organisation it became clear that the culture was primarily characterised by fear, blame and negative reinforcement. People would do what they needed to do to meet the requirements of their roles, keeping their heads down and trying as hard as possible to avoid the blame and recrimination that would inevitably follow any problem. People were overloaded, morale was low and the level of performance was not where it needed to be.

Upon leaving, I reflected that many people perhaps didn't realise how aversive the culture was. They had spent most of their working years there. They did what they needed to do to survive in an organisation that was doing them a real disservice. Unfortunately, these dynamics reflect the working environment of many corporate organisations.

On a more positive note, I have also been in teams that have achieved high levels of performance in environments fuelled by positive reinforcement. As a young manager, I was responsible for a market segment of a regional business unit. The unit was growing quickly in a competitive market. I was part of the leadership team, in one of my first senior leadership roles. The unit leader adopted a challenging but supportive approach, encouraging us to push forward, to try new things and take complete ownership of our individual areas. There was no micromanagement. No apportioning of blame when things did not go to plan. Our successes were rewarded with encouragement and potential for advancement. In turn, each of the leadership team members were incredibly supportive of each other. We discussed and learned from the things that didn't go to plan. It was often challenging, but we were energised by the environment and having fun. The leader, whether consciously or not, positively reinforced the behaviours which drove significant success.

Applying positive reinforcement

Leaders can easily learn to use positive reinforcement to unlock the discretionary effort of their people. Through a deliberate approach to planning and implementing the right consequences for specific behaviours, they can drive collaborative performance. A few key things to consider are:

- **Pay attention.** Show people that you are interested in and value what they are doing. This is a simple yet underused way to achieve positive reinforcement. Just like children and pets, employees suffer if they receive zero attention from their 'superiors' (managers, owners, bosses). Saying 'thank you' is free and has perhaps the highest return on investment of any leadership activity.

- **Make it individual.** Effective positive reinforcement is different for everyone. Some people love to be openly praised in group meetings. For introverts (like me), a quiet conversation would be much more comfortable. Taking the trouble to understand what people need, rather than making assumptions, pays dividends.

- **Capitalise on relationships.** Strong working relationships between peers are inherently reinforcing. As social beings, we are evolutionarily wired to collaborate. Doing so successfully will automatically lead to people wanting to do it more. As a leader, modelling and fostering effective working relationships builds the collaborative foundation.

- **Try things and learn what works.** Rather than engaging in detailed consultation, analysis and planning, simply attempt to empathise with individuals in their roles. Try something that you think might work and observe the result. If the behaviour you want increases, you will know you have positively reinforced it. If not, try something else.

- **Bribery and rewards are not positive reinforcement.** Be careful not to confuse other forms of extrinsic incentive with positive reinforcement. Bribery is something offered in the context of a problem behaviour, to attempt to influence behaviour in the moment – for example, offering a child an ice cream to try to stop a tantrum. This may stop the behaviour in the short term, but the approach can be problematic: the child now knows exactly how to get an ice cream.

The home environment can be a good arena for leaders to test ideas for influencing desired behaviour through positive reinforcement. My daughter plays the saxophone, attending weekly lessons, at which it is clear to her teacher whether she has put in enough practice to maintain her progress. I realised that, as parents, our default method of influencing the desired behaviour – regular practice – was to nag. This is negative reinforcement. My daughter would only do the minimum amount of practice required to stop the nagging. We experimented with a few other ideas. My daughter loves to play her saxophone late at night, as if she is playing in a jazz club. Rather than nagging parents, we became her audience. She finds this both relaxing and conducive to concentration, regularly playing for far longer than the 'expected' minimum. She *enjoys* it. Her practice is positively reinforced in a way that works for her.

Our nagging was the default, ineffective 'leadership' behaviour. This is analogous to how some leaders attempt to cajole the behaviour they want from their people. They instruct. They berate. They micromanage. But through a considered, individualised approach to creating positive reinforcement, it is possible for leaders to transform the behaviour of their people.

Consider your own approach. How can you increase the level of positive reinforcement you give your team? Your family? Yourself?

Chapter takeaways

- **Establish psychological safety:** Psychological safety is foundational for high-performing teams, allowing people to take risks without fear of humiliation or retribution, fostering an environment where innovative ideas can thrive. To create it, actively work to build an open, trusting environment where you encourage candid feedback, admit mistakes and learn from each other. Regularly assess the level of psychological safety within your team through anonymous surveys or facilitated discussions to identify areas for improvement.

- **Mind your language:** The language used within teams can significantly impact psychological safety and, by extension, collaborative performance. Negative or dismissive language can stifle innovation and engagement, so monitor and adjust your communication style to ensure it is inclusive and encouraging. Ask for opinions from quieter or lower-level team members first and never shut down ideas, comments or constructive challenges: say 'Yes... and...'.

- **Unlock discretionary effort:** The effort team members choose to give beyond what is required is a key indicator of engagement and motivation. Individualised positive reinforcement can significantly increase this kind of effort, so acknowledge achievements and provide opportunities for professional growth. Experiment to find what works best and continuously adapt your approach. Say 'thank you'.

- **Exemplify:** Leaders play the crucial role in establishing a 'fearless' environment. Discrepancies between a leader's statements and their actions can undermine psychological safety and trust, so consistently model the behaviours you wish to see in your team. This includes being open about your own mistakes, actively listening and visibly supporting team members' efforts and ideas.

FIVE
Adaptive

S uccessful species are those that can adapt. They learn from and morph with their environments to survive and thrive. This relentless adaptation, so crucial in the natural world, has parallel implications for enterprises, organisations and teams. Unlike the gradual progress of natural selection, the organisational landscape demands immediate and deliberate adaptation processes. Real-time situational awareness of both internal and external dynamics is critical for growth, innovation and resilience against threats.

Leaders are the architects of this organisational evolution. Their role transcends mere oversight; they become the facilitators of understanding, learning and adaptation. By delving deep into the sub-surface currents shaping their organisations, leaders unearth insights that are otherwise hidden. They champion the cause of enterprise learning, encouraging a culture in which knowledge flows freely. Resistance to change, often a formidable adversary, is met with empathy and addressed with tact, turning potential obstacles into steppingstones towards organisational resilience.

This adaptive approach is not just about survival; it's about thriving in the face of perpetual change. Great leaders cultivate environments where learning is continuous, change is embraced and adaptation is swift, ensuring that their organisations, much like the most resilient species in the wild, not only survive but flourish.

This chapter explores how leaders can:

- Understand what's *really* going on

- Cultivate learning and knowledge sharing

- Understand and address resistance to change

Find out what's *really* going on

As a leader, do you know what's going on in your team? Not what they tell you, but what's *really* going on? How would you know? Do you really *want* to know?

An executive recently shared with me her experience of working with her new CEO. The CEO had asked the team to keep him informed of critical issues and challenges, but when one team member shared a particularly thorny issue, the CEO berated him. The rest of the team observed this and kept quiet. Now the CEO only hears what the team think they want to hear. This all too common dynamic persists even when leaders receive 'bad news' in a positive manner.

A leader should be able to trust their team to be honest with them. But people often hold back in group settings, afraid to speak up, worried about what their colleagues will think and concerned about the consequences of what they reveal. Even in environments high in psychological safety, there is almost always a degree of filtering and political spin on the 'truth' that is presented to leaders. Leaders should make a working assumption that they are not receiving a full and accurate picture. To get to the *whole* truth needs their extra effort – collecting and cross-checking data, gathering feedback and asking powerful questions.

The power of anonymous data

By providing safe and anonymous ways for people to share their thoughts and feelings, leaders can tap into a deeper level of insight that might otherwise be hidden. Surveys are a great place to start. They allow the collection of a lot of data, quickly and easily, and the results can be used to identify trends and patterns. For example, if you ask people to rate their level of satisfaction with their job, you might discover that a particular team is consistently scoring lower than the rest of the organisation: a red flag that something is amiss.

But even with anonymous surveys, there can be suspicion and reticence. Many organisations carry out regular 'engagement' type surveys. Often, these are not trusted to be completely anonymous and confidential. People assume, reasonably in most instances, that they could be identified by the specifics of what they share. The response rates reflect this mistrust.

Using an independent third party can help. I often play this role, gathering perspectives from team members and sharing key findings in ways that ensure individual confidentiality. I often use surveys. Of course, these have limitations: they can be superficial and it's not always easy to interpret the data. That's where one-on-one interviews come in. By sitting down with team members individually, I can get a deeper understanding of their perspectives and experiences.

When conducting such interviews, it's important to create a safe and welcoming environment. Let people know that their feedback is valued and that you're genuinely interested in hearing their thoughts. Ask open-ended questions. Listen more than you talk. Resist the urge to be defensive or dismissive if someone shares something you don't want to hear.

One benefit of interviews is that they allow you to follow up on survey data. For example, if the survey indicates that people feel like they don't have enough opportunities for professional development, you can ask them to elaborate. You might discover that they're specifically interested in learning more about a particular area or that they feel like their manager isn't providing enough support.

Increase feedback intensity

We love to use sports analogies to inspire better business performance. Comparing our collaborative efforts to Formula 1 pit crews or Premier League football teams is compelling and fun. But there is a critical difference between such elite environments and the typical business team. The salience and immediacy of feedback are orders of magnitude greater than in typical workplaces. Every technical, physiological and psychological factor is measured, analysed and worked on, and the results are immediately clear. This fast iteration and learning drives performance.

Construction sites and operational facilities offer tangible and immediate feedback on many aspects of their status and performance. Real things are happening in real time. Concrete is being poured. Widgets are being attached to other widgets. Skilled site agents and operational managers can intuitively 'feel' how things are going and take immediate action when necessary. It's different in office-based, knowledge- and professional expertise-based organisations. It is much harder to get clear, real-time, shared perspectives on progress and performance. The post-pandemic hybrid working environment has exacerbated this disconnect. Results may not be visible for months. In many organisations, people receive feedback once a year – the dreaded performance appraisal – so opportunities for learning and improvement are late or lost altogether.

'Let me give you some feedback,' is not a phrase that's commonly heard. When it is, the reaction is often a reluctant wince. We know we need it – we just don't want it. 'Please give *me* some feedback' is even rarer. Here are some things that I have found help to increase the quality and usefulness of feedback:

- Recognise the importance of giving feedback on both *performance* and *behaviour*. The basic behaviours of a functional environment described in Chapter 3 are a good place to start.

- Pick a simple model for giving feedback and stick with it. Which model you choose is less

important than your commitment to using it.
I like the AID model:

- Action(s): The specific action that led to the
  feedback being delivered. 'You were three days
  late in sending this piece of information that
  the client requested.'

- Impact: The implications of the specific action,
  for whom. 'This meant that the client could not
  complete their report to the board on time.'

- Do/do differently: Explain what needs to be
  done or done differently in the future. 'Please
  ensure you provide client information on
  time or contact them immediately if there is
  potential for delay.'

- Balance *positive* with *developmental* (rather than
  negative) feedback. Pointing out an action
  that had a good impact is massive positive
  reinforcement. 'When you were concise and to
  the point in that meeting you came across very
  well to the client. Please, keep it up.'

- Be aware of the fine line between feedback
  and criticism. A former colleague used to say,
  'Criticism is a gift.' He was most generous with
  his 'gifts'. The problem is that criticism is, by
  definition, negative. It implies failure and infers
  blame. It is focused on the past rather than
  improving the future.

- To build up your confidence, start small and share feedback on individual actions, comments or behaviours.

- Most importantly, for leaders: seek feedback on your own behaviour and performance. Whatever feedback you get, say 'thank you'.

James, a business partner of mine, shared this story as an example of important feedback, delivered terribly. As a young board member, he was keen to make an impression. In particular, he would make a conscious effort to speak up in board meetings. During one meeting, as he began to speak, the chair slammed the table. 'James, would you ever shut the [expletive] up?' Rather shocked, James did. 'The problem with you, James, is that when you have something in your head you feel you *must* say it. Often, the conversation has moved on. Or someone else just made the same point. It can be frustrating and distracting for everyone.' Of course, this public reprimand exemplifies exactly the wrong way to give feedback. The chair apologised after the meeting for how the feedback was delivered, trying again: 'James, you often make contributions that are out of context for where meetings have moved to.' (Action) 'This can take the meeting off course and make others feel frustrated.' (Impact) 'Please consider the timing of your contributions. It may be better to wait for the end of the meeting or pick up issues offline.' (Do differently) James said, 'Thank you.'

Ask powerful questions

For me, one of the most important – and liberating – leadership lessons is: leaders do not need to *know everything*. Early in my leadership journey, I made the mistake of thinking that I had to have all the answers. It was up to me to know what a client's principal challenges were. To understand every aspect of any problem. To always know what to do next. Over time, I came to understand the limitations of this ego-driven mistake. I realised that one of the most critical tools for a leader, or a consultant, is asking great questions. *Powerful* questions. You know you have asked a powerful question when the other person stops in their tracks and has to really think. They don't have a prepared response. Their answer is enlightening for both of you and the discussion moves to another level. Here are some examples of powerful questions I have found useful:

- What are we not seeing?

- What assumptions are we making?

- What if our assumptions are wrong?

- What if someone in our team has something important to share, yet is too afraid or embarrassed to do so?

- What might be the unintended consequences of this course of action?

- What is the evidence to suggest we are wrong?

- How does this approach align with our values?

- What will we stop doing?

- What would it take to ensure that this is a success?

Jeff Wetzler suggests, 'questions are the world's most powerful and underutilised all-purpose, everyday learning tool.'[21] In a situation where opinions differ and emotions run strong, Jeff Wetzler advises that you ask *yourself*, 'how does *their* story/position/action make sense to *them*?'

All of the above are open-ended questions: they cannot be answered with a simple 'yes' or 'no'. Using powerful questions to best effect takes preparation and practice; there needs to be a relationship of openness and trust. Used well, they increase trust and connection. Powerful questions demonstrate curiosity; they are non-judgemental; they empower and build confidence in the way forward.

Cultivate learning and knowledge sharing

As the saying goes, 'Knowledge is power' – and you can multiply that power by sharing it. In a world increasingly defined by the speed of change and the complexity of new challenges, the capacity of teams and organisations to not just acquire, but rapidly share and apply knowledge, becomes the linchpin of innovation and success. This ethos stands in stark contrast to environments where knowledge is hoarded, wielded as a tool for individual advantage, rather than a shared asset. The transformation from a culture of competitive gatekeeping to one of collaborative knowledge sharing isn't just beneficial, it's essential for career advancement and organisational vitality.

Innovation, at its core, is the art of applying 'new knowledge' – new, that is, at the point of application, even if it originates from disparate contexts or geographies. The transfer and application of knowledge not only fuels innovation but ensures the organisation remains agile and resilient in the face of evolving challenges. It is this shared quest for knowledge, leveraged collectively, that distinguishes truly revolutionary teams and organisations from mere assemblies of individuals.

How do we know what we know?

Most organisations, most of the time, have access to the knowledge and capability to tackle the challenges they face. It's in there, somewhere, hidden within reach. The challenge is to find it and apply it to the point of need, at the right time.

For many years I was involved with knowledge management (KM) for a global technical organisation, initially as a participant and ultimately as the executive responsible for the ongoing development and implementation of the KM strategy. This was one of the most rewarding journeys of my professional career.

What exactly is knowledge management? How is it possible to 'manage' knowledge, when most of it resides inside people's heads? A useful definition of KM proposed by Girard and Girard is: 'the process of creating, sharing, using and managing the knowledge and information of an organisation'.[22]

Increasingly, we are working in 'enterprise' arrangements involving multiple organisations collaborating to achieve outcomes. For example, infrastructure programmes in the UK may involve many of the largest global engineering consultancies, multiple 'Tier 1' construction companies and any number of specialist suppliers. As each organisation connects into the enterprise, the knowledge and learning potential increase exponentially. The challenge is to tap into this. The client organisation, in theory, has access to all the knowledge and learning residing within this far-reaching enterprise. For any challenge faced, someone, somewhere in the enterprise will have tackled something similar and thus has a potentially valuable contribution to make. A successful solution; a painful lesson learned; a key risk to be managed; a particular critical expertise. This is all knowledge, with the potential to be shared to add value in some way. The issue is not whether such knowledge exists, it is how it can be located, shared and applied when it is needed.

A few definitions are useful at this point:

- **Individual knowledge** comprises facts, information and skills acquired through experience and education.

- **Enterprise knowledge** is the sum of all the knowledge contained within the enterprise that can provide value in support of achieving outcomes.

Individual knowledge, and by extension enterprise knowledge, can be *explicit*, *implicit* or *tacit*.

- **Explicit knowledge** can be articulated, written down, communicated and stored. Data sheets, reports, research papers and numerical analyses are all examples of explicit knowledge.

- **Implicit knowledge** is generated by the practical application of explicit knowledge. Examples include methods of working, best practices and specific skills that can be demonstrated, shared and transferred for application by others.

- **Tacit knowledge** is generated and refined through personal experience and context and is the hardest form to articulate, capture and share. Master practitioners of any discipline develop a 'feel' for their craft through years of experience that cannot be written in a book or captured in a procedure. Tacit knowledge is the submerged, unseen part of the iceberg of enterprise knowledge. It is tacit knowledge that leaves the building when people retire or move to another organisation.

- **Innovation**, I like to think of as the practical application of 'new' knowledge. It is new at the point of application, as it may have been successfully applied in a different context, sector or country.

Of the above types, only explicit knowledge has the potential to be captured and separated from the people in an enterprise. Until technology advances to be capable of downloading the entire contents of our brains, we must rely on relationships and interactions between *people* to learn and share knowledge effectively. The behavioural aspects are as important as the system- and process-related aspects of an enterprise-wide learning and knowledge-sharing strategy, if not more so.

In the table below are some examples of ways in which different forms of knowledge can be 'managed', based on the work of Nick Milton.[23]

Example attributes of an enterprise approach to learning, managing and sharing knowledge

	Explicit knowledge	Implicit knowledge	Tacit knowledge
Systems	Data and information storage systems	Communication technologies	

	Explicit knowledge	Implicit knowledge	Tacit knowledge
Processes	After-action reviews Questionnaires/surveys Audits Checklists	Structured training programmes Project processes to plan and learn from previous projects	Apprenticeships Mentoring Masterclasses Succession planning Industry conferences
People and behaviours	Asking and responding to questions	Presentations and demonstrations	Collaborative working relationships
	People, networks and communities responsible for capturing, communicating and sharing knowledge		
	Roles, career paths and key processes with specific behavioural expectations relating to learning and knowledge sharing		
	A culture of enterprise learning and knowledge sharing (ie, a high-performing collaborative environment)		

Detailing the process of crafting and executing a comprehensive enterprise KM strategy is beyond the scope of this book. Critical though, is the recognition that such a strategy is fundamentally *behavioural*. Sophisticated data-management systems and business processes alone cannot achieve enterprise-wide learning and knowledge sharing. What is needed is an environment in which the right behaviours are modelled, reinforced and are ultimately career enhancing.

Knowledge sharing is career enhancing

At the heart of a transformative approach to enterprise learning and knowledge sharing is a simple shift in people's perspectives from 'knowledge is power' to 'knowledge sharing is career enhancing'.

In many, if not most, organisational cultures the natural tendency can be to keep our knowledge to ourselves. By doing so we may feel we are maintaining our advantage over others, with whom the culture has put us in competition. We are also limiting the risk of negative feedback, or even ridicule, associated with potentially being proved wrong, inexperienced or naïve. Common organisational barriers to knowledge sharing include:

- **An environment of low psychological safety** in which the perceived risks of sharing ensure people keep what they know to themselves

- **Destructive organisational politics** leading to fears of one-upmanship, credit stealing or back-stabbing

- **It's simply too hard** – the organisational structure, processes and technology get in the way of rather than accelerating knowledge sharing

- **Lack of trusted relationships** – when we don't know people's roles, goals and needs, we don't

know how we may be able to help them, or how
they may be able to help us

- **Lack of feedback** – when we don't know how
  what we have shared has been used, the lack of
  positive reinforcement reduces the likelihood
  that we will share again

- **Lack of clarity of expectations** – it's simply
  not clear in leadership communication, role
  definition and business process that knowledge
  sharing is expected for the benefit of individuals
  and the entire organisation

Behavioural aspects of knowledge sharing

Social connectivity plays a crucial role in knowledge
sharing, as people tend to gravitate towards their
'tribes'. I have observed process engineers form their
own tight-knit community within larger engineering
organisations. Loyalty often lies more with the peer
group than with the wider organisation. Trusted social
connections are the foundation for meaningful support and knowledge exchange. Promoting such communities, or knowledge networks, can spark magic: a
'hive mind' where collective intelligence thrives and
amplifies the ability to solve problems collaboratively.

Intrinsic motivation, as discussed in Chapter 2, is the
fuel for knowledge-sharing engines. Effective knowledge communities offer individuals opportunities
to master their craft, giving them the autonomy and

support to apply their expertise for wider influence, in pursuit of meaningful purpose. Recognising and celebrating contributions to the shared knowledge pool adds a layer of extrinsic motivation, further catalysing community accomplishment.

Reciprocity is a game-changer in knowledge sharing. When people are directly approached for help, they are more likely to be open about and share their knowledge. In turn, they feel comfortable to ask when they need help, knowing support will be willingly offered. Formal knowledge management systems and processes are well and good, but sometimes a personal touch is all it takes.

Rewarded curiosity. For an organisation to thrive, it must respond to changes in its environment and then adapt. By definition this requires change. The old ways won't work indefinitely. The first step to working out how and what to change is to shift to a curious mindset. Leaders need to demonstrate and reinforce behaviours that seek to explore, ask questions and challenge the status quo.

Role definition and career paths matter. Recognising the distinct contributions of key groups (such as technologists and managers) to knowledge sharing is crucial. What are the specific behaviours for each group that enhance collective learning? How are these behaviours encouraged, reinforced and measured?

Informal connectivity – the hidden strategic asset of knowledge-based organisations

At the organisational level, knowledge sharing is a strategic asset with far-reaching implications for competitiveness, talent retention and client value. Why, then, does this asset remain hidden and its benefit unrealised in so many organisations? A simple mindset shift could help. As leaders and managers, we tend to think about the structure of our teams in the linear, clearly defined hierarchy of the classic 'org-chart'. But people don't actually work this way. We connect and build informal relationships way beyond the lines that join our 'box' to others' on the org-chart. Knowledge, ideas and support flows most effectively through the most trusted connections. I no longer appear on any org-charts, but I am highly connected within the networks of several global organisations.

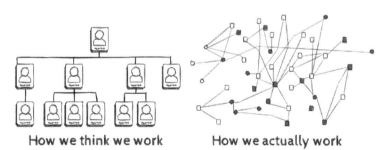

How we think we work   How we actually work

Sometimes people who are 'low' in the hierarchy of the corporate org-chart have the highest level of trusted social connectivity. They are the people you go to when you need support. They know who to connect you with. These are the people who make a knowledge-based enterprise work. Do you know who they are? What are you doing to protect and build the precious strategic asset that is the informal connectivity across your organisation? Much of what I see organisations doing under the banner of 'transformation' (particularly digital transformation) I believe threatens this hidden connectivity.

Understand and address resistance to change

As leader, I know what the team needs to do differently. That's why I'm the leader. I tell my team what to do, then the team do it. That's their job. Easy, right?

Except, of course, it's not. Leaders I work with are frustrated. They ask:

- 'Why won't they do what I tell them to do?'
- 'Why won't they follow my strategy?'
- 'Why won't they collaborate?'
- 'Why won't they change?'

Don't read this section

Anyone who has looked after children knows the frustration of them doing precisely what you have told them *not* to do. Our teenage son cracks his knuckles.

It drives my wife mad when she has just told him not to do it. If we are being honest, most of us feel an immediate adverse reaction to being told what to do. We dislike restrictions on our autonomy or freedom to choose. This 'psychological reactance'[24] leads us to action, or inaction, to attempt to regain our freedom.

It is critical for anyone seeking to initiate change to take psychological reactance into account. Issuing instructions is likely to be met with an equal and opposite reaction. This might be direct, through simply ignoring or re-interpreting the instructions, or there might be unwilling compliance combined with negative sentiment towards the leader. People can also feel this reactance in response to persuasive dialogue. Being told what we *ought* to do, *should* do or *need* to do, no matter how logical it may be, can trigger negative feelings towards the message and the messenger. Often this will strengthen resolve against *both*.

This fundamentally challenges attributes associated with leadership. 'A leader should give instructions, orders and commands. My team should just do what I say, I am the leader.' As people step up into leadership positions, it's easy to make the mistake of thinking like this. I know I did.

Why won't they change?

Leading change can be incredibly difficult, a task fraught with perils and the success of which is always uncertain. According to Niccolò Machiavelli, this is in no small part due to the fact that 'the innovator has for enemies all those who have done well under the old conditions, and lukewarm defenders in those who may do well under the new.'[25]

These words, written in the sixteenth century, encapsulate the dynamics that anyone who has been involved with leading change will have felt. There seems to be inevitable and significant resistance to *any* change, no matter how logical, beneficial or cost effective the intent. It is especially evident among those who benefited from the previous way of doing things and those for whom the proposed new way represents more risk. This resistance can manifest as obvious and even hostile intransigence, which is pretty easy to identify, but in many cases it shows up as quiet, passive inertia. People agree, nod, smile and simply do nothing, telling themselves, 'This too shall pass.'

You may have experienced the positive energy associated with the early stages of a new initiative, applying concepts learned at a training event or innovative ideas for a new way of working. Those involved are fired up, with genuine intentions to implement the changes and then... *absolutely nothing happens.*

Resistance to digital technology

I have observed an unlikely resistance among technical people to change involving digital technology.

Industries such as utilities and manufacturing must continually improve the efficiency of their systems to remain competitive. They describe how they need to move from being reactive to being proactive and even predictive. Instead of waiting for a problem, then rushing to fix it, they need to get ahead of the game. Where is the system operating sub-optimally? What component will fail next? Digital technology is at the heart of this. As with weather forecasting, the combination of historic and real-time data and analysis using AI generates increasingly accurate predictions of what will happen next. It seems obvious that this technology will be jumped on by the system operators, right? Perhaps not.

I have heard versions of the same story from many different people involved in developing such AI-driven solutions, where they get an opportunity to run a 'pilot' on an element of the system to prove its effectiveness.

'That's not how we do things round here!'

The issue is that *this is not how things are done round here*. Operators respond to problems and fix things. They know their system. They trust their gut feeling. They don't trust an AI-driven black box. Particularly one they feel threatens their job. They find a way to shut it down. 'I'd rather spend the money on more widgets.' From a strategic perspective, this resistance feels like Canute fighting against the tide. From a behavioural perspective, it is understandable and predictable.

The power of loss aversion

Why does there seem to be such predictable resistance to change, even when it makes sense from a rational perspective? There is an evolutionary factor that contributes to this. Our hunter-gatherer ancestors inhabited the African savannah. Whilst hunting, they had to leave protective cover to go after a target, which exposed the hunter to attack from other predators – perhaps even the fabled sabre-toothed tiger. This was an asymmetric situation – the negative consequences of loss (injury or death) outweighed the positive consequences of success. This asymmetry is encoded into our psyche as a strong and consistent behavioural bias; we call it 'loss aversion'.

The amount of pain we feel from a loss is typically greater in magnitude than the positive feelings from a similar-sized gain. Essentially, losses loom larger than gains, and we are unconsciously influenced by our paranoid perception of potential loss. This perception is subjective, context-specific and highly vulnerable to influence and manipulation.[26]

The impact of loss aversion on our behaviour is hard to overstate. Skilled negotiators, for example, carefully consider the feelings associated with losses and gains for the other party as they make offers on price or other aspects of a potential deal. They will give concessions one at a time, to maximise the instances of positive feelings for the other party. By contrast, they will aggregate their demands requiring concessions from the other party to minimise the instances of negative feelings associated with loss.

Loss aversion and resistance to change

Imagine that you are a leader seeking to implement a major change to how your organisation works. You share your plans and its benefits with your people: they will be able to make better use of limited resources; to focus on the areas that need their expertise. It makes perfect strategic sense, doesn't it? How exciting. Let's go!

Now consider your audience's perspective. They have minimal understanding of *your* context, but full and complete awareness of their own. This unconscious contextual filter results in what they hear perhaps being different to what you said. What they infer (from what they unconsciously choose to hear) diverges considerably from what you meant to imply. They are currently hiding in the bush, safe from predators. This is the 'status quo' that they understand. It hasn't killed them. What you describe is different. They could be exposed, the outcome is uncertain – it *might* kill them. Better to watch someone else go first.

Evolutionary coding leads us to treat *any* change in the environment as a potential threat, so even *imagined* losses loom larger than possible future gains. The unconscious mental comparison between the safety of the status quo and the inherent uncertainty of anything new, creates emotional resistance. Your people understand the common-sense logic of your plan. Yet a nagging, negative voice chips away at the back of their minds. Those who feel they have something to lose fight harder and longer than those on the side of change. Even if the numbers of people 'for' and 'against' are equal, the weight of resistance will likely be greater than the positive intent and progress will grind to a halt. Machiavelli was right.

Addressing resistance to change

The realisation that leadership is not as simple as issuing instructions is as profound as it is challenging. Your people have been psychologically and evolutionarily coded to resist you when you tell them what to do; to perceive a threat in any change you propose. Some leaders never realise this; they keep instructing and pushing harder directly on their people. This book is not for them.

Creating change calls for a profound shift in leadership mindset, one that moves away from enforcing change to nurturing it. Key leadership behaviours to address the inevitable resistance to change include:

- **Clarity of meaningful intent:** Clearly articulate the 'why' behind the change and define the parameters for success (as discussed in Chapter 2).

- **Empathy and connection:** Listen to and understand the team's perspectives on the change.

- **Involvement in the process:** Find ways to give team members a say and get their fingerprints on the design of the change.

- **Shaping the environment:** Create conditions that encourage individuals to work out the rationale for change and how to achieve it for themselves.

Your primary leadership responsibility is to create the right working environment, one that influences and reinforces the right behaviours. Your task is to change the environment, not the people – to make it *revolutionary*.

Chapter takeaways

- **Embrace honest feedback and deep insight to increase situational awareness:** Leaders must transcend surface-level understandings and dig deeper into their teams' experiences, concerns and challenges. Encouraging anonymous feedback mechanisms, like surveys and one-on-one interviews, allows leaders to capture honest insights and understand team dynamics.

- **Intensify feedback mechanisms:** Leveraging the immediacy and salience of feedback can significantly enhance learning and performance. Adopt real-time feedback tools and conduct after-action reviews to facilitate immediate learning and adjustment.

- **Foster a culture of knowledge sharing:** Knowledge is a strategic asset and should not be hoarded. Cultivate an environment where knowledge sharing is viewed as career enhancing by promoting and rewarding it, for example by integrating it into performance metrics. Establishing and encouraging informal and formal networks, such as knowledge communities, enhances such an environment.

- **Ask powerful questions:** Leaders don't need all the answers but should master the art of asking insightful questions that provoke thought and innovation. Build a repertoire of powerful questions to foster a culture of curiosity and deeper analysis.

- **Acknowledge and address resistance to change:** Understanding the psychological underpinnings of resistance to change, such as loss aversion, is critical. Direct commands often meet with resistance due to an innate preference for autonomy and fear of loss. Rather than mandating change, involve team members in the decision-making process, focusing on creating an enabling environment that naturally encourages the desired behaviours.

SIX
Revolutionary

Leaders are frustrated. Their people aren't doing what they want them to do. Organisations aren't changing fast enough. They've tried to change their people and it hasn't worked. The tendency is then to change the processes or add yet more, to reorganise, implement 6-Sigma, hire management consultants to implement the new processes. Their mistake is to treat change as an event or intervention, rather than an intentional, consistent and ongoing leadership discipline.

Revolutionary leaps in performance are achieved not just by refining processes, but through the leadership discipline of *defining and consistently reinforcing the behaviours that support collaborative performance.* To be revolutionary leaders, we need to draw not just from management science, but also from behavioural science.

This chapter explores why leaders must:

- Change the environment, not the people, to get the results they want

- Apply behavioural insights to change behaviour, using influence powered by STEAM

- Adopt a 'test and learn' mindset to manage risk and build on what works

Change the environment, not the people

I work with leaders who are seeking to define and execute their strategies. To grow their businesses. To achieve significant outcomes from the collaborative efforts of individuals and teams. To transform their organisations. Their missions have something in common: they need people to change; to do different things; to do things differently. If people don't change their behaviour, organisations don't change their results.

Leaders tell me, 'Instead of doing X, they need to be doing Y. I've done the presentations. I've sent the memos. I've told them to do Y and *why* they need to be doing Y. So why are they still doing X?'

Imagine frustrated parents wanting to improve the behaviour of their kids. They post a notice that clearly sets out the behaviour change they want. They even arrange a follow up presentation.

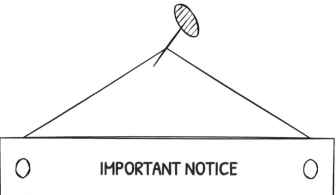

IMPORTANT NOTICE

To: Children
From: Mum & Dad
Subject: Behaviour Change – Urgent

It has come to our attention that recently there has been a significant level of unacceptable behaviour. Please ensure that you follow the guidance in the Family Operating Manual, with particular attention to the following points:

1. All verbal and written instructions must be complied with in full.
2. We may contradict each other. It's up to you to work out what we mean.
3. Bedrooms and sleeping areas must always be kept neat and tidy.

Ridiculous, right? But often this is exactly how we behave in organisations. The leader shapes the narrative, sends the memo and broadcasts the webinar. Perhaps presents in every location. People turn up and listen. For a moment, they might even *believe*.

The leader's rare visit ends. People return to work, motivated but unsure what to do differently. They sit at their desks and look around. Nothing has changed. The tried and tested behaviours that have always made things work around here still seem to do so. The local managers are behaving as they always have. The leader's message fades in their minds. The corporate posters sag on the walls.

CASE STUDY: How not to achieve change

A client shared this experience with me, which is typical of how change efforts fail. A global environmental organisation, known for its ambitious expansion through acquisitions, embarked on an initiative to unify its commercial approach. The aim was to harmonise processes and harness synergies, whilst preserving the distinct characteristics of the various 'tribes'.

An individual was appointed to spearhead this change. Armed with a singular vision, he attempted to enforce it across the business units. His approach, devoid of engagement, ignored the perspectives of each entity. Instead of a shared journey towards a common goal, the initiative morphed into a top–down push.

The result was predictably disastrous. The initiative failed to gain any meaningful buy-in or traction from the individual units. It was perceived not as a shared opportunity for improvement but as an unwelcome imposition. A critical error was the assumption that the inherent value of the change would be universally recognised, negating the need for inclusive dialogue and consensus-building. Each business unit simply retreated into their foxholes, kept their heads down and waited for the storm to pass.

Environment shapes behaviour

Consider a trip to the supermarket for a pint of milk. You enter the store with this single item on your mind. As you navigate the aisles, your basket gradually fills with an assortment of goods – snacks you suddenly crave, a new brand of coffee on sale, exotic fruits that catch your eye. Before you know it, your basket is brimming with items. You might even exit forgetting the very thing you came for.

This outcome does not come about by chance – it's the result of meticulous planning. Every element of the supermarket, from the layout of the aisles to the shelf arrangements, is carefully curated to maximise consumer spending. The bright, inviting lighting enhances the appeal of products. Enticing smells from the bakery waft through the air. Eye-catching signs and tempting pricing strategies draw attention to unmissable offers.

Why is the milk often located at the far side of the store? This is deliberate. As you traverse the length of the supermarket to reach the dairy section, you're exposed to an array of other products, increasing the likelihood of impulse purchases. This journey is not just a physical one; it's a carefully orchestrated psychological manipulation designed to influence you to buy. We feel that we have made all of our own choices, and we have: except we have been 'nudged' to make some that may or may not be in our best interests.

At all times we are aware of our surroundings and the behaviour of people nearby. Consciously or unconsciously, we adapt our own behaviour based on the dynamics around us. As we move between environments, our behaviour adapts accordingly. We behave differently at a football match to in a hospital waiting room. How we act with our friends at a restaurant is different to how we act with strangers on a bus.

The implication? Environment shapes behaviour. To create change in their people's behaviour at work, leaders need to design and implement change in the workplace environment.

The workplace environment

Workplaces are, and should be, variable and diverse, with unique blends of physical, managerial and cultural attributes. There are myriad factors in any work environment that influence our behaviour. Let me offer a simplification. The typical workplace environment comprises people, place and process.

People

We pay attention to the people around us and what they are doing and saying. We pay most attention to the people with most influence, who may or may not be the most senior leaders. Their influence might come through the strength of their personality, or their hard-won experience. The most senior leaders in an organisation can be much less front of mind for their people than they would think. Executives appear infrequently, perhaps on webinars or on an annual location visit. It is the 'local' leaders, line managers and strong characters who have the influence, and it is their behaviours that are most visible and determine 'how things are done around here'.

Place

The physical space in which we work influences our behaviour, our mood and our productivity. Well-managed sites and factory floors improve safety. Well-designed offices encourage collaboration. When Steve Jobs was designing Pixar's new headquarters, he placed the bathrooms and the café in the central atrium. Though this increased the distance people needed to walk, it also increased the frequency of chance connections and conversations, contributing to the sharing and combining of ideas.[27]

For a significant proportion of the global population, the COVID-19 pandemic fundamentally changed the work environment, almost overnight, and the ramifications of lockdown are still being felt. The development of 'hybrid working' is an ongoing process and there seems to be no consistently effective model. A significant proportion of the workforce now spend a significant proportion of their time working from home, or locations other than their core workplace. Their environment has changed to be a combination of online and their home (or wherever they connect from). This massive shift has various important implications.

When I watch my teenage son gaming with his friends, he is transported into the online environment. His behaviour is determined by the design of the virtual world and the behaviour of others within it – both 'real' and computer-generated. Whilst perhaps not as engaging as the latest video game, the online work environment has similarities. Laptops and smartphones provide the interface with all aspects of the workplace – how we access information, how we follow processes and how we engage with people. As with video games, virtual working environments can be welcoming, easy to navigate and supportive. They can also be frustrating, unproductive, even hostile.

We behave differently in our virtual workplace to how we do in the 'real' workplace. Back-to-back meetings have become the curse of our calendars. More people attend more meetings now, and for longer. It is so much easier to set them up and just takes a click to 'attend'. In an office, meetings are constrained by the availability and size of meeting rooms. It also takes time to get there. Online, we don't have these problems.

Leaders tell me that group discussions online tend to be 'lower level' and more focused on day-to-day issues. It's hard to elevate the discussion to higher-level strategic thinking and planning. They suspect that the attendees are multi-tasking – emailing on their smartphones whilst trying to follow the conversation, and doing both poorly. One of the most distracting things in online meetings is having our own image on the screen staring back at us. In your next meeting, try not to look – or better yet, turn off the self-view.

When people are in the same physical workplace, they have a shared experience of the environment. With remote working, everyone is in a unique environment. Some have home offices with minimal distractions, good connectivity and comfortable ergonomic chairs. Others are perched on the sofa, surrounded by unfinished housework and energetic pets. The point is not how conducive to working each of our locations are – it is that everyone is in a *different* environment and, therefore, having a different experience, leading to different behavioural responses.

Process

Forgive me, I am using the term 'process' here as a hugely simplified collective term for all the 'stuff' that is put in place to run an organisation. This includes things relating to:

- **Structure:** The hierarchy, organisation chart and reporting lines / chain of command. Project teams, committees, regular meetings etc.

- **Work processes and systems:** How tasks are managed – protocols; pathways; checklists; procedures; management systems for quality, safety and many other areas.

- **Information flow and decision-making:** How information is shared, when and with whom. How decisions are made and who participates. How feedback is given and received.

- **Measurement:** What is measured, reported on and the associated consequences.

This is the 'infrastructure' of an organisation, designed, built and operated by 'management'. I have deliberately over-simplified and grouped these elements under the term 'process' to make a key point. The only way any of this can show up in the workplace and influence the behaviour of an individual in a team or organisation is through the physical and / or online environment that they are in, and through the behaviours of other people in that environment.

Environment trumps 'the rules'

'It's on the system.' This is a phrase often heard in large organisations as they become increasingly digitally enabled. Whatever it is may well be on the system, somewhere, but if it's more than one or two intuitive clicks away, it may as well not exist. Busy, distracted and stressed individuals don't always follow the rules. They navigate their environment as best they can, conserving precious time and energy. They look around and see what other people are doing and follow them. This may not be how things *should* be done – but it becomes how things *are* done. It's not right. It may not be safe. Leaders are exasperated. Yet the observed behaviours are a result of the environment as it is, rather than what the environment needs to be to reinforce the right behaviours.

CASE STUDY: Leaders shape the environment for change

I worked with a group of senior leaders responsible for influencing change in their organisation. They wanted their people to collaborate and innovate more effectively, taking advantage of digital technology to develop new, more sustainable solutions. They clearly saw the competitive advantage that would be gained by getting this transformation right, and they could articulate a compelling story regarding the benefits of the changes. They were travelling round their offices giving presentations and briefings, people were nodding along and seemed to be supportive. It felt like progress. Yet how much real change was happening?

I challenged them to consider something. I pointed to some people working at their desks just outside the glass-walled meeting room we were in. What would influence those people to change? Right now. Without waiting for an office briefing or needing to be chased. What specifically would we see them doing differently? This thought experiment prompted the realisation that unless these people's environment changed in some way, their behaviour was unlikely to change.

We looked out of the window, which overlooked a busy crossroads. Work was being carried out to upgrade the pavements and traffic lights. A system of temporary lights and fenced off walkways was in place so that pedestrians could safely navigate from one side to the other. The problem was, due to the pavement on one side being closed, getting from one side to the other involved three road crossings instead of just one. As we watched, many pedestrians simply ignored the clearly signposted, safe route and instead stepped into the road and walked between cars waiting at the traffic lights to take the most direct route. The next people simply followed their lead.

I asked the team to consider a better solution. They suggested that a simple re-organisation of the temporary barriers would create a direct route for the busiest stream of pedestrians. This simple change in the environment would most likely result in greater compliance and safety. They also saw how the situation was analogous to their organisation. 'Often,' they said, 'we make it difficult for people to do what we want them to do and much easier to do what we don't.'

Change the environment to change behaviour

Changing organisations requires changing *individual behaviours*. If people don't do something different then nothing has changed. If nothing in the environment changes, behaviour won't change. No behavioural change, no organisational change. For leaders, the key is to pinpoint specific behaviours that will bring the desired organisational change to life. What, specifically, will people be doing differently when the change has been successful? What, specifically, are they doing *now* that is getting in the way of the desired change?

Imagine your strategy relies on increased collaboration and knowledge sharing across organisational boundaries to improve efficiency and competitiveness. Your leadership narrative stresses the importance of acting as 'one team' in the best interests of the overall organisation. This messaging alone is unlikely to stop silo behaviours. The key is to identify *specific* target behaviours that, if changed, would have most impact on cross-boundary collaboration. For example, there may be key decision points in a solution development process where insights from the wider business would lead to better outcomes. At that moment, the specific target behaviour would be for teams to ask questions such as, 'Who has done this before?' and 'What can we learn from their experiences?' You can then use the STEAM-powered influence model to identify changes that could be made to nudge this target behaviour and improve the team's output.

Influence powered by STEAM

Behavioural science tells us that *context matters* (see Chapter 1). Our state of mind, our physiology and our personality are all part of the context that influences our behaviour These are all highly individual, private and clearly not appropriate things for a leader to try to influence. This means that influencing the environment that people are working in is the most powerful tool available to leaders seeking to change the context within which people behave and make decisions.

Research has identified many ways in which our environment influences our behaviour.[28,29,30] Five of the most powerful 'levers of influence' in the workplace environment are included in the STEAM model below. Something is influential if it is:

- **Social:** We are strongly influenced by social norms – ie what other people do and what they think about us

- **Timely:** Timing matters – we respond differently depending on when we are prompted

- **Easy:** How easy is it for people to do what you want them to do?

- **Attractive:** How can you attract people's attention in a busy, crowded and distracting environment?

- **Messenger:** Who is the right person to communicate your message?

Let's look at each of these levers of influence in more detail.

Lever of Influence 1: Social

Humans are social creatures, significantly influenced by the actions and opinions of those around us. Earlier in our history, exclusion from the tribe would mean almost certain death. We are wired to build and protect our position in whatever groups we are members of, including in our workplace. Understanding the profound impact of social norms and leveraging them wisely can facilitate positive change, fostering environments that encourage desired behaviours through subtle cues and the endorsement of influential community members.

Examples of ways in which social dynamics can be harnessed include:

- **Comparison:** Show that other people perform the desired behaviour. Signs in hotel bathrooms state, 'Most of our guests re-use their towels'. Performance reporting compares the results from one business unit with another.

- **Connection:** Create networks, groups or communities of like-minded individuals. For example, knowledge communities connect professionals from the same disciplines and facilitate sharing of knowledge and ideas.

- **Shared commitments:** Encouraging people to make a commitment to others will significantly increase the likelihood of them following through.

- **Requests for help and involvement:** As we've established, people don't like being told what to do, but generally respond positively to requests for help, support or advice.

- **Reciprocity:** We tend to respond to others in ways that mirror how they engage with us, for example openness, respect, kindness and recognition.

Lever of Influence 2: Timely

We have all made the mistake of picking the wrong moment to ask for something we want from someone, whether that's our boss or our spouse. By getting our timing wrong, we stand a good chance of not getting the response we want, no matter how reasonable our request. We are more responsive to certain prompts at certain times. Consider the sweet treats placed at a child's eyeline beside the supermarket checkout. At the hectic moment of packing and paying for our groceries, we perhaps have less mental energy to resist demands for chocolate. It may be disconcerting to realise just how susceptible key decisions are to seemingly arbitrary timing-related factors, but it is important to be on the lookout for moments when we may be vulnerable.

For example, I can recall my purchase of a lovely 'approved used' Audi. I played it cool, did my homework and negotiated what I thought to be a good deal. But I also ended up purchasing insurances for the paintwork, the wheels and several other things. Only later, when I had time to think about it, did I consider the prices of these extra policies (a lot) and whether they were good value for money (they weren't).

This example also shows how our perspective can be influenced by preceding events. I had just bought the car in 'showroom perfect' condition – of course it made sense to protect my beautiful new toy. The extra few hundred pounds for the insurance seemed minimal in comparison to the purchase price. These factors combined, in that specific moment, meant I bought the insurance. Few such policies are sold separately from the purchase of the main item, because the salespeople know it's all in the timing.

Below are some more examples of ways in which timing can be used to influence behaviour:

- **Present bias:** We tend to be more influenced by consequences, costs and benefits that are certain and immediate than those that are possible and in the future. Good negotiators know that offering terms that give an immediate benefit to their counterpart will increase their chances of success. For example, cash buyers offer a more certain, quick house purchase, which may allow them to negotiate a better price. Presenting the immediate benefits of your plans will have more positive impact than offering 'jam tomorrow'.

- **Build it into the process:** Rather than relying on people to remember the specific things you want them to do at specific times, make them explicit at key points in processes. For example, the right time to engage experts to share their knowledge in the development of a project is as early as possible. How can the project development processes be amended to prompt this to happen? Checklists are used by pilots and even surgeons to ensure that basic, yet critical, activities are carried out at the right time.

- **Deadlines:** Nothing galvanises action like a deadline. Even artificial deadlines can be effective at pushing people through the inertia of a project or a change. Deadlines and intermittent milestones help us to counteract the effect of Parkinson's Law, which holds that work will expand to fit the time available for its completion.

- **Fresh starts:** There are certain times when a change or a new way of working will make more sense and get more traction, for example at the start of a new project or financial year. New Year's resolutions are the classic example.[31]

Lever of Influence 3: Easy

There is so much inertia created in organisations (and in life) by bureaucracy that it can be unclear, difficult and time consuming for people to do what you want them to do. It is often much easier for people to do the things that you *don't* want them to do.

There is perhaps no greater opportunity for accelerating change, or indeed achieving any objective, than simply making it *easy* for people to do what you want them to do.

For example, I worked with a large utility organisation that changed its structure and then struggled with performance. I asked people to explain the new structure, how it should work and their place in it. There was zero consistency in their answers. The 'launch' communication had not been followed up to create understanding of what needed to be different, and why, at the coal face. Managers either made their own interpretation of the way forward or continued to operate in the way they always had. Performance suffered due to confusion, unnecessary complexity and demotivating inertia.

A good leader makes the environment as easy as possible to work in. In physics, the term 'entropy' describes the level of disorder in a system. The second law of thermodynamics states that a closed system will gain in entropy over time. Disorder *always* follows order. The incontrovertible evidence for this is the state of my teenage son's bedroom. Unless acted on by a positive outside force (me, or much more likely my wife), the state of the room will always increase in entropy (disorder). Think also of a garden. If you don't keep on top of maintenance, what happens?

Many leaders fail to address the implications of this law, and they inexorably allow the organisation to increase in bureaucracy, complexity and inertia. It becomes harder and harder for people to collaborate to achieve their collective goals. To counter this, Timpson, the largest service retailer in the UK, has only one standing committee. The 'cut the crap' committee strips out unnecessary and ineffective processes.[32]

The wider business environments are similarly increasing in complexity, speed and interdependence.

We are nostalgic for the simplicity and slower pace of life gone by.

In my view, leaders need to ask themselves:

- Are my actions likely to increase the complexity and inertia of the environment my people are operating in?

- How can I help my people see the wood from the trees by making things 'elegantly simple'? What stories will bring my strategies to life?

- How can I make it as easy as possible to get the right things done? What obstacles do I need to remove?

'The devil is in the default'

Recently, I reviewed my pension arrangements with a financial adviser. She noted that all my investments were in the 'default' funds selected by each provider. This was perhaps OK, but perhaps not. The point was that at no time had I made any conscious decision regarding fund allocation. I suspect I am not the only one to behave in this way.

The default option is the one that you choose by doing *nothing*. Doing nothing is the easiest thing for us to do, hence the power of the default. Defaults can be designed to promote behaviours that we want. Company pension schemes now have auto-enrolment, meaning that eligible employees automatically join, whilst still having the option to opt out. A construction company wanted to increase the number of projects that underwent a 'digital rehearsal', a process of creating a digital model of the proposed solution to be reviewed with the clients to identify design improvements and safety issues. They changed their project development process to make digital rehearsals the default. It was still possible to avoid carrying one out, but it required a justification process. This dramatically increased the adoption of digital rehearsals.

As a leader, have you considered the power of defaults in your organisation?

Lever of Influence 4: Attract attention

Are you paying attention? In our modern world, we are constantly bombarded by interruptions, distractions, information and other cues from our environment. There is a war to capture and keep our attention to influence how we think, what we buy, whom we vote for. We cannot take it all in, so we make choices, conscious and unconscious, about where to allocate our limited and precious attention.

The term 'paying attention' is appropriate, as there is a high mental cost associated with consciously directing our attention. Focusing on a particular mental task takes effort and quickly uses up our available mental working capacity. It is hard to hold more than five pieces of information in our working memory at any one time. When we are paying attention in one area, it is entirely likely that we fail to observe other things that may be right in front of us.

The implications of our selective attention are significant. Studies have shown that the mere presence of a mobile phone can negatively influence our driving performance, even when it is switched off.[33] Any time that we are immersed in a task, a thought process or a course of action, we are potentially blind to risks and opportunities that present themselves in the wider environment.

In behavioural science, things that have these attributes and capture our attention and interest are described as being 'salient'. If we are seeking to influence people's choices and behaviour, we first need to capture their attention through increasing the salience of our approach. There are a few different ways to do so.

Novelty

We notice changes in our environment – things that are new or different. Have you ever had the experience of only noticing the office air conditioning in the moment that it switches off? Images and information that are vivid, shocking or out of place tend to capture our attention and stand out against the background, potentially disproportionately to their importance.

A great example of an attentional nudge was the simple addition of the image of a fly to the urinals in Schiphol Airport in Amsterdam. The effect of having a 'target' impact was to significantly reduce the cleaning costs associated with 'human spillage'.[34] How can you make your change message stand out in a crowded and distracting environment?

Simplicity

We have discussed the ever-increasing complexity of the modern workplace. People simply don't have the time or energy to translate, unpick or infer what a complicated leadership message means for them. Simplicity is key. Often, a well-selected story or case study is what brings a complex strategy to life.

Framing

Much of the information we receive is *framed*, usually in an attempt to influence us in one way or another. The same information can be presented with a negative/loss frame (eg 20% fat) or a positive/gain frame (80% fat free). Our tendency to be loss averse (described earlier) means that a negative frame can induce an emotional reaction and influence our choices and actions. The Brexit slogan, 'Take Back Control' is a great example, influencing a choice to mitigate an implied 'loss'.

Consequences

As we discussed earlier in the book, the course of action we choose is influenced by its consequences (real or imagined). Incentives, rewards and sanctions all tend to get people's attention.

Lever of Influence 5: The right messenger

When seeking to drive change or influence behaviour, the tendency can be to focus on the message itself. The key words for the memo, the killer slides, the main points for the briefing. Less consideration is given to *who* should deliver the message for maximum impact.

In 2017, the *Blue Planet II* documentary series was shown on BBC Television. The series drew attention to the threats to the aquatic environment caused by human behaviour. The heart-breaking footage of turtles entangled in plastic bags and sea birds regurgitating plastic debris had a dramatic impact, and the scale of raised awareness became known as the 'Blue Planet effect'. The impact came from a combination of the shocking pictures and the narrative of the messenger, Sir David Attenborough.

As a boy in 1979, I marvelled at Sir David's groundbreaking series, *Life on Earth*. For over forty years, his work has been part of my Sunday evening viewing. This long-term connection built my perception of him as a passionate, trusted expert.

Sir David Attenborough is the perfect example of an effective messenger.

What are the specific attributes of an effective messenger? Authority and expertise in the specific field are, of course, hugely significant. Trustworthiness is also critical, which may be associated with the messenger's reputation, or arise from their personal connection to members of the audience. The other important factor, but one that is often missing, is *similarity*. We are more likely to listen to people like us, or people whom we aspire to be like. Importantly, these attributes must be perceived by the recipients of the message.

The experience of one of my clients highlights the importance of the right messenger. Andy is a contract manager in a major utility company. As in many organisations, the guidance on the handsfree use of mobile phones whilst driving was being changed and it was now against company policy. This had been communicated to all staff via the usual channels of emails from the HR function and senior management briefings. But with the amount of travel between sites and his workload, Andy felt the pressure to remain available for phone calls even when driving. He told me that what finally changed his behaviour was when his direct supervisor, Vanessa, made a point of saying that she put her own mobile phone in the back of the car when driving, so she would not be tempted to take calls. The message was the same – don't use mobile phones when driving – but the impact on behaviour was much greater when delivered by a familiar leader, Vanessa, than by HR or head office.

The people who have influence are not necessarily those with the most prominent position on the organisational chart. In large organisations, it is often people in 'lower status' positions who have the most influence, due to the strength of their connections and relationships. They have the social capital that is key to sharing messages and driving change.

Who are the best messengers for what you want to achieve in your organisation?

STEAM checklist

Below is an example of how to use the STEAM Levers of Influence to affect a specific behaviour.

Applying STEAM

Make it social – we are strongly influenced by social norms, ie what others do and what we think they think of us	• Show that most people like them perform the desired behaviour • Harness the power of peer groups/networks • Encourage people to make a commitment to others • People respond to requests for help

Applying STEAM

Make it timely – timing matters, we respond differently depending on when we receive prompts	• Prompt people when they are most likely to be receptive • Consider the immediate costs and benefits • Help people plan their responses to events
Make it easy – how easy is it for people to do what you want them to do? (The easiest thing for people to do is nothing)	• Harness the power of defaults • Reduce the 'hassle factor' of taking action • Simplify messages as much as possible
Make it attractive – how can you attract attention in a crowded and hectic environment?	• Increase salience to attract attention • Design incentives, rewards and sanctions for maximum effect • Personalise it, use people's names
Use the right messenger – we are heavily influenced by who communicates information	• Perceived authority and knowledge • Perceived trustworthiness • People like us (or people we want to be like)

Test and learn

When new initiatives and changes are introduced in organisations, there is rarely any form of testing to determine the impact of the proposed change in comparison to alternatives, or to doing nothing at all. They are simply rolled out with no way to measure their effectiveness with any degree of certainty, as there is no way to compare the impact with what would have happened had the initiative not been introduced.

Experimentation is core to scientific method; through it, the consequences of alternative courses of action can be compared and understood, which allows resources to be allocated efficiently. Testing and learning from what works and what doesn't, mitigates the potential for large-scale failure.

Not failing is not an option

The word 'failure' strikes fear into many of us. Failure is an anathema for many professionals, particularly us engineers. The word conjures up catastrophic images of collapsed bridges, crashed computer banking systems or other nightmare scenarios with grave implications for lives, careers and reputations. Of course, when we design and create infrastructure and systems that people rely upon, they must be safe. We must do all we can to mitigate the potential for and consequences of failure. Yet many of us carry this aversion to failure and making mistakes into other aspects of our lives and work, with negative implications for our learning, development and potential.

Any time we learn something new we must expose ourselves to failure and its consequences. When we learn to ride a bicycle as a child, there is a point when we must just 'go for it'. The first time we are on our own, without stabilisers, we wobble, move tentatively forward, too slowly to keep ourselves going. We topple. There is no completely risk-free way to learn. We must be confronted by the gap between our current level of competence and our desired level of expertise. As children, we simply get on with it, feeling no stigma associated with making mistakes as we create, learn and grow.

But for many of us, as we move into professional life, our relationship with failure changes. We might go through structured training processes such as apprenticeships and professional qualifications. At some point, we consider ourselves to be 'beyond' the learning phase. Mistakes and failures no longer feel acceptable. We have more on the line and are unwilling to risk our professional status or capital. We begin to play it safe, doing all we can to avoid being associated with things that go wrong, lest the exposure damages us.

The issue is that nothing of value is created without an iterative learning process which, by definition, exposes us to risk. We cannot learn, grow, innovate and drive value without this exposure.

The 'test and learn' mindset

In Chapter 2 we discussed the important realisation that leaders don't need to know all the answers. It takes self-awareness and humility for leaders to counter their misplaced beliefs that the outcomes of a change, new initiative or new product can and should be completely knowable, that they can confidently predict what will happen. Sometimes they can, but often they can't.

Instead of trying to predict the unpredictable, I suggest the adoption of a test and learn mindset, which requires you to:

- **Embrace calculated risks:** Acknowledge that some level of failure is inevitable. Be willing to test ideas on a smaller scale to manage the risk of large-scale failure. This allows you to learn from mistakes cheaply and avoid more costly missteps.

- **Focus on learning over winning:** Prioritise learning from every iteration, regardless of the outcome. Be open to unexpected results and view them as valuable insights. Don't get discouraged by setbacks; focus on what you've learned and use it to improve your approach.

- **Seek continuous improvement:** This is an ongoing process, with a commitment to continuously iterating and adapting your approach based on the learnings from your experiments. Be prepared to adjust your strategies as you gain new information.

CASE STUDY: A tale of two business lines

I experienced two contrasting approaches to new product development through contrasting experiences within a single company.

The first initiative focused on complex client system modelling. It was developed in isolation, with no client interaction or internal feedback. The grand unveiling at a launch event showcased intricate models that proved overly complex and confusing. The lack of testing with potential clients had resulted in a product that failed to capture their attention and meet their needs.

In contrast, the second embraced a 'test and learn' philosophy. They began with open communication, building an understanding of the clients' challenges through dialogue with them. This client insight informed the creation of Minimum Viable Products (MVPs) – simplified, initial versions of the product. These MVPs were then tested with clients, creating a continuous feedback loop, which allowed for quick 'debugging' and addition of features, ensuring the product addressed the clients' needs. This iterative approach, emphasising 'testing' and 'learning' from clients, led to a highly successful software line.

Chapter takeaways

- **The power of environment over behaviour:** Emphasise redesigning both physical and virtual workspaces to guide employee behaviour towards collaboration and efficiency. This holistic approach can significantly influence positive outcomes by fostering environments conducive to desired behaviours.

- **Influence through social norms and expectations:** Utilise the power of social cues and the actions of peers to shape behaviour. Leaders can cultivate a positive environment by recognising achievements that align with organisational goals and encouraging the sharing of success stories.

- **Make desired actions easier:** Simplify processes and make changes easy to execute to eliminate barriers to desired behaviours. Adjusting workflows, policies and tools to align with organisational objectives can enhance the effectiveness of change initiatives.

- **Timely and attractive messaging:** Ensure that messages about change are not just clear but delivered when employees are most likely to be receptive. Using stories and aligning announcements with significant events can make communication more engaging.

- **Using the right messengers:** The effectiveness of communication depends heavily on who delivers it. Empowering credible individuals within the organisation to advocate for change can improve the message's reception and impact.

- **Embrace a 'test and learn' mindset:** Recognise that not every initiative will succeed initially. Encouraging experimentation and viewing failure as a learning opportunity will accelerate innovation and adaptability.

SEVEN

Transformative Mindset Shifts For Collaborative Leadership

For leaders, the journey to fostering excellence and a high-performing collaborative environment begins with a shift in their own mindset. Imagine the organisation as a garden. The leader nurtures and cultivates an ecosystem in which each plant thrives in harmony with the others, contributing to the garden's overall beauty and productivity.

Embrace the idea that leadership is not about commanding from the front but empowering from within. In this journey, adopt a mindset that values empathy as giving a competitive advantage, being aware that the roots of genuine collaboration and innovation lie in the deep soil of mutual respect and understanding. As you shift your focus from changing people to transforming the environment in which they operate,

197

you create a fertile ground for growth, innovation and sustained high performance.

Below are eight 'Mindset Shifts' that I believe help a leader to drive their organisation towards unprecedented heights of success.

FROM: **TO:**

Directive → Empowering

Expert → Facilitator / coach

Siloed thinking → Networked thinking

Relying on logic → Increasing influence

Presenter → Storyteller

Fixed mindset → Growth mindset

What we see is all there is → What are we not seeing?

Directing change → Exemplifying change

Mindset Shift 1: From directive to empowering

Traditional stereotypes of leadership are based on control through commands, and top–down decisions. 'My way or the highway.' As the challenges we face in the modern world become more complex and interdependent, we can no longer rely on directive styles of leadership to achieve successful outcomes. This is for two principal reasons. First, no individual party has the breadth of perspective and capability to develop and deliver effective solutions; the collaborative input and efforts of many different parties are needed. Second, transferring information 'upwards' so that decisions can be made and flow 'downwards' is too slow and limits initiative and spontaneous collaboration beyond direct instructions.

In *Turn the Ship Around*, David Marquet recounts his transition from traditional command to 'intent-based leadership' during his tenure as captain of the USS *Santa Fe*, a nuclear submarine he unexpectedly commanded without prior familiarity.[35] Initially prepared for a different submarine, Marquet faced the challenge of leading a crew more knowledgeable about the ship than himself. This prompted a shift in leadership style towards articulating clear mission objectives and empowering his crew to make decisions aligned with these goals. The crew was encouraged to declare their intended actions in support of the mission, rather than simply awaiting instructions, fostering a culture of trust and autonomy. This significant deviation from the norm led to unprecedented performance levels.

Technical professions involve the application and mastery of complex systems, equations and processes, which in turn generate complex and unique language and methods of communication. But to lead the collaborative efforts of groups of people requires clear, unambiguous and consistent communication – a very different style. Most importantly, the leader's intent must be crystal clear. What's the mission? As we've already discussed, without a clear leadership narrative that can be easily translated across the organisation, people are left turning the handles of their day-to-day activities without an understanding of why they are doing so, or where they are collectively going. To effect this mindset shift, leaders should ask themselves four questions:

1. Do I have a clear message regarding the direction for my team?

2. Do my people know what this message is?

3. Could each of my team members repeat this message if asked?

4. Do each of them know what it means for them?

With the mission clear, the leader can get out of the way and focus on ensuring that the team have the tools and support they need to achieve it. There will be obstacles to be removed, resources to be procured, risks to be mitigated and course corrections to be made when necessary. This is what the leader should focus on.

This shift from a directive to an empowering style can be difficult. In every interaction with the team, it will be tempting to tell them what you think they should do. Instead, adopting an open, questioning and supportive approach will help the team shape their own – better – approach to achieving your mission.

Mindset Shift 2: From expert to facilitator/coach

The shift from an expert/problem solver to a facilitator/coach is a pivotal transformation in leadership, especially in the context of fostering collaborative performance. This transition to a leadership role is not merely a change in title but a deep-seated change in behaviour and mindset that directly influences collaborative outcomes. There are certain key behaviours of a facilitator/coach that are critical to nurturing an environment where collective intelligence and teamwork flourish, many of which are based on the concepts we've explored throughout the book.

Convening the right people at the right time

Leaders must act as architects of collaboration, skilfully bringing together diverse groups of individuals to tackle complex issues. This requires an acute understanding of the unique strengths within the team and the broader organisation. By ensuring that the right mix of skills and perspectives are at the table, leaders facilitate a richer, more comprehensive dialogue, directly impacting the quality of collaborative efforts. This is not just about gathering people; it's about curating environments where the collective intelligence can exceed the sum of its parts.

Creating psychologically safe environments

As we discussed in Chapter 4, psychological safety is the bedrock upon which collaborative performance is built. Leaders must cultivate spaces where team members feel safe to express ideas, challenge norms and admit mistakes without fear of retribution. This openness fosters trust and respect, allowing innovation to thrive. By demonstrating vulnerability and encouraging risk taking, leaders set a precedent that empowers others to contribute their full selves to the team's objectives.

Ensuring diversity of thinking

To combat groupthink and status quo bias, leaders must actively seek out and value differing viewpoints. This involves challenging one's own assumptions and fostering an environment where contrarian views are welcomed and explored. By leveraging cognitive diversity, teams can uncover novel solutions and approaches, enhancing the quality and creativity of collaborative work. This requires leaders to be facilitators of dialogue, encouraging open discussions that bring hidden assumptions to light and pave the way for innovative solutions.

Asking powerful questions

Shifting from providing answers to facilitating discovery is a hallmark of the coach mindset. By asking powerful, open-ended questions (see Chapter 5), leaders guide their teams to insights and solutions that they own. This approach not only builds the team's problem-solving skills but also deepens their engagement with the work. Leaders must master the art of inquiry, creating a culture where questions are valued as much as answers. This behaviour signals a shift from leader-as-expert to leader-as-guide, speaking to the collaborative nature of performance and learning.

Capturing and simplifying key thoughts and concepts

During complex discussions, the leader's role in distilling and clarifying key points becomes crucial. This not only ensures alignment among team members but also makes complex ideas more accessible. By synthesising discussions into actionable insights, leaders help the team focus on what matters most to them, building momentum. This behaviour supports the collaborative effort by ensuring that all team members are working from a shared understanding.

Mindset Shift 3: From siloed to networked thinking

Traditionally, we've viewed our organisational habitats as well-ordered structures with clear hierarchy and rules. This perspective, whilst offering clarity and a semblance of order, inadvertently shackles us to a myopic view that stifles innovation and collaboration.

At the heart of this transformation is the recognition that, despite appearances, we don't merely function within rigid frameworks or isolated compartments. Instead, we are part of a vibrant network of relationships, a dynamic web through which knowledge, ideas and value flow with the potential to create transformative outcomes. This network transcends the conventional boundaries of individual teams, organisations and even broader enterprises, linking us to a much larger system of interdependent entities and interests.

The challenge and opportunity before us are to navigate beyond the 'silos' – those familiar zones demarcated on organisational charts that can become fortresses of insularity. Silos, by nature, represent a segmented approach to organisational thinking, each focusing inwardly on its own goals and metrics of success. But in a world that demands agility, resilience and innovation, the silo mentality is a relic of the past, a barrier to the cross-pollination of ideas and collaborative synergy that fuels progress.

To cultivate a networked mindset, we must begin by expanding our cognitive horizons, striving to understand the needs, challenges and aspirations of those beyond our immediate sphere. This broader perspective enables us to appreciate the interdependencies that exist within the organisational ecosystem and see that our collective success relies on our ability to function cohesively across traditional boundaries.

Defining collective success beyond the narrow confines of individual or departmental achievements also becomes paramount. This involves establishing a shared vision of success that encompasses the entire enterprise, aligning goals and incentives in a way that promotes cooperation over competition, synergy over segregation.

Addressing and mitigating misaligned incentives and silo-focused behaviours is crucial. These are often the root causes of friction and fragmentation within organisations, impeding the free flow of information and collaboration. By identifying and systematically dismantling these barriers, leaders create an environment that encourages openness, mutual respect and shared purpose.

In essence, the shift from siloed to networked thinking is not merely an operational adjustment but a transformation in the very ethos of how we conceive and conduct our collective endeavours. It's a journey from isolation to integration, from compartmentalisation to connectivity, charting a course towards a future where collaborative performance and shared success are the hallmarks of enterprise-wide excellence.

Mindset Shift 4: From relying on logic to increasing influence

At the heart of every organisation is a dynamic web of emotions, beliefs and relationships that drives decision-making as much as, if not more than, logic and reason. The transition from a reliance solely on logic to harnessing the power of influence marks a critical shift in the mindset of successful leaders. This change reflects a deeper understanding of human nature, acknowledging that collaborative performance requires not just strategic brilliance but the ability to connect, persuade and inspire.

Consider Mark, a leader and former colleague with a vision to revolutionise how engineering projects are managed through a new management system. He put forth a proposal that was a strategic masterpiece, backed by a solid business case that demonstrated clear benefits over costs. Yet, when I witnessed Mark presenting to the board, his logical fortress crumbled under the weight of emotional and political dynamics he hadn't accounted for. The ensuing chaos was not a repudiation of his idea's merit but a stark lesson in the limits of relying on logic alone to garner support and drive action.

Such political failures are common scenarios in corporate governance. They illustrate a key lesson from behavioural science: humans are swayed more by emotion than by reason. The implications for leaders are profound. It necessitates a shift towards understanding and leveraging the emotional and relational landscapes within which decisions are made. In this context, the art of influence becomes a critical skill set, encompassing the ability to read the room, engage with empathy and build coalitions of support that underpin the strategic and logical arguments.

Influence in this context is not about manipulation or coercion but about connecting with others on a deeper, emotional level. It's about understanding their motivations, addressing their concerns and aligning your proposal with the broader organisational vision in a way that resonates. It involves pre-emptively building relationships and alliances, engaging in dialogue to understand the political and personal dynamics at play and crafting messages that speak to both the head and the heart.

For leaders like Mark, this means stepping out of the comfort zone of spreadsheets and presentations to engage in the messier, more nuanced world of human interaction. It involves listening as much as talking, asking questions to uncover hidden agendas and demonstrating how a proposal supports not just the organisational goals but the personal aspirations of those whose support is needed.

This mindset shift, from relying on logic to increasing influence, does not diminish the importance of having a solid business case or strategic rationale. Rather, it enriches the leader's toolkit, enabling them to navigate the complex interplay of logic, emotion and power dynamics that the corporate landscape imposes. In doing so, it opens new pathways to collaborative performance, grounded in a shared vision and fuelled by a collective passion to achieve remarkable outcomes. This is the essence of modern leadership:

blending the precision of logic with the art of influence to drive transformational change.

Mindset Shift 5: From presenter to storyteller

The essence of the transformation required in the world of business and leadership is captured in the shift from 'traditional presenter' to 'evocative storyteller'. When collaborative performance is not just desired but essential for success, the art of storytelling emerges as a vital skill for leaders and teams alike.

Why is this shift necessary? Stories are not just a means of entertainment; they are the fabric of human connection, weaving together the threads of vision, values and action. When we gather, whether in a meeting room or a pub, it's not dry, bullet-pointed slides that captivate us; it's stories. Stories have the power to engage our senses, evoke emotions and inspire actions. They move beyond the surface, delving deep into our shared human experience, making the abstract tangible and the complex understandable.

Consider the example of a CFO client who wanted her finance team to transcend the numbers. The challenge was clear: 'How do we communicate the importance and impact of our work to the rest of the business?' The solution was found in storytelling. By training the team to tell the story behind the numbers, they began to illuminate the hidden narratives of effort, strategy and impact. This approach not only brought the figures to life but also forged deeper connections among colleagues.

Selecting the right stories is key to bringing strategies to life. Just as a good novelist selects themes that resonate with their readers, leaders must choose stories that align with their vision and values. These stories should not be random or superficial but carefully curated to embody the principles and objectives of the organisation. They should serve as beacons, guiding the team through the complexities of the business landscape, highlighting challenges, celebrating achievements and showing the way forward.

The shift from presenter to storyteller is not merely a change in technique but a transformation in mindset. It recognises that at the heart of effective leadership and collaboration is the ability to connect on an emotional level. To do this, leaders must embrace vulnerability, authenticity and empathy – all qualities inherent in great storytellers. They must see themselves not as disseminators of information but as weavers of meaning, crafting narratives that inspire, motivate and unite.

Through storytelling, organisations can forge stronger bonds to unite its people under the umbrella of a shared journey. As leaders, the stories we choose to tell are not just narratives of the past but the tools with which we sculpt the future.

Mindset Shift 6: From a fixed mindset to a growth mindset

Carol Dweck's seminal work describes the 'fixed mindset' as one where abilities are seen as static and unchangeable, whereas a 'growth mindset' embraces challenges, learns from criticism and perseveres in the face of setbacks, viewing capabilities as improvable through effort and learning.[36] This distinction is not merely academic; it is critical to how leaders can drive – or hinder – collaboration within their teams.

The correlation between a growth mindset and superior collaborative performance is both intuitive and empirically supported. A growth mindset leads to an environment where mistakes are viewed as learning opportunities rather than failures. This perspective encourages open dialogue, innovative problem-solving and a willingness to experiment, all of which, as we have seen, are essential for effective collaboration. By emphasising learning and development, leaders can cultivate an environment in which team members feel valued and supported, leading to higher engagement, creativity and collective problem-solving prowess.

To nurture a growth mindset, leaders can adopt specific behaviours, including:

- **Encourage learning and curiosity:** Emphasise the importance of learning and exploration over merely achieving results. By rewarding curiosity and the process of learning, you can create an atmosphere where team members feel safe to ask questions, seek feedback and innovate.

- **Model resilience and adaptability:** By openly sharing your own challenges and how you've learned from them, you can set a powerful example of resilience. This behaviour from a leader shows that setbacks are not failures but steps in the learning process.

- **Create psychological safety:** An environment where team members feel comfortable expressing their ideas and concerns without fear of reprisal is crucial. This requires you to actively listen, acknowledge contributions and make sure all voices are heard.

- **Embrace and learn from failures:** Shift the organisational culture from one that fears failure to one that sees it as simply a part of innovation. Celebrate the lessons learned from 'failures' and encourage team members to share their experiences and takeaways in a non-judgemental setting.

- **Promote collaborative goals:** Set goals that require collective effort and interdependence, encouraging team members to work together, share knowledge and support each other's growth.

- **Provide constructive feedback:** Focus your feedback on efforts and strategies rather than innate abilities. This approach helps individuals understand that their skills can grow with effort and persistence.

An example of a fixed mindset impeding collaboration is seen in situations where leaders attribute the lack of team success to unchangeable traits of team members, such as labelling someone as 'not a team player'. This not only demotivates the individual but also creates a culture of blame rather than one of collective growth and improvement.

My MSc dissertation on negotiation underscored the practical benefits of adopting a growth mindset. I found that negotiators with a growth mindset were more inclined to seek additional information, understand the other party's needs and explore mutually beneficial solutions. This approach resulted in negotiations that were not only more successful but also benefited from a spirit of collaboration and value creation. Such findings further substantiate the argument that a shift towards a growth mindset is not just beneficial but essential for leaders aiming to drive collaborative performance in today's workplace environments.

Mindset Shift 7: From assuming 'what we see is all there is' to asking 'what are we not seeing?'

In the ever-evolving theatre of leadership and collaborative performance, the shift from a myopic, single perspective to a broader, elevated viewpoint is not just advantageous – it's imperative. This transformation enables leaders to harness the collective power of their teams, driving the kind of innovation and efficiency that can only arise from a united front. It's a journey from seeing the trees in meticulous detail to appreciating the vastness of the forest and the ecosystem it supports, a critical transition for those at the helm of change.

The story of Abraham Wald during World War II serves as a poignant metaphor for this necessary shift in perspective. Wald understood the need to reinforce the *undamaged* parts of returning bombers, rather than the visibly damaged sections because he realised the significance of what he was *not* seeing – the damaged areas of planes that *didn't* make it back. This insight underscores the importance of considering what isn't immediately visible – the uncharted territories of opportunity and risk that lie beyond a conventional viewpoint.[37] It teaches us a valuable lesson in leadership: the need to question the completeness of our perspective, to ask ourselves, 'What are we not seeing?'

Similarly, the work of Daniel Kahneman illuminates the peril of assuming that what you see is all there is, a cognitive bias that narrows our view and, thus, decision-making capacity.[38] As leaders, we must actively challenge our perspectives and encourage our teams to do the same, playing the devil's advocate or conducting a pre-mortem to unearth potential blind spots. Such practices are not just exercises in critical thinking; they are safeguards against the overconfidence that can lead to strategic missteps.

To move towards this elevated perspective, leaders must engage in specific actions and behaviours. First, they must prioritise establishing a collective direction and understanding the big picture before diving into the details. This approach ensures that every team member is aligned in their efforts towards a common goal, fostering a sense of purpose and direction. Leaders should facilitate open forums for discussion, where challenging the status quo is welcomed and diverse viewpoints are sought and valued. By doing so, they not only democratise the decision-making process but also capitalise on the cognitive diversity within their teams.

Encouraging the team to adopt a 'big-picture' mindset involves not just periodic reminders of the overarching vision but embedding this perspective into the fabric of the team's operations. Regularly revisiting the strategic objectives, celebrating milestones that contribute to the larger goal and contextualising day-to-day tasks within the broader mission are all crucial.

Moreover, leaders themselves must model the behaviour they wish to see. This means demonstrating an openness to feedback, a willingness to change course based on new information and a commitment to lifelong learning. It's showing that leadership is not about having all the answers but asking the right questions.

Just as I learned to see beyond the narrow perspectives of my upbringing in Northern Ireland, leaders must learn to see beyond what is immediate and familiar to them. They must recognise their own and their team's blind spots and strive to comprehend the unseen forces shaping their environment. Only by embracing this elevated perspective can leaders truly inspire and drive collaborative performance, navigating their teams through the complexities of the modern business landscape with vision, empathy and strategic acumen.

Mindset Shift 8: From directing to exemplifying the change

The journey of leadership is fraught with misconceptions and missed opportunities, particularly when it comes to driving and embodying change within an organisation. A common pitfall for many leaders is the belief that simply articulating a vision and putting initiatives in place is sufficient for change to occur, when in fact a total system shift is needed. Such a realisation is not just an acknowledgement of the design of the workplace environment but a call to action for leaders to look inwards and evolve their approach from leading change to exemplifying it.

The essence of this shift lies in understanding the profound impact a leader's behaviour has on their team's performance and collaboration. It's a transition from the impersonal directives of 'do as I say,' to the

215

personal embodiment of 'do as I do'. This transformation requires leaders to become acutely aware of their visibility and the scrutiny their actions invite, a realisation that may come slowly but is essential to a culture of trust and mutual respect.

For leaders, particularly those transitioning from technical roles, this visibility and the subsequent analysis of their actions by their team can be an uncomfortable and daunting challenge. But the dynamics of leadership extend beyond technical expertise, requiring a nuanced understanding of how to navigate and influence the organisational landscape effectively. Missteps in this area often stem from a lack of awareness about the impact of one's actions and the critical mistake of failing to model the behaviours essential for the team's success.

In the context of promoting collaborative performance, specific actions and behaviours become pivotal. Leaders must actively demonstrate the value of collaboration by engaging in and promoting cross-functional teamwork, openly sharing information and recognising and rewarding collaborative efforts. They must not only set the standard for expected behaviour but also dismantle silos, building a more integrated and cohesive work environment.

Moreover, the transition to exemplifying change shows the importance of *consistency* over *intensity* in driving organisational transformations. Simon Sinek emphasises that whilst organisations often initiate change with great fervour, the absence of a sustained effort and a clear framework for accountability leads to initiatives that fizzle out without effecting real change.[39] Just as brushing our teeth requires daily attention to prevent decay, organisational health and collaboration demand ongoing, consistent efforts rather than sporadic interventions.

The shift from leading to exemplifying change highlights the leader's role in creating an environment where collaborative performance can thrive. It challenges leaders to reflect on their actions, ensuring they align with the collaborative behaviours they seek to instil in their teams. By embodying the change they wish to see, leaders will both inspire their teams and catalyse a culture of collaboration and collective success. The renewed sense of purpose and direction they will gain paves the way for an overall more collaborative, innovative and resilient organisation.

Chapter takeaways

To lead effectively in this new era, you must embrace the role of a guide rather than a commander. Encourage your team to share insights, make decisions and take ownership. Cultivate an environment where every voice is heard and valued, ensuring your mission and objectives are understood and passionately pursued by all. Trust in the collective genius of your team, and watch as they navigate challenges with creativity and resilience, in ways you had not imagined. Your belief in their potential will unleash unprecedented levels of innovation and commitment. To do these things, you will need to make eight challenging but essential shifts in your leadership:

1. From directive to empowering

2. From expert to facilitator/coach

3. From siloed to networked

4. From relying on logic to increasing influence

5. From presenter to storyteller

6. From a fixed mindset to a growth mindset

7. From assuming 'what we see is all there is' to asking 'what are we not seeing?'

8. From directing to exemplifying the change

Embrace this transformation. Shift your mindset. Empower your team. Watch extraordinary things happen.

Conclusion

What sets companies apart in our modern VUCA world? Knowledge-based organisations all have access to the same pool of people. All implement similar processes and systems. There is, though, an untapped source of competitive advantage, but it's *behavioural*. It's a deliberate effort to build, reinforce and improve a high-performing collaborative environment. Such an environment attracts and retains the best people. It supports them to grow, learn and share their knowledge. They know how to collaborate, and through their collaboration they innovate and create value.

As leader, you can't simply instruct, push for or demand the behaviour you want. The workplace environment you create is the primary controllable influence on behaviour. If you want high performance, you must build an environment in which the behaviours that drive it have a chance of showing up.

The challenge for leaders, particularly those with professional backgrounds in fields governed by clear cause-and-effect relationships, is to embrace the 'fuzziness' of human behaviour. Recognising that beneath the surface of logical decision-making lies a mess of emotions and unconscious dynamics, leaders can still shape the environment to encourage desirable behaviours. This calls for a conscious, deliberate approach, where the workplace itself is engineered to foster collaboration, learning and adaptation.

As a leader, you must consider the profound impact you have in shaping the environment of your organisation. It is within your grasp to cultivate an ecosystem where collaboration, innovation and high performance are not just aspirations but daily realities. This involves a commitment to understanding behaviour, a willingness to experiment and learn and a resolve to create a workplace where every individual feels valued, heard and empowered. In doing so, you will not only move more effectively through the modern business landscape but also leave a lasting imprint on your organisation, shaping its culture for the longer term, building its resilience and securing its place at the vanguard of innovation and excellence. The path is set before you, rich with opportunities to forge a legacy of leadership that transcends the boundaries of traditional business paradigms, embracing the untapped potential of behavioural innovation as the cornerstone of competitive advantage. Embark on this journey with openness, courage and a spirit of discovery. It is in the cultivation of human potential that the future of organisational excellence truly lies.

This book has shared an approach to driving collaborative performance through engineering behaviour change. It is my testimony, constructed from what I have applied and seen work in successful organisations. It has summarised the ways in which I've seen leaders shape, influence, nudge and reinforce collaborative behaviours that have been and will be differentiating. It is also my response to the frustration of serving in dysfunctional environments.

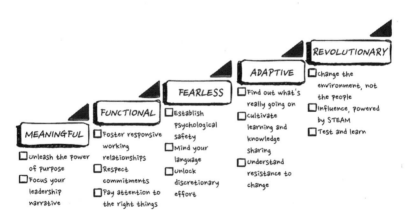

The high-performing collaborative environment

My call to action for you as a leader is to listen, explore, understand and adapt with humility, empathy and curiosity. To engineer an environment that is meaningful, functional, fearless, adaptive and revolutionary. To *be the change*.

Notes

1 WG Bennis and B Nanus, *Leaders: Strategies for taking charge* (HarperCollins, 1985)
2 Oxford Learner's Dictionaries, 'Collaboration' (OLD, nd), www.oxfordlearnersdictionaries. com/definition/american_english/ collaboration, accessed April 2024. Incidentally, another definition of collaboration is 'the act of helping the enemy during a war when they have taken control of your country'. This may resonate for some people working in siloed, bureaucratic organisations.
3 YN Harari, *Sapiens: A Brief History of Humankind* (Vintage Books, 2015)
4 D Kahneman, *Thinking Fast and Slow* (Farrar, Straus and Giroux, 2011)

5 This equation for collaborative performance builds on the work of Ryan Olson. His equation for an *individual's* performance is: Performance = Ability + Motivation – Obstacles. Skills are not enough to achieve high performance; the individual must have the motivation to achieve the desired level of performance, and obstacles to achieving success must be navigated or removed. R Olson, 'First things first: Priorities for creating protective and positive workplaces' (Oregon Health & Science University, nd), www.ohsu.edu/sites/default/files/2019-04/OIOHS-Outreach-Symp-May17-Olson.pdf, accessed May 2024

6 RM Ryan and EL Deci, 'Self-determination theory and the facilitation of intrinsic motivation, social development, and well-being', *American Psychologist*, 55/1 (2000), 68–78, https://doi.org/10.1037/0003-066X.55.1.68

7 DH Pink, *Drive: The surprising truth about what motivates us* (Riverhead, 2009)

8 T Husson, 'Embrace storymaking to change your sustainability brand narrative' (Forrester, 20 October 2023), www.forrester.com/blogs/embrace-storymaking-to-change-your-sustainability-brand-narrative, accessed May 2024

9 D Kahneman, *Thinking Fast and Slow* (Farrar, Straus and Giroux, 2011)

10 JH Gittell, *The Southwest Airlines Way* (McGraw-Hill, 2003)

11 D Kahneman and A Tversky, 'Intuitive prediction: Biases and corrective procedures', TIMS Studies in Management Science, 12 (1977), 313–327

12 B Flyvbjerg and D Gardner, *How Big Things Get Done* (Currency, 2023)

13 Office of Rail and Road, 'Inquiry into May 2018 network disruption' (ORR, 7 December 2018), www.orr.gov.uk/monitoring-regulation/rail/investigations/may-2018-network-disruption, accessed May 2024

14 AC Daniels, *Bringing Out the Best in People: How to apply the astonishing power of positive reinforcement* (McGraw-Hill, 1999)

15 V Govindarajan and S Srinivas, 'The innovation mindset in action: 3M Corporation', *Harvard Business Review* (6 August 2013), https://hbr.org/2013/08/the-innovation-mindset-in-acti-3, accessed April 2024

16 C Duhigg, 'What Google learned from its quest to build the perfect team' (*The New York Times Magazine*, 25 February 2016), www.nytimes.com/2016/02/28/magazine/what-google-learned-from-its-quest-to-build-the-perfect-team.html, accessed June 2024

17 A Edmondson, *The Fearless Organisation: Creating psychological safety in the workplace for learning, innovation, and growth* (John Wiley & Sons, 2019)

18 A Edmondson, 'Psychological safety and learning behavior in work teams', *Administrative Science Quarterly*, 44/2 (1999), 350–383, https://doi.org/10.2307/2666999

19   J Renck, Episode 1: *Chernobyl*, Sky Atlantic
(2019)

20   AC Daniels, *Bringing Out the Best in People:
How to apply the astonishing power of positive
reinforcement* (McGraw-Hill, 1999)

21   J Wetzler, *Ask: Tap into the hidden wisdom of
people around you for unexpected breakthroughs in
leadership and life* (Hachette Book Group, 2024)

22   J Girard and J Girard, 'Defining knowledge
management: Toward an applied compendium',
Online Journal of Applied Knowledge Management,
3/1 (2015), 1–20

23   N Milton, *Knowledge Management for Teams and
Projects* (Chandos Publishing, 2005)

24   BD Rosenberg and JT Siegel, 'A 50-year review
of psychological reactance theory: Do not read
this article', *Motivation Science*, 4/4 (2018), 281–
300, https://doi.org/10.1037/mot0000091

25   N Machiavelli, *The Prince* (Viking Classics, 2023)

26   D Kahneman and A Tversky, 'Prospect theory:
An analysis of decision under risk', *Econometrica*,
47/2 (1979), 263–291

27   G Gavett, 'Think carefully about where you put
the office bathroom', *Harvard Business Review*
(nd), https://hbr.org/2013/07/think-carefully-
about-where-yo, accessed May 2024

28   P Dolan et al, 'Mindspace: Influencing behaviour
through public policy' (Cabinet Office, 2011),
www.instituteforgovernment.org.uk/sites/
default/files/publications/MINDSPACE.pdf,
accessed April 2024

29 D Halpern et al, 'EAST: Four simple ways to apply behavioural insights', *Annual Review of Policy Design*, 5/1 (2014), 1–53, https://ojs. unbc.ca/index.php/design/article/view/1658, accessed April 2024

30 RH Thaler and CR Sunstein, *Nudge: Improving decisions about health, wealth, and happiness* (Yale University Press, 2008)

31 H Dai, KL Milkman and J Riis, 'The fresh start effect: Temporal landmarks motivate aspirational behaviour', *Management Science*, 60/10 (2014), 2563–2582, https://doi. org/10.1287/mnsc.2014.1901

32 J Timpson, *The Happy Index: Lessons in upside-down management* (HarperCollins Publishers, 2024)

33 P Chee, J Irwin, JM Bennett and AJ Carrigan, 'The mere presence of a mobile phone: Does it influence driving performance?', *Accident Analysis & Prevention*, 159 (2021), 106226, https://doi.org/10.1016/j.aap.2021.106226

34 J Hayward, 'How Amsterdam Schipol reduced toilet cleaning costs by 8% with fake urinal bugs' (Simple Flying, 21 August 2021), https://simpleflying.com/how-amsterdam-schipol-reduced-toilet-cleaning-costs-by-8-with-fake-urinal-bugs, accessed April 2024

35 D Marquet, *Turn the Ship Around: A true story of turning followers into leaders* (Penguin, 2012)

36 C Dweck, *Growth Mindset: Changing the way you think to fulfil your potential* (Robinson, 2017)

37 M Mangel and FJ Samaniego, 'Abraham Wald's work on aircraft survivability', *Journal of the American Statistical Association*, 79/386 (1984), 259–267, https://doi.org/10.1080/01621459.1984.10478038

38 D Kahneman, *Thinking Fast and Slow* (Farrar, Straus and Giroux, 2011)

39 S Sinek, *The Infinite Game* (Penguin, 2019)

Further Reading

MH Bazerman, *Judgment in Managerial Decision Making* (Wiley, 2020)

JR Boyd, *Destruction and Creation* US Army Command and General Staff College (1976)

Z Chance, *Influence is Your Superpower: The science of winning hearts, sparking change, and making good things happen* (Crown, 2021)

RB Cialdini, *Influence: The psychology of persuasion* (HarperCollins, 1984)

P Dolan, *Happiness by Design: Finding pleasure and purpose in everyday life* (Allen Lane, 2014)

N Duarte, *DataStory: Explain data and inspire action through story* (Duarte Press, 2019)

A Edmondson, *Right Kind of Wrong: The science of failing well* (Atria Books, 2023)

G Gigerenzer, *Risk Savvy: How to make good decisions* (Viking, 2014)

A Grant, *Think Again: The power of knowing what you don't know* (Viking, 2021)

R Greene, *The Laws of Human Nature* (Viking, 2018)

G Klein, *Seeing What Others Don't: The remarkable ways we gain insights* (PublicAffairs, 2013)

K Leonard and T Yorton, *Yes, And: How improvisation reverses "No, But" thinking and improves creativity and collaboration – lessons from The Second City* (Harper Business, 2015)

J Maeda, *The Laws of Simplicity: Design, technology, business, life* (MIT Press, 2006)

DH Maister, CH Green and RM Galford, *The Trusted Advisor* (Free Press, 2000)

C Newport, *Slow Productivity: A practical guide to reducing stress and enhancing performance* (Penguin Random House, 2023)

S Sinek, *Start with Why: How great leaders inspire everyone to take action* (Penguin, 2009)

R Sutherland, *Alchemy: The dark art and curious science of creating magic in brands, business, and life* (HarperCollins, 2019)

M Syed, *Black Box Thinking: Why most people never learn from their mistakes – but some do* (John Murray, 2015)

M Syed, *Rebel Ideas: The power of diverse thinking* (John Murray, 2019)

RH Thaler and CR Sunstein, *Nudge: Improving decisions about health, wealth, and happiness* (Yale University Press, 2008)

Acknowledgements

This book could not have been completed without the support and input from an amazing group of people. My deep thanks to all of them.

To my parents, Ian and Ann, for their unwavering support and encouragement. To my wife, Sarah, and our kids, Amalie and Arran, for their patience and love throughout this process.

To my beta readers, Howard Lees, Mark Sweeney, Jaspal Mundh and Mark Ashton, whose critical insights helped shape the manuscript.

I appreciate the intellectual and professional guidance provided by my business partners and fellow behavioural explorers: James Beazley, Michael Taylor, Neil Fachie, and Tianne Croshaw. I have been shaped by the wisdom and mentorship of Bob Uhler, Don Smith, David Nickols, Ian McAulay, Betsy Redfern, Professor Adam Greenstein and the late Vic Gulas.

Thank you to my colleagues, collaborators and clients: Tania Flasck, Scott Jackson, Paddy Brow, Craig McMaster, Jugal Choudhary PhD, Alex McCluckie, Colin Cumming, Professor Tony Conway, Tracey Gee, Kevin Fowlie, Ulrike Fehr, Daressa Frodsham, Tim Griffiths and Pia Aaltonen-Forsell for their contributions, challenges and inspiration.

A special mention to my peers from the LSE Behavioural Science cohort – Kate Webster, Indrajeet Ghatje, Guilherme Lima – and also to the LSE faculty members who inspired us all to explore how life really works, including Paul Dolan, Matteo Gallizzi, Barbara Fasolo, Heather Kappes and Dario Krpan.

I'm also thankful for the inspiration I've gained from many thought leaders including Amy Edmondson and the late Daniel Kahneman who have guided my thoughts through their groundbreaking work.

A heartfelt thanks to Justin, Diana and the team at California Coffee & Wine and Mark Lee-Kilgariff at Tatton Perk for keeping me caffeine-fuelled and sane.

Also, to Chris Nicklin and the Nxtep 7am crew for helping me stay resilient and energised.

To everyone who supported me in any way, your generosity has not gone unnoticed, and I am profoundly thankful.

The Author

 Garry Sanderson is a leadership and behavioural consultant. He is the founder of Visualyze, which supports leaders and teams to increase collaborative performance in support of delivering major strategies and transformation programmes. Garry specialises in the practical application of behavioural science through consulting, coaching and digitally enabled facilitation.

Through his former executive-level roles in global professional service organisations, Garry successfully led significant operations, major growth initiatives and global change programmes. In doing so, he became passionate about the human, social and behavioural aspects that are key to organisational success yet are so often poorly understood.

Garry has a distinctive academic background, having studied engineering at Queen's University of Belfast, business leadership at Harvard Business School and Behavioural Science at London School of Economics.

In 1999, Garry was winner of the UK Young Consulting Engineer of the Year Award, presented by the Association of Consulting Engineers and the Worshipful Company of Engineers.

Combining this learning with more than thirty years of industry experience, Garry brings a unique blend of practical solution development, global leadership skills and the application of cutting-edge behavioural insights.

Garry's six-word story that represents his approach to his work is *There must be a better way.*

You can find out more at:

⊕ www.Change-Engineer.com

CW01083732

CO
VE
RT

Also by A.S. Dulat

Kashmir: The Vajpayee Years
(co-authored with Aditya Sinha)
The Spy Chronicles: R&AW, ISI and the Illusion of Peace
(co-authored with Gen. Asad Durrani and Aditya Sinha)
A Life in the Shadows: A Memoir

Also by Asad Durrani

The Spy Chronicles: R&AW, ISI and the Illusion of Peace
(co-authored with A.S. Dulat and Aditya Sinha)
Honour Among Spies

CO
VE
RT

THE PSYCHOLOGY
OF WAR AND PEACE

**A.S.
DULAT** | **ASAD
DURRANI** | **NEIL K.
AGGARWAL**

HarperCollins *Publishers* India

First published in India by HarperCollins *Publishers* 2024
4th Floor, Tower A, Building No. 10, DLF Cyber City,
DLF Phase II, Gurugram, Haryana – 122002
www.harpercollins.co.in

2 4 6 8 10 9 7 5 3 1

Copyright © A.S. Dulat, Asad Durrani and Neil K. Aggarwal 2024

P-ISBN: 978-93-5699-942-8
E-ISBN: 978-93-5699-618-2

Typeset in 12/17 Berling LT Std
Manipal Technologies Limited, Manipal

Printed and bound at
Thomson Press (India) Ltd

Contents

Foreword
   A.S. Dulat   ix

Introduction   xi

1. Life after *The Spy Chronicles*   1
2. The Psychological Foundations of Track II,
   People-to-People Diplomacy   40
3. Case Studies in How We Become Indians
   and Pakistanis   84
4. Making Peace Can Be as Hard as War: Why Some
   Initiatives Succeed and Others Fail   140
5. An Honest Assessment of Future Peacemaking   190

   Notes   231
   Index   247

Foreword

A.S. Dulat

<hr />

It all began as a joke; or so it appeared at the time.

Late one October evening in 2021, Sundeep Waslekar, our friend from Mumbai, walked into our home. With him was Karan Sawhney. Not having met for a couple of years, we began by exchanging pleasantries before settling down to a glass of Merlot. Waslekar had barely taken his first sip when he burst into sudden laughter.

'What's tickled you, Chief?' I asked. 'Chief' is my moniker for him.

Waslekar continued to laugh. Finally, he said, 'There is a group of shrinks in New York who are going to discuss your book [*The Spy Chronicles*] next month.'

I too was amused when I heard this. 'How do you know?'

'They are part of a book club [Bloomsbury] that discusses a different book every month,' Waslekar explained. 'One of the guys, a bearded fellow called Chuck, wanted me to join in the debate.'

I had first met Waslekar—author, strategic thinker, peacemaker—through a colleague in Mumbai in 1994 when I was seeking a way forward in Kashmir. People in Mumbai, including some prominent businessmen, showed interest in Kashmir in those days, more than elsewhere. In 1995, Waslekar was to lead a fact-finding delegation, which included, among others, Rahul Singh, Teesta Setalvad, Karan Sawhney, a couple of doctors and an academician. They would meet with Kashmiri separatist leaders in Srinagar and bring us information in Delhi—where any crumb was more than useful.

Waslekar's initial focus was South Asia, and during this time he developed many contacts in Pakistan. Interestingly, his friend Abdul Sattar, then Foreign Minister of Pakistan, reached out to Waslekar to seek his advice in dealing with India prior to the Agra summit. Since 2002, Waslekar has spread his wings, enlarging the compass of his work. It was while he was serving as a senior fellow at the Centre for the Resolution of Intractable Conflict in Oxford that he met Chuck.

In 2016, Waslekar was in Delhi to follow up with his publishers [HarperCollins] on his book *A World without War*, which brought him to our place. And in 2021, it was his offer to get General Durrani and me to join in the shrinks' discussion on *The Spy Chronicles*, moderated by Neil K. Aggarwal, that led to this book on 'The Psychology of War and Peace', which has virtually turned out to be *The Spy Chronicles* Part II, once again pointing to a way forward between India and Pakistan—perhaps a fantasy, but always on our minds since history has put us side by side.

I have known and engaged with General Saheb for some years now, but it has been a fascinating interaction with Neil. One can lie to the world, but not to oneself—and to a psychiatrist, even less!

Introduction

If you ask A.S. Dulat and Asad Durrani how they got into the intelligence field, they will tell you that it was by accident. Accident also characterizes how we three—General Asad Durrani, former chief of the ISI, Amarjit Singh Dulat, former chief of RAW, and Dr Neil Krishan Aggarwal, psychiatrist and social scientist—met.

In August 2021, Aggarwal recommended *The Spy Chronicles* to a group of psychoanalysts who meet monthly to discuss the psychology of war and peacemaking. The moderators of this group—Dr Chuck Strozier and Lord John Alderdice—enjoyed the book. Alderdice, a psychiatrist and psychoanalyst with a lifetime peerage, had been a lead negotiator in the Irish Peace Talks. As a sitting member of the House of Lords, he offered to explore possible connections to Dulat and Durrani. Alderdice contacted a colleague, Sundeep Waslekar, who was Dulat's friend. Dulat and Durrani agreed to participate in a November 2021 book discussion with psychiatrists and psychoanalysts on the psychology of peacemaking. Strozier and Alderdice

graciously permitted Aggarwal to lead a discussion based on
The Spy Chronicles.

Aggarwal suggested to Dulat and Durrani that he write
up their conversation as a manuscript for submission to a
prominent psychiatry journal. Scholarship on the psychology
of peacemaking has been dominated by the perspectives
of psychiatrists and psychologists who have participated in
Track II negotiations, but never before had foreign policy
experts at the highest levels of intelligence agreed to share
their reflections on the technical aspects of peacemaking. We
discovered an intellectual niche, along with the realization
that the three of us enjoyed each other's company. In
February 2022, we met to marvel at the quick passage of
our manuscript through the academic peer-review process.
Aggarwal suggested another project. Dulat challenged him
to consider a book. Aggarwal agreed, provided that the book
would not repeat *The Spy Chronicles* and that he would
have full liberty to ask the men any questions. Durrani was
intrigued. By March 2022, HarperCollins India graciously
came on board. To our knowledge, no other book has
explored the inner lives and motivations of spy chiefs, let
alone former rivals.

Given this project's origins, this book is inherently
psychological. Aggarwal's fields of academic specialization
are in three disciplines: cultural psychiatry, psychiatric
anthropology and South Asian studies. This book sits at the
intersection of these disciplines. From the outset, we have
wanted to make contributions in two main areas: (1) using
psychiatry and psychology to understand conflict, intelligence
and peacemaking, and (2) offering specific, practical strategies
for peace-building between India and Pakistan. Hence, this

book can be helpful for all people who are invested in peace in South Asia. It also offers a roadmap for peacemakers interested in adopting a psychological approach in other contexts.

We adopted the ground rules that Peter Jones offers in his book *Track Two Diplomacy in Theory and Practice*:[1]

- Participants will interact civilly, listen actively with attention and respect, not interrupt, and allow each other to present all views fully.

- Participants will speak from their hearts and minds, knowing that their emotions and ideas will be acknowledged.

- Participants will respond as directly and fully as possible to all points while attempting to put themselves in each other's shoes.

- Participants will try to learn from each other to increase the complexity of their thinking.

However, we did not adhere to one of Jones's rules—on observing time limits—so that each person could speak as completely as possible, as the situation warranted. We met for seven formal sessions over Zoom, each for about two hours. We recorded each session, all of which produced nearly 150,000 words of text. These sessions were transcribed to produce chapters and we supplemented drafts with text from phone calls and emails when our conversations spilled into other forums.

The book is laid out in the following chapters. These can be read in order or separately.

Chapter One describes the reactions of both men to *The Spy Chronicles*, examining enduring domains of psychological interest such as self-perception, self-esteem, trust, stress, vulnerability, coping and perceptions of others.[2] This chapter also assesses their perspectives on regional developments after 2018 to serve as context for the rest of our discussions.

Chapter Two explores the childhood, adolescent and early adulthood experiences of both men. We outline their professional trajectories, focusing specifically on intelligence work.[3] We also reflect on their transitions from seeing each other as enemies to allies in peacemaking.

Chapter Three dives into how the men developed their cultural, ethnic, religious and regional identities. We trace the sources of these identities, along with their evolutions throughout life. We contemplate the relationships of these identities to being Indian and Pakistani, and why such similarities and differences matter when discussing peace.[4]

Chapter Four discusses how both men view the foreign policy establishments of India and Pakistan through questions that come from experiments in the psychology of international relations.[5] We assess why the Governments of India and Pakistan collaborate in certain areas and compete in others.

Chapter Five concludes with an honest appraisal of next steps for peacebuilding. We sit with the discomfort of knowing that conflict is inherently programmed into the India–Pakistan bilateral relationship. We review scholarship on the psychology of intractable conflicts to propose realistic, incremental ways that foreign policy professionals in both countries could resume meaningful negotiations.

We thank Dr Strozier, Lord Alderdice and Sundeep Waslekar, who were instrumental in bringing us into contact.

At HarperCollins India, we thank Udayan Mitra who suggested the dialogue format to retain the tone of our conversations and Ananth Padmanabhan who supported this project from its inception. Finally, we thank our families for allowing us to sneak away at all times of day and night to continue this dialogue.

1

Life after *The Spy Chronicles*

> Sometimes we have to do a thing in order to find out the
> reason for it. Sometimes our actions are questions, not answers.
> —John le Carré, *A Perfect Spy*

In 2018, HarperCollins published *The Spy Chronicles: RAW, ISI and the Illusion of Peace*. The book presented transcripts of dialogues that the Indian journalist Aditya Sinha moderated between two former foreign intelligence chiefs: Amarjit Singh Dulat, who ran India's Research and Analysis Wing from August 1999 to December 2000, and General Asad Ahmed Durrani, who ran Pakistan's Inter-Services Intelligence from August 1990 to March 1992. The novelty of rival spymasters from two of the world's most secretive and dreaded organizations publicizing their conversations captivated the political establishments in both countries.

The book was launched by A.S. Dulat in New Delhi on 24 May 2018. Former Prime Minister Manmohan Singh and former Vice President Hamid Ansari came as chief guests.[1] Former Foreign Minister Yashwant Sinha—then a member

1

of the Bharatiya Janata Party (BJP)—denounced the Modi government's approach to Jammu and Kashmir, saying, 'They are using this so-called muscular policy in Kashmir, and we all know that a policy that uses brawn lacks brains.'[2] Former Chief Minister of Jammu and Kashmir Farooq Abdullah skipped a Bengaluru meeting with chief ministers and the Gandhi family in order to attend the launch.[3]

The Government of India blocked General Durrani from the event. In a pre-recorded message, he joked, 'By denying me a visa they have saved me from the wrath of my hawks.'[4]

The book received warm reviews in prominent Indian newspapers. Sushant Singh wrote in the *Indian Express* that 'the idea of getting a former Pakistan intelligence chief and a former Indian intelligence chief together in a dialogue format is powerful and enticing'.[5] In *Business Standard*, Praveen Swami praised the 'warm, reassuring timbre' of both men.[6] Rezaul Laskar noted in the *Hindustan Times* that the book managed to 'capture the zeitgeist' and 'tap into a subject that is central to the lives of millions of people', namely India–Pakistan relations.[7]

Pakistani journalists were more ambivalent. Aisha Saeed paid a compliment in *Daily Pakistan*, writing that 'the book is a rare piece, almost fictional and a bait for many', which 'encapsulates the general human aspect by offering a rare glance into [a] comfortable conversation.'[8] But there was criticism too. In *Daily Times*, Nyla Ali Khan highlighted a controversial position that General Durrani took, which criticized the Pakistani deep state's 'complete disregard for the narrative of an independent and secular Kashmir'.[9] Imad Zafar contended in the *Express Tribune*, 'Nothing revealed by Durrani has come as a shock to anyone; the only shocking aspect of it all is the seniority of the person revealing it.'[10]

Pakistan's military leaders hit back. On 28 May 2018, four days after the book's release, military spokesperson Major General Asif Ghafoor announced that General Headquarters (GHQ) had summoned General Durrani 'to explain his position on views attributed to him in [the] book *Spy Chronicles*'.[11] According to a military statement, General Durrani's authorship was 'taken as a violation of [the] Military Code of Conduct applicable on (*sic*) all serving and retired military personnel.'[12]

After his summons, the Interior Ministry released a statement: 'It has been decided to place the name of Lt Gen. (retd) Muhammad Asad Durrani on the Exit Control List under Section 2 of Exit from Pakistan (Control) Ordinance, 1981, on the recommendation of Military Intelligence Directorate Rawalpindi due to his involvement in an ongoing inquiry.'[13] An intelligence agency once helmed by General Durrani turned against him. The Government of Pakistan placed him on a no-fly list.

Leaders in opposing political parties found a common target. Former Prime Minister Muhammad Nawaz Sharif from the Pakistan Muslim League demanded a national commission to probe General Durrani's disclosures,[14] the most serious being that Pakistani officials mishandled the case of Indian spy Kulbhushan Yadav and had struck a deal with the American military to apprehend Osama bin Laden in Abbottabad.[15] Former Senate Chairman Raza Rabbani from the Pakistan People's Party raised concerns of hypocrisy, contending, '[If] politicians and civilians had [done this], they would've been booked for treason as a result of their "revelations".'[16]

Dulat defended his co-author, telling a reporter, '[The] things written in [the] book are his memories. Even former

Pakistan Foreign Secretary Riaz Mohammad Khan said that
26/11 Mumbai attacks destroyed Pakistan's credibility in
Kashmir. If a former foreign secretary can get away with it,
why not [an] ISI chief?'[17]

In February 2019, the Islamabad High Court ruled that
General Durrani's name must be removed from the Exit
Control List within the month.[18] By June 2019, Durrani
filed a contempt case against the Interior Secretary for failing
to comply with the court's orders.[19] In October 2020, the
government restored his pension and other post-retirement
benefits.[20]

In late 2020, HarperCollins published Durrani's novel
Honour Among Spies. He acknowledged that the book is
'essentially about the events that followed the appearance
of *Spy Chronicles* in May 2018—and how they guided me to
understand the rancour some in the military hierarchy had been
harbouring against me for the last many years'.[21]

Pakistan's military leaders persisted in their legal case
against him. In January 2021, the Ministry of Defence
submitted a statement to the Islamabad High Court,
insinuating that General Durrani had acted treasonously:
'The petitioner is affiliated/interacting with hostile elements,
specially Indian RAW, since 2008. During an interview before
respondents [the ministries of defence, interior and the State
of Pakistan] the petitioner rendered an affidavit committing to
refrain from such activities which is still not seen in tangible
terms.'[22]

Finally, on 4 March 2021, the Islamabad High Court
ordered General Durrani's removal from the Exit Control List,
declaring, 'Like all citizens, this retired three-star general also
has rights.'[23]

Psychoanalysts have approached diplomacy by exploring how the inner psychological worlds of foreign policy professionals intertwine with the external world.[24] In this chapter, we take up John le Carré's challenge of doing a thing in order to find out the reason for it. A.S. Dulat and General Durrani reflect on personal developments since *The Spy Chronicles*. They discuss events since 2018, such as Jammu and Kashmir's legal status in India and the Taliban's conquest of Afghanistan. Both men have spoken candidly about their emotional investments in these regions as spy chiefs. Their reflections reveal psychological themes of conflict, coping, resilience and perseverance, with everyone aware of the high costs involved in peacemaking.

1. Personal Reactions in the Aftermath of *The Spy Chronicles*

Neil Krishan Aggarwal: This book is in conversation with *The Spy Chronicles*, but it is not *The Spy Chronicles 2*. I'm not a journalist. I'm a psychiatrist who specializes in the psychology of cross-cultural misunderstandings, conflict and peacemaking. But because so much has happened publicly to both of you, and especially to General Durrani, we need to ask about how that book was received. The first question is, how do you now feel about the reception of the book?

Asad Durrani: Initially, I was puzzled—frankly, I did not expect what happened. But over time, I have been amazed by how people have reacted. Some people found merit in this book, and the venture: that the two of us joined hands to write that book.

There have been many different consequences. One, of course, is your project. I never expected that one day the two us would be subjected to a psychiatrist. But I'm actually quite pleased about it.

In Pakistan, there are people who, after first looking askance, later said, 'Sir, this was a good idea. How did you come up with it?' These were the few, mostly in academia and the establishment, who had actually read the book.

Aggarwal: Dulat Saheb, how do you feel about the reception of the last book?

A.S. Dulat: We were surprised by the reception it got, though we knew it was unique when we started on the book. General Saheb had a harder time of it in Pakistan; the deep state goes deeper there. But I faced negative reactions here, too. Very few people said they saw merit in it; they were more concerned that a former chief of RAW collaborated with a former chief of ISI. But I got off relatively lightly. I was more worried for General Durrani. He told me, 'You worry about me more than I worry about myself.' He was cool as a cucumber, as always —I think that's why people in Pakistan have started seeing merit in the book.

Aggarwal: What surprised you both about the reception?

Dulat: I was shocked by the adverse reaction. We knew the book was unusual but the reaction was worse than expected. It wasn't a conspiracy between two spooks. What we have done, as we have throughout in Track II and particularly 'Spooks Track II', is to stick as close to the truth as possible.

Quite often, General Saheb and I used to sit side by side and joke around, to the surprise of the diplomats. We had fun talking, and we always talked honestly. That's how it went with the book too. It may not be full of facts and figures, but it is an honest book.

Aggarwal: General Saheb, what surprised you most about the book?

Durrani: The day of the launch, I was watching, sitting here [in Pakistan]. The discussion was very well done. The participants were top notch in India—Manmohan Singh, Hamid Ansari, Farooq Abdullah, some union ministers and, of course, Mr Dulat and his friends. Their conclusion was that this book tells you the right way forward. I never expected that from them. I thought there would be criticism. This was the best outcome that I could have expected.

People here started looking at me positively mostly because of what we said about Kashmir. Someone serving at that time whispered to me, 'Sir, I think this book is very good—I am a Kashmiri and I think the book would help solve our dispute.' I have always said, 'Mr Dulat knows Kashmir much better than I do.' When there were discussions on India, Pakistan, Pulwama or Kashmir, Mr Dulat was invited almost every time. That was encouraging.

The discourse that took place at the launch said how useful they found the book. It created the conditions to make real progress in peace but because some idiots raised a hue and cry, that favourable moment was lost. We both feel we must

recover that lost moment. But even that cacophony was helpful
because I saw how things that happened years ago continue to
impact decisions made today.

Aggarwal: What did not surprise you about the reception of
the book?

Durrani: I did expect that some people would say, 'Why did
you do that?' or 'You know these so-and-so Indians, the designs
they have,' or 'You're not supposed to be talking to someone
like Dulat.' That is the usual way of looking at things.

It took a long time for the sceptics to take a back seat, and
some started to write reviews. But we hardly had a review
for a year. All the reviews were from India or elsewhere. The
surprise was that there was no negative review from India—
they were all encouraging.

Aggarwal: Dulat Saheb, what did not surprise you about the
reception? And I'm going to ask you a follow-up question. You
mentioned twice that you heard about people in India who are
not happy with the book. We tend to hear more about General
Durrani's struggles on the Pakistani side, but what were people
here were unhappy about?

Dulat: Both of us understood this was an unusual book. But I
didn't for a moment think that there was anything that people
could take objection to. But that I was talking to a former ISI
chief—yeah, that did not go down well with some people. But
we had been talking, and doing Track II together, for years.

When I heard that General Saheb had been denied a visa to
attend the launch, I realized there were some who were not

happy that this was happening. Fortunately for both of us, it went off well.

Aggarwal: I want to understand how the book may have been a source of self-esteem. Tell me about a time when you heard something positive about you or the book. How did it make you feel?

Durrani: The book has reached far and wide. I was told a few days ago that some countries in the Maghreb—Morocco, Algeria and some other places—have heard of this and said, 'If this is the path to resolve some conflicts out in the open and to make peace, why not do it?' So this model has been widely accepted.

Aggarwal: And when you say that the model for the Maghreb countries has been inspired by the book, do you mean specifically about intelligence chiefs communicating?

Durrani: I think so. Someone said that if in chronically hostile countries like India and Pakistan, their former chiefs of intelligence agencies, which have been blamed for so much mischief, can come together, then why can't we? This idea of working jointly seems to have caught on.

Aggarwal: Dulat Saheb, how has your book helped your self-esteem?

Dulat: At the launch, to have Dr Manmohan Singh there! It was a very touching moment for me. So, I called him up a couple of days later and thanked him profusely. And he said,

'No, no, no! I learned a lot that evening.' You can't get humbler than that. At that time, this mattered more to me than what anyone else said. It gave me a lot of heart.

Durrani: Some unexpected things did happen. One was that very often, instead of talking about what I had said, they would take out a ruler and measure how much space I took in the book compared to him. They seemed to think that one should speak less and let the other blurt out a little more, so they let out state secrets. But it was never about that.

The other surprising thing that happened a couple of years later is that the diplomatic corps also caught up with the book. Many of them said, 'We appreciate how both of you have shown respect for each other. You haven't gone for the jugular. He gave his point of view; you gave yours.' I said, 'Yes, that was the idea: to let the two versions come out, not to prove myself right and the other person wrong, but because both versions must be heard.'

Dulat: In most things, we agreed. Where there was disagreement, we respected each other's point of view, so there was no argument. We were adversaries who respected each other. When it came to Kashmir, General Saheb would concede graciously that 'Dulat knows a little more'. And if Afghanistan came up, I would say, 'Nobody knows more than General Saheb.'

Also, we shared the conviction that we need to try and work together. General Saheb would say, 'You're an optimist.' I would say, 'Yeah, I'm an optimist.' He is more of a realist. But that was our hope—that somebody would understand that we need to move together at the earliest.

Durrani: For example, I heard some criticism from many people: 'Why didn't you rebut?' 'Why didn't you explain?' 'Why did you let him get away with that?' I have always ignored them. Some types of questions cannot be answered. Otherwise, this would become a squabbling match.

Aggarwal: Did the book's reception change your perception of what you can accomplish by way of peacemaking?

Durrani: Yes, it did in my case.

Aggarwal: How so? Please tell us, General Saheb.

Durrani: When people said that I was a peacemaker, I replied, 'I am not in that business. I am in the business of blowing up bridges.'

I went to Oslo to study how peace is made. I also carried out my own analysis of [former Indian Prime Minister Inder Kumar] Gujral's formula of composite dialogue.[25] I started to understand something about how to make peace. But I never thought about *being* a peacemaker. I'm happy if the book gave me that honour. No one wants to go down as a warmonger or a hawk. There's one thing for which I can take credit: when I said, 'The only solution that I can think of is that Kashmir becomes a bridge, from confrontation to cooperation.' And Mr Dulat said, 'Yes.'

Just to connect this to what is happening now in Europe, [former US Secretary of State Henry] Kissinger is no peacemaker. He is a hardliner who practises realpolitik. But he also said that the best thing is to make Ukraine a bridge between the East and the West.[26]

But this recommendation has no chance under the current circumstances.

Dulat: You know, it had the opposite effect on me. As you know, I'm an optimist; call me a peacenik if you like. But I think things are much tougher now than I had thought. I suffer from no illusions.

I have realized that peace between India and Pakistan is becoming increasingly difficult. I'm not suggesting that we are going to go to war or any such thing. But the status quo will continue. Everything becomes an excuse for not moving forward. Whether it's Imran Khan's possible no-confidence vote,[27] the next election here, or the one in Pakistan, and so on and so forth.

It's strange that people don't believe that the best chance for peace, especially for Kashmir, was during the time of Atal Bihari Vajpayee and Pervez Musharraf, or Dr Manmohan Singh and Musharraf. All who followed have lacked that kind of conviction. India has changed a great deal in the last eight to ten years. If I'm sitting here or I collaborate with the General again, it's only because of my great respect for him, not because I see it doing any good anytime soon.

Aggarwal: One doesn't often hear about spies or spymasters facing the sort of negative reactions you both described. I want to ask you both one question. Tell me about a time when you heard something negative about you or the book. How did it make you feel?

Durrani: The negative opinions were unsubstantiated. Every time I asked them, 'Have you read the book?' they would say,

'No.' Now, hardly anyone says such stuff. But even in the initial days at the height of the hue and cry, surprisingly, among the retired services, people would give me a thumbs up [*gesturing*] and say, 'Good! Well done! This is something new!' The negative things were a little unkind. That was to be expected.

Looking back, I feel a little amused. People reacted the way they did because I enjoyed a high profile, I was invited to Doha and Oxford—they felt jealous and envious. But it's not up to me. You get invited because some sponsor thinks, 'I should talk to you about it.' I got invited to Russia so many times even though my past was suspect.[28]

Aggarwal: But General Durrani, you faced some pretty heavy consequences. You were put on the Exit Control List. You were stripped of your pension and retirement benefits. This from an establishment to which you had devoted decades serving. How did you feel?

Durrani: You just hang in there for a year or two. It was in the court. Oh God! When the charge came: 'He's a RAW agent!' 'He's a RAW affiliate!' I had a big laugh. I said, 'How are these people going to prove this charge? How are they going to proceed?' Luckily, I recovered.

All the pension, the exit, etc., everything is back to normal. And at this age, I'm not looking for more. I said, 'Fine. You did it for your reasons.' I paid a price for a while. I am the winner. This is a closed chapter as far as I'm concerned.

It's happened to better people than me, and considering the environment, I got off lightly, even benefitted. I repeat: I am the winner. Everyone else realized when they read this book that it is significant. Some people told the establishment: 'Don't press with your line because this man is not going to give in. He's not an unknown person.'

Aggarwal: I appreciate you sharing that with us. Dulat Saheb, how did you feel when you heard negative things about the book?

Dulat: They said a lot of negative things. I wouldn't have minded if the purpose of the book had been served—if it had made *some* difference. But I don't think it has. That's why I feel disillusioned. So, although I'm a great believer in peace, right now I'm not very optimistic about it—it would be delusional. *Hun kuj honvala nahin* [Right now, nothing will happen].

Durrani: Isn't this very strange, what happened after the book with the two of us? We've turned around: he's more realistic; I'm more hopeful. That reminds me of a very old verse: *Hum hue kafir, toh woh kafir Musalman ho gaya* [We became infidels, that infidel became a Muslim].[29]
[*All three laugh.*]

Durrani [*laughing*]: I became a kafir. I became a non-believer in so many things. And Mr Dulat, he became ...

Dulat [*laughing*]: General, *mainu jehri tusi gall karni hai, kar lo* [General, say whatever you want to say to me].
[*All three laugh.*]

Dulat: Neil, India has changed. India is changing. The world needs to take note of it. I think in India and Pakistan we need to realize that now it's different. The decision-makers want to know they will benefit from what they do, and how it will affect election results. Winning elections and gain are the main considerations.

Aggarwal: I'm going to ask you both to share a little about your inner worlds. I want to ask you about trust. To whom did you turn for support when you heard negative things about yourselves or the book?

Durrani: Frankly, to no one. When someone criticized, I would say, 'Read the book, and then go climb a pole.'

I was not going to ask someone for support. I might send him [Dulat] a message and get encouragement. Shivshankar Menon, who was High Commissioner here[30] and is now a recognized scholar, said that General Durrani is recommending a formula for peace processes that seems to make sense—that was encouragement. I had come up with something that the other side found acceptable. I didn't go looking for local supporters or try to create lobbies.

Aggarwal: Dulat Saheb, who did you turn to for support when you heard negative things about yourselves or the book?

Dulat: At times like this, very few people stand by you. Fortunately, I had a colleague who thought it was a good book and supported me. I invited him and he said, 'I'll come but I won't speak.' I said, 'Please, you have to speak.' So he spoke, and he praised the book.

But it's not easy. So, ultimately, what is your fallback position? Your fallback position is your wife. She was undoubtedly a pillar of strength. And to cheer me up she said, 'Why are you worried? Who are these people anyway, only those who are jealous.' She was really aggressive at the time. She even picked a few fights.

But it's not very pleasant, and in one's head it's like a sad refrain: 'What are you all about?' 'Where are you headed?' 'What have we been doing all along?' 'What is this whole tamasha [spectacle] about?'

Aggarwal: I'd like to understand your ability to see the situation from other people's views. What do you both wish you could say to your sceptics now?

Dulat: I wouldn't know what to say to them. Anyway, it's not worth it. As I said, things are changing. It's sad, but honest people are hard to find. I'm not talking India; it's all over the world. Somebody says something to you today, but ten days later they deny it.

Now a lot of people say that the Russian attack on Ukraine saved Boris Johnson his job.

Durrani: I agree with that.

Dulat: If that is the kind of thread your job depends on, then you can imagine what's happening. And is one's job the most important thing? Where is *din-iman* [faith and integrity]?

Durrani: You can't go and convince these people.

Dulat: These are the thing we keep asking Pakistan. *Ke tuhadi niyat ki hai* [What is your intention]?

Durrani: Some will come around on their own.

Dulat: Like I said, *koi chanan pao. Sanu daso. Sadi apni niyat ki hai* [Someone enlighten us. Tell us: what is your intention]?

[*Both men laugh.*]

Durrani: I have an old friend, a very sensible man. He heard about the book. He was furious. He said, 'This man [Durrani] should be court marshalled.' After he read the book, he sent apologies and said, 'This is a very good book.'

People need to come to that conclusion themselves. I am not going to argue that we're right—it's not worth it. I won't try to change their opinion. Let them find out for themselves; they'll suffer more from the realization.

Aggarwal: How did the events that followed the book change the way that you see each other?

Dulat: My view did not change except I saw he is much tougher and has even more spine than I thought. But I worried for him. When he wrote *Honour Among Spies*, the first thing I asked him was, 'General Saheb, I hope you have a good lawyer.' And he said, 'The very best.' So I said, 'You need to. You've already been in trouble. You'll land yourself in a bigger soup.'

Since it was fiction, he was saved from repercussions. But what is fiction? We all know it is born of facts. Fiction is much truer than a lot of facts.

Durrani: I don't think how I saw him changed in any way. We already knew each other well, had worked on papers before. We had chemistry, we had compatibility on so many different fronts. That was why we started on the book together.

My family has met him. Mr Dulat helped my son back in 2015.[31] So all of them were already a part of his fan club. No one said, 'Oh look! This chap has gotten us in trouble.' Instead, we simply stood by each other. So, there was no change except for a reinforcement of my assessment of him.

———

2. *The Spy Chronicles*'s Impact on Policies in India and Pakistan

Neil Krishan Aggarwal: Are you aware of any recommendations from the book being adopted either by the Government of India or the Government of Pakistan?

A.S. Dulat: Not to my knowledge.

Asad Durrani: Yes, in a way, and for which we have been credited. In the last three or four years, many people in Pakistan have told me that the idea of a back channel has been accepted. The idea was being credited to us. I should be very grateful if it is so.

There's also a very obscure part in the book: how to react to certain accidents. We even talked about choreographed responses if neither country was primarily responsible for a particularly bad episode, orchestrated to make us fight more, widen the gap. Instead of reacting the way someone might have wanted, we can respond sensibly. We can talk to each other about how to carry out certain essential political responses.

Now every time something like that happens, like after the 2019 Pulwama attacks, and there is no big reaction, people say, 'They must have taken a page out of your book.'

Dulat: Right.

Durrani: Take a certain base in Iraq. Iran bombed it because it was empty.[32] Iran did it to show that there was a response and not to cause any damage. People said, 'They must have taken this from your book.'

Some people even gave us credit for an event in which an empty Syrian base was bombed; I don't know by whom. My old German friends said that Moscow, Tel Aviv and Washington were all on board, and had decided this was how they would do it.

These things may have happened for any number of reasons. But it is Allah's kindness that people say, 'I think you suggested that.'

Dulat: What has benefitted from this book is Track II diplomacy. This book was born of Track II. If the idea of possible peace on the subcontinent has caught people round the world, it's not so much because of the contents of the book but the very idea that two spooks, reckoned to be adversaries, could sit down, talk amicably and produce a book. That points the way forward. If there had been no Track II, there would have been no book.

Also, both of us have argued for institutionalizing spook-to-spook dialogue, that is, intelligence chiefs meeting regularly and openly. Possibly, make station chiefs on both sides open posts, because it would benefit both sides. I think that is possibly one of the deals that could come out of this book if people are thinking on the right track.

3. Developments in Afghanistan and Kashmir after *The Spy Chronicles*

Neil Krishan Aggarwal: When it comes to international relations, we know that people often develop emotional attachments to regions. In going through *The Spy Chronicles*, I saw General Durrani's attachment to Afghanistan and Dulat Saheb's attachment to Kashmir. By attachment, I mean somebody spends much of their career focused on something, investing a great deal of time and emotion. These two territories have changed significantly from your last book when you both gave very clear recommendations for these areas. I want to see how your assessments have evolved since 2018.

Let's turn to Afghanistan first. In *The Spy Chronicles*, General Durrani thought that Afghanistan could be a focus of collaboration between India and Pakistan. How do you assess recent events in that regard? For instance, we see that Pakistan has recently allowed Indian humanitarian aid to be transported overland. And yet, there are still concerns within India about recognizing the Taliban. Can both of you please tell us whether you still think about Afghanistan as a possible focus of collaboration for India and Pakistan, and if so, how?

Asad Durrani: I said at the time that despite the basic wisdom and soundness of the plan devised in the 1997 Composite Dialogue, the environment was bad after the 26/11 Mumbai attacks, that it was not possible to work on it. It's brought up every time, but there's no chance now that we can do it together.

That's why I recommended this: if both countries are sensible—just to ensure that this time is not completely wasted [because the effects of Mumbai will last a very long time]— why not work on some other tracks? One, of course, is the hydroelectric project in Doda in Kashmir.[33]

The second is Afghanistan. It is a level playing field for both countries. Here, India's size and power don't give it an advantage like in Kashmir, as it has no direct access. We have the advantages of being the neighbour, but we have certain disadvantages as well.

India happily exploits those disadvantages. It reaches out to the Afghans; Bollywood is there. It keeps telling them, 'These Pakis are the ones who keep creating problems for you,' or 'You ruled us for four hundred years, so we are quite all right with you.' I used to describe this policy as one of 'our neighbour's neighbour'.[34] The neighbour's neighbour is whom you're trying to get to.

India initially thought that it could do whatever it wanted because the Americans were there. However, nothing's forever. After the Americans left, things changed. But I said that if India is clever, it will take advantage of the difficulties Pakistan might be facing and the errors we have committed, and jump the gun: it will recognize the Taliban and get that much ahead of the game. India would recreate that space for itself while we are still confused and hedging our bets.

India didn't do that, but something better happened. They wanted to send humanitarian aid and Islamabad agreed. This is fantastic because besides geopolitics, humanitarian concerns are important. I think it's 50,000 tonnes of wheat and one-third has been delivered so far. I'm happy they're doing it. They should do it. But it's not for the love of cooperating with Pakistan. They can tell the Afghans, 'Didn't we tell you? We are your real friends.'

Now where is the Pakistani MEA [Ministry of External Affairs] in all this? We've sent only one consignment. India can say, 'Haven't you seen these people are dragging their feet? Not recognizing you?' I'd have said, recognize the Taliban from day one. What are we afraid of? This is about Afghanistan, not the Americans or something else.

In this context, anything that India would do, like the humanitarian aid, would be very good. Sceptics—not me— sceptics would say, 'They are going back into the region.' But if you look at things together, it is not just India–Pakistan, but India–Pakistan–Afghanistan–Iraq and so on. Now these are the arguments. Mr Dulat?

Dulat: The point is: what is the problem between India and Pakistan? Lack of trust. As General Saheb said, why shouldn't we cooperate in Afghanistan, a level playing field? There are many areas for cooperation.

When the Americans left and the Taliban came in, there were apprehensions that we'd have Taliban in Kashmir now. I said, 'Nothing doing! Why should the Taliban come to Kashmir? They're seeking recognition from India. They'll never do anything to incur India's wrath.' And they haven't. The Taliban were not in Kashmir earlier either, as far as I know.

I was happy to hear that the trucks containing aid were allowed to pass through Pakistan. But again, why can't we just institutionalize this? Afghanistan isn't the only thing now. The pandemic was an opportunity. There's climate change. There are many things where India and Pakistan could cooperate, but we see obstruction instead.

Aggarwal: Dulat Saheb, in *The Spy Chronicles* you were pretty critical of India's policy towards Afghanistan. What do you think the policy should be? Like General Saheb mentioned, if India were clever, it would recognize the Taliban. Do you think that—

Dulat: I've always maintained that we should. It was 2012 and there was a big tamasha in Berlin, organized by our Pugwash friends. I met one of these Talibs there. He went out of his way to say that the Taliban would like a relationship with India. So why would we not want a relationship with the Taliban?

Recall when the hijacking of Flight 814 happened.[35] We were handicapped because there was nobody to talk to. The Taliban refused to talk and our relationship with Pakistan was also not at its best. I agree with General Saheb that India needs to have a better relationship with the Taliban. It's not like we don't talk to them, but we need to do it better and oftener.

Aggarwal: General Durrani, you mentioned in *The Spy Chronicles* that you saw an axis forming between Pakistan, Iran, Russia and China with respect to Afghanistan. Do you still see this axis emerging or are there new configurations?

Durrani: All these countries—China, Russia, Iran, Pakistan, probably Turkey—didn't want to see continued American presence. After all, who wants a powerful extra-regional force in your stomping ground? Unless you want to use that power to fight your rival, which is stupid. Yet we do it all the time.

Soon after the Partition, Pakistan saw the US as a counterweight vis-à-vis India. But when its presence became a problem, we looked at other actors, such as China and Russia. So, after a particular objective is achieved, we may consider fresh alignments.

Now that America is gone, we are all pursuing our go-alone individual policies. We haven't gotten together to give Afghanistan humanitarian aid or recognize it. Pakistan is doing its bit; Iran is going its own way, of which I know little. The big player in Afghanistan is China. It has the clout, the money and many good people. It can happily expand CPEC [the China–Pakistan Economic Corridor] to Afghanistan.

As a group, we were sometimes called the Gang of Four or the Gang of Five, but I don't think we are working together. But overall, things on the western front have turned in our favour; at least they're less troublesome than when the US was there.

Aggarwal: I want to ask you both about China because you just mentioned it. To what extent have the COVID years impacted India–Pakistan relations? Both with China being vilified as the source of the virus and the India–China rivalry on the eastern border now? In your assessment, have you seen the China factor affecting India–Pakistan relations and their capacity for peace?

Dulat: It does affect the India–Pakistan relationship. Pakistan is very close to China, and as an 'all-weather' friend, China will always come to Pakistan's aid; meanwhile we have problems with China on our eastern borders. COVID and where it came from is not a big problem: what's happened in eastern Ladakh is. It's a serious issue that has needed resolving for a long time now. We need to engage, to talk. There's no other way.

Yesterday in the papers, I read that the Pakistan Army Chief has suggested tripartite China–India–Pakistan peace. I agree with him.

There used to be a diplomatic triad once upon a time: India, Russia and China. Where that is now, I don't know. The Pakistan, Iran, Russia and China configuration is a reality and we should be concerned. They all have a good relationship with Taliban. They are better placed in Afghanistan than us, because we aligned our policy with the Americans for too long and then they left. They'd been talking about it for quite some time but we ignored it and kept banking on them.

I think we need to rethink our own policy, not just in Afghanistan but in the whole region.

Aggarwal: General Saheb?

Durrani: There is much we do not understand about the Chinese, and we have not dealt with them closely or deeply, except as 'Iron Brothers'. We're still not sure how to deal with them, except learning that one needs finesse.

Lately, India took a position on the Ukraine crisis that suited Russia, similar to what China predictably did. We are nowhere there. Similarly, we misread the Kashmir situation when Modi did this to [Articles] 370[36] and 35A.[37] The change of status of territory next door may have alarmed the Chinese. It was all right so long as it was technically a disputed area. Now that it was going to be part of a union territory, it had to be viewed differently. That would be their thinking.

I don't think the Pakistanis have understood how the Chinese think. We may not even have understood this with CPEC. When people like us say, 'CPEC is not only economic.

It also has strategic implications,' the Chinese pretend not to hear. That's strange, because if you have good economic relations, it follows that it has strategic implications. The Chinese keep silent at best and sometimes even joke about it. That means we have a problem.

I agree with Mr Dulat. We need to use every occasion, despite everything, to talk to each other—India, Pakistan, Afghanistan, America, China ... for heaven's sake, if China and India can come to a certain understanding, it would then be the easiest thing in the world.

When the Quad [Quadrilateral Security Group of Australia, India, Japan and the United States] meets, if India is not careful, it will suffer the fate that befell other countries that bet on America despite knowing the odds, knowing things can and will shift and change. If the US and China come to a new relationship, India and Pakistan will both be dumped.

We never claimed that we had that sort of finesse. We always thought that the Big Brother has a better understanding. India also thinks more tactically—it looks beyond its nose.

Aggarwal: General Saheb, you mentioned Articles 35A and 370. That's a great segue to Kashmir, which has also changed since you both co-wrote *The Spy Chronicles*. The Pulwama attack happened in 2019; both countries deployed their air forces; Abhinandan[38] had chai in Pakistan; and both those articles were revoked. How do you both assess the future of Jammu and Kashmir from your vantage points—not just of the territories within your own countries, but also the territories across the border?

Durrani: Here is the master of Kashmir.

Dulat: I have no problem talking about Kashmir. It's my favourite subject. What happened in August 2019 is sad. But this was waiting to happen. The BJP, or the NDA [National Democratic Alliance] as they call themselves, came back with a thumping majority in 2019. They felt this was the best time to do whatever they wanted to do.

Otherwise, there was nothing left in Article 370. It had been lost long ago, back in 1975 in the accord between the Sheikh Abdullah and Mrs Indira Gandhi when the Sheikh recognized that accession was irrevocable.[39] Actually, he pleaded very strongly for a revision of certain acts passed since 1953, but nothing happened. The erosion was taking place. These guys just smacked it off.

I spoke against it. I wrote against it. Former Union Minister Chidambaram spoke very passionately against it in Parliament. Ghulam Nabi Azad may have muttered something against it in the Rajya Sabha. But everybody knows that 370 is not going to come back now.

I spoke to a gentleman from RSS [Rashtriya Swayamsevak Sangh] at a lit fest in Chandigarh in the winter of 2020. He assured me Kashmir's statehood would be restored soon. It was not. There is talk now—I don't know how serious it is—that finally elections might be held in Kashmir before next winter [2023].

That is the best thing that could happen in Kashmir, provided there is a level playing field, because Kashmir needs to return to its political and democratic process. However good or bad a system is, when you have outsiders ruling your state, a part of the political process is lost. The Kashmiri has realized for the first time the importance of having one's own government, however much one criticizes it.

It's difficult to predict what might happen in an election. There has been some delimitation of constituencies. In terms of arithmetic, it is not easy to change too much in Jammu and Kashmir. Some people believe that Jammu means Hindus. No—Jammu is not all Hindus; there are a lot of areas that have a Muslim majority.

Kashmir is simply a bad mess, although infiltration has almost stopped. It's minuscule compared to whatever there was earlier. The most positive thing to happen was the ceasefire on the Line of Control since February of last year [2021]. I hoped it would open a door for moving forward, but unfortunately that didn't happen. It got stuck. Again, it is made conditional on waiting for possible future leaders, on the absence of leaders of the past.

There are so many imponderables, but I think Kashmir needs that healing touch again. It needs a government of its own.

Aggarwal: General Durrani, how do you assess events in Jammu and Kashmir?

Durrani: People on the Indian side of Kashmir sent messages to Mr Dulat and me that we can solve their problem—that made me feel quite happy. But they also sent messages that Pakistan made no good response to abrogation.

Paralysed or pathetic or indifferent, Pakistan did not know what to do. They redrew a map, renamed a road. This feeble reaction made me furious, which got me a few more supporters from the Indian side of Kashmir.

Even those thinking only in terms of realpolitik should worry about the humanitarian aspect. Kashmiris will suffer, but hopefully Modi's policy will not alienate that area forever.

I mean, Modi's abrogation was an unwise reaction, but it was going in that direction for the last many years.

When I see Mr Dulat worried, Kapil Kak worried, Yashwant Sinha worried, I believe it is because their policies are not working for India. Yashwant Sinha said, 'We have lost Kashmir. We can only keep the territory now. Hearts and minds are gone.'

I can be happy because this may ultimately work in Pakistan's favour—or it may not. But everything is not about politics and status; we should talk about how the people are suffering there.

In this situation, some Kashmiris believe that people like Dulat and me can help—why not give such people the task? After all, the final decision will be taken by Delhi and Islamabad, not by us. But if we try, we can make a good assessment, bridge the gap and bring a little hope to those people.

Aggarwal: In India, the movie *The Kashmir Files* has animated debates about the suffering of Kashmiri Pandits. That raises the question of why politicians in both countries have been silent on the plight of minorities in Jammu and Kashmir, whether it's Kashmiri Hindus, Kashmiri Sikhs or Muslim Gujjars and Muslim Bakerwals. Neither country has discussed a dispensation that would accommodate the minorities in the entire territory.

Durrani: My answer will be very brief; the stage goes to Mr Dulat because I know how he has reacted lately to that film. My answer is that people here have no idea about certain aspects of Kashmir. The scholars and academics do not know;

the government certainly hasn't a clue. So here, it is ignorance, but people are more aware on the other side.

Aggarwal: To be clear, is it your understanding that the Government of Pakistan has been silent on the situation of minorities in Kashmir because government officials are ignorant of different communities living there, like Hindus, Sikhs, and Muslim Gujjars and Muslim Bakerwals? Or do you think there are other reasons for that silence?

Durrani: They do know that these communities live there, but have no idea—and may not even have thought of—how to tailor their policy accordingly.

Dulat: Neil, I was in Kashmir when all this happened. I was there from 1988 to 1990. The winter of 1989 to 1990 was terrible. I've written about it in my first book, *Kashmir: The Vajpayee Years*.

Yes, the Kashmiri Pandits did suffer. They were targeted. But they were not the only ones, and they weren't the first to be targeted.

There were categories of people who were targeted. It started with political workers, and the main target was the National Conference party because it was in power—its leaders and workers. Then the J&K Police and Special Branch were targeted. The Intelligence Bureau was targeted. We lost four officers in the space of three weeks.

Pandits were also targeted. It created a huge panic among them. There is a narrative that Governor Jagmohan[40] was responsible for driving the Pandits out of the Valley. I'm no great admirer of Jagmohan, but I don't think he was a villain or that he made them go. He would certainly have been relieved that they were leaving by the time he arrived in Srinagar on 21 January 1990. Militancy was taking such a toll all around that he had to come down hard, and he didn't want Pandits to be at the receiving end. A couple of very nasty incidents took place. One was the Gawkadal massacre:[41] there was a protest, the protesters were shot at, and about fifty people were killed. It was a terrible time.

This movie is extremely one-sided. It is only going to polarize Kashmir further. A lot of people blame former Chief Minister Mufti Mohammad Sayeed[42] for bringing the BJP into the Valley by going into a poll alliance with it. But Mufti Saheb had very few options in 2014; he didn't have the numbers, and every mainstream leader knows better than to get on the wrong side of Delhi. But the problem is Mufti overestimated himself and underestimated Modi, and landed himself in a soup.

That is why after Mufti Saheb passed away, his daughter didn't take up chief ministership right away. She knew how much her father had suffered. At Mufti Saheb's funeral, there were hardly three or four hundred people. It was a sad end to someone who was not a bad man. Mufti had his qualities. When he became chief minister in 2002, he did a lot of good and provided what he called 'the healing touch'. It was a good chief-ministership. Unfortunately, the Congress didn't allow him to sit clear; they insisted that after three years it was their turn.

But then, Kashmir changes very quickly. If you talk to a Kashmiri, he tells you that he is always at the crossroads. It can change overnight. It can be great one day, and it can be terrible the next. That's what happened with the kidnapping of Rubaiya Sayeed. She was kidnapped on 8 December 1989,

and released five days later in exchange for imprisoned men.
There was jubilation in Kashmir. The JKLF [Jammu Kashmir
Liberation Front] boys thought independence was round the
corner. Even Pakistan was taken by surprise. Kashmir can still
change for the better, but it requires imagination. It requires
a heart. You need to understand the Kashmiris. Nothing in
Kashmir is in black and white. It's grey. As General Saheb said,
there is a humanitarian side to all of this.

If the Kashmiri heart throbs, it throbs because of
Kashmiriyat [the sense of Kashmiri identity], which is above
any other distinctions of religion or region. So when there's talk
of genocide of Kashmiri Pandits, I say they don't understand
Kashmir and Kashmiriyat, because there are plenty of Kashmiri
Pandits who have said this movie is bunk.

Durrani: One reason that I agreed to the first project was that
I read Mr Dulat's first book *Kashmir: The Vajpayee Years*. It
made me aware that there is someone who knows Kashmir,
things I had no idea about.

About *The Kashmir Files*, Mr Dulat's other remark went viral
in Pakistan: that the Muslim population in Kashmir helped
the Kashmiri Pandits. Now everyone is looking at the problem
differently.

We have started to realize that there is something called
Kashmiriyat. It isn't just about India or Pakistan.

Similarly, when it comes to Afghanistan, there is something
called Afghaniyat that sometimes people here do not
understand. They think, 'If we get the Pashtuns on our side,
we can dominate Afghanistan.' Others say, 'These people
were not up to it, but there are people in the north who will
make better partners.' The point is that regardless of their

differences and factions, there is something deeply ingrained, and that is Afghaniyat. No one can divide them for very long. We can divide them on certain other lines like, for example, who will we collaborate with, who will get money, who are the militants. But not on ethnic or any other lines because deep down, they all remain Afghans like all Kashmiris remain Kashmiris.

Aggarwal: Do you think this kind of movie challenges the idea the governments of India and Pakistan have had—that the All Parties Hurriyat Conference is the sole representative voice for Kashmiris? Will more stakeholders now wish to join the political process because there's more knowledge about other groups involved in the territory?

Dulat: Not at all. That would promote more polarization.

Aggarwal: General Durrani, do you think that this changes the decision-making in Pakistan about seeing the All Parties Hurriyat Conference as the sole representative voice for Kashmiris now that other groups such as Kashmiri Hindus are looking for recognition and greater civic discourse?

Durrani: Hurriyat is supposed to be the political arm of the resistance, inspired by what used to happen, for example, in Vietnam with Ho Chi Minh[43] and the Viet Cong to complement each other. To expect that all parties in the Hurriyat believe in the same solution would be foolhardy. Of course, due to some very smart moves by my friend Mr Dulat to create dissensions among them—
    [*Both men laugh.*]

Dulat [*laughing*]: I think the Hurriyat took us over, sir.

Durrani: At that point, when he said that the Hurriyat was the Pakistani team, I felt a little better because it was created in my time—

Dulat: I called it the Pakistani team. But the thing is, if only we had converted that Pakistani team and made it our team. An effort was begun, but then, it didn't happen.

Durrani: We have not formed a policy on a direction- or shape-steering mechanism. Some blame should be taken by us as well as by the Indians. Generally, on Kashmir, people have taken rash decisions. When they acted deliberately, constructively, it was not sustained. It was usually a one-off thing and then given up. We lack sustained action. In fact, now one is not even sure if it is wanted. The interest has gone down. That's our problem.

Aggarwal: Final question to you both before we set the next appointment. How do you both now assess the status of Azad Kashmir and Gilgit-Baltistan in Pakistan, given the changes in 2019 that have taken place with the abolition of Articles 370 and 35A?

Asad Durrani: Their status is just one more illustration of how stupid some people can be. This problem has been going on for the last sixty or seventy years. It needs to be resolved in a way that our locus standi remains and is clear to the people, and at the same time, we address the problems of the people in Azad Kashmir and Gilgit-Baltistan.

So, there were some suggestions. I can talk about one of them. The premise is 'Kashmir will be all ours one day. So, in our assembly, we will have so many seats. Some will be kept vacant because they cannot be filled until there is a plebiscite there.' But we can hold elections in Azad Kashmir and Gilgit-Baltistan. We could say, 'You are provisionally here until the final solution.' Something like that.

And people said, 'It makes sense, but we can't do it.' Why? Because the politics in Kashmir, in Gilgit-Baltistan, present us with the worst of all options. I do not think that we found the correct solution to address the genuine grievances of our side of the Kashmiris and the Gilgit-Baltistanis.

Sometimes by default, these people are with us. They have nowhere else to go. Sometimes because of politics, they continue to be with us because Pakistan does give a lot more budget and resources to these areas.

Aggarwal: Dulat Saheb, do you see the changes in Jammu and Kashmir in India from 2019 having any kind of real-world impact or bearing on how the Government of India claims Azad Kashmir and Gilgit-Baltistan in Pakistan?

Dulat: Is there a solution of the kind we're looking for? That is the question. I have concluded that there is not. The only kind is a very basic one: sooner or later, we'll have to settle on the Line of Control. Musharraf's four-point formula[44] touted all over was really a one-point formula to settle on the Line of Control with cosmetic changes.

I agree with General Saheb regarding the India–Pakistan relationship: a stable status quo is good enough. That's the best that can happen.

As General Saheb mentioned, when Durrani and Dulat talk, it gives the Kashmiri hope that these two mad guys are still talking. Possibly, something will happen—without realizing that these two guys themselves are unimportant.

When Article 370 was abrogated, I felt sad. We're only rubbing the Kashmiri nose into the ground. 370 was long gone, and now remained only a psychological and emotive issue— much like Kashmir itself.

But now that it's gone, I've been arguing with myself about how to justify it to Pakistan. General Saheb was disappointed that Pakistan didn't really react to the abrogation. I remembered Musharraf. I still believe that he was the most reasonable Pakistani leader in a long time. He realized that one must come to terms with certain realities. And what Musharraf used to say was, 'Whatever is acceptable to Kashmiris would be acceptable to Pakistan.'

So, I was thinking, if the Kashmiri accepts abrogation, then what objection could Pakistan have? I think that what Musharraf said was fair enough. He was in a sense toeing the Kashmiri line, which sometimes unwittingly I also do because I'm attached. Because when you work in a place for a long time, when you know people for a long time, there is a certain attachment.

4. The Psychology of Coping and Adapting to Stress

Neil Krishan Aggarwal: I've asked you both a lot of questions. Do you have any questions for me?

A.S. Dulat: You know, Neil, I'm curious as to what you think about us. One of the things that attracted us to this project was your expertise in psychology.

Aggarwal: I appreciate you saying that. When we first met, I mentioned to both of you that you were advancing the theory and practice of applied psychology by being a part of Track II diplomatic efforts. Psychiatrists and diplomats invented this mechanism so that people outside of government could build peace.

Dulat: Yes. I did not know that psychiatrists came up with Track II.

Aggarwal: I've been reluctant to share my psychological assessments with both of you for several reasons. First, we are not in a clinical setting. While I am a psychiatrist and use the tools of psychiatry and psychology to understand conflict and peace, I'm not your psychiatrist. Second, I recognize that you are both public figures, and I want to make sure that you are both comfortable with having certain types of personal information out in the open. Third, I will share my assessments with you only if we agree that I am presenting hypotheses about you both, not definitive statements. None of us can ever know what is in anyone else's heart or mind, and this would have to be a collaborative process. You have every right to disagree and reformulate my assessments, either in our sessions or separately.

Dulat: I am quite comfortable with that, Neil.

Asad Durrani: By all means, Neil.

Aggarwal: There are many ways to think about psychological domains. One is how we all adapt to stress. In psychiatry and psychology, we talk about defence mechanisms, which are the ways we block out thoughts and emotions. We can do this knowingly or consciously, and unknowingly or unconsciously.

One major source of stress has been the negative reactions to *The Spy Chronicles*. General Saheb exhibits the use of rationalization as a defence mechanism, which is the ability to explain conflicts in a logical manner. Discounting his detractors by reasoning that they have not read *The Spy Chronicles* and challenging his opponents in court to prove through evidence that he is a RAW agent reflects logical thinking. Also, he has not used others to validate his self-esteem. For instance, when he describes how he did not turn towards others for support, he is communicating how he autonomously handles threats or vulnerabilities to his perception of himself. I would speculate that General Saheb interprets his experiences of the world primarily through ideas and intellect. An interesting question is whether he gravitated to intelligence work because of this cold, calculated approach to information or whether the act of perfecting assessments made him who he is today. So, it's a chicken and egg issue here.

Dulat Saheb is different. He describes seeing himself within his social relationships. For instance, he blamed himself as a defence mechanism for the blowback that General Saheb faced in Pakistan after *The Spy Chronicles*. We get a sense of how deeply those series of events affected him because he blamed himself several times. He also turned to a colleague and to his wife for support when he heard negative reactions about the book. Finally, one source of self-esteem came from how dignitaries like former Prime Minister Manmohan Singh praised the book. So Dulat Saheb seems more extroverted and willing to share his emotions in a social way.

Neither approach is good or bad, since we are all different. You are both extremely high-functioning individuals who served your countries at the top of your fields. Clearly, you can both handle stress. A psychological approach to peacemaking reminds us that individuals are front and centre when it comes to war and reconciliation. It's easy to get lost in the processes of peacemaking with all these tracks, laws, treaties and procedures. Psychology puts the individuals back in this narrative to see how we can all work together, normalizing the fact that we all have fears and anxieties, hopes and fantasies about what we can and wish to accomplish. Our next sessions delve more into your backgrounds before we start to talk about peacebuilding.

2

The Psychological Foundations of Track II, People-to-People Diplomacy

In the last chapter, A.S. Dulat mentioned that one benefit of *The Spy Chronicles* has been to reignite Track II initiatives. Here, psychiatrists have made a unique contribution to diplomacy. In 1982, psychiatrist William Davidson and diplomat Joseph Montville co-authored a scientific article on the role of psychology in resolving international conflicts. They were realistic in their assessment, writing, 'Political psychological analysis will not eliminate such concrete problems as territorial boundary disputes or allocation of water and mineral sources. But it can help illuminate human barriers to the resolution of human problems.'[1] Davidson and Montville introduced the concept of Track II diplomacy as unofficial meetings among people with access to government policymakers, through which 'actual or potential conflict can be resolved or eased by appealing to common human capabilities to respond to good will and reasonableness.'[2] As former spy chiefs who are no longer in government service but have access to policymakers,

A.S. Dulat and Asad Durrani have participated in Track II initiatives since 2008.

It was decades after Davidson and Montville's 1982 paper that Track II diplomacy caught on in psychiatry. The reasons for the delay go back farther. On 30 July 1932, theoretical physicist and Nobel Prize winner Albert Einstein wrote a letter to Sigmund Freud, psychiatrist and founder of psychoanalysis. Einstein asked a question that remains pertinent even today: 'Is there any way of delivering mankind from the menace of war?'[3] Frustrated at political leaders refusing to sacrifice their national interests for international peace, Einstein wondered whether psychology could uncover new solutions: 'Is it possible to control man's mental evolution so as to make him proof against the psychoses of hate and destructiveness?'[4]

Freud's response came two months later. He took a grim view: 'The most casual glance at world history will show an unending series of conflicts between one community and another or a group of others, between large and smaller units, between cities, countries, races, tribes and kingdoms, almost all of which were settled by the ordeal of war.'[5] Freud dismissed psychology's possible contributions to peace, responding that, 'There is no likelihood of our being able to suppress humanity's aggressive tendencies.'[6] In fact, Freud saw war as a natural state of human affairs, asking Einstein: 'Why do we, you and I and many another, protest so vehemently against war, instead of just accepting it as another of life's odious importunities? For it seems a natural thing enough, biologically sound and practically unavoidable.'[7]

Still, a generation of psychiatrists did protest war vehemently and found inspiration in Davidson and Montville's approach.

From 1979 to 1986, the American Psychiatric Association convened groups of Egyptian, Israeli and Palestinian psychiatrists, psychologists, diplomats and journalists for Track II negotiations.[8] A psychiatrist who participated in these discussions described how psychology revealed a whole host of interesting issues among participants, such as their moods, how they react [defence mechanisms], why they react similarly across situations [repetition compulsions], the relationship between their inner psychic lives and how they see their place in the world, the ways that leaders and followers imagine each other, and issues about identity.[9] The tools of psychiatry helped people move towards peacemaking, as Neil Krishan Aggarwal continues to show in moderating sessions with Durrani and Dulat. In our very first session, in fact, we discussed the exchange of letters between Einstein and Freud to reflect on how peacemaking has eluded some of the most brilliant minds in human history.

Track II initiatives between India and Pakistan began in the 1990s.[10] The Partition of British-governed South Asia into India and Pakistan in 1947 has produced enduring territorial disputes, leading to wars in 1947, 1965, 1971 and 1999. While Track I or official diplomacy works within the assumption of realpolitik, zero-sum power considerations, Track II initiatives between India and Pakistan have successfully reframed dialogues from managing conflicts to promoting peace.[11] One reason could be that Track II's diverse formats allow for flexibility: public meetings can be convened to disseminate creative ideas and pressure Track I negotiators towards resolutions, while one can also have secret meetings which guarantee the kind of confidentiality that is necessary to discuss unconventional solutions to longstanding conflicts.[12] Track II can also maintain back channels of communication during political crises when one side refuses official Track I negotiations due to policy changes or public pressure.[13]

Despite a very promising start, collaborations among psychiatrists and international relations experts have waned in recent years. By 2018, one psychiatrist wrote, 'Psychoanalysts have written on a variety of topics relating to the diplomatic and political realms, but their contributions have thus far been mostly theoretical in nature, and of little practical use to diplomats and politicians.'[14] Here, we seek to make a practical contribution for diplomats, politicians and peacemakers by exploring how life details relate to peacemaking. Dulat and Durrani describe their childhood and adolescence, their professional aspirations and the skills they acquired during their years of government service. They discuss their decisions to enter diplomacy after decades of intelligence work, and their assessments of the current state of India–Pakistan relations. Psychology reveals how aspects of human personality— motivations, capabilities and life experiences—inform both men's approaches to peacemaking.

1. Childhood

Neil Krishan Aggarwal: A psychological approach to peacemaking tries to understand several dimensions. It's not just about what is on the table—in terms of options—while devising solutions to problems. It's also about understanding the backgrounds of the peacemakers themselves.

A.S. Dulat: In your reckoning, are we more interested in the singer or the song?

Aggarwal: We are interested in both. One cannot have the song without the singer, right? One cannot have peace without the peacemakers.

Dulat: That's exactly it.

Aggarwal: This is why all our questions—especially those for this session and the next—are intended to understand both of you at a deeply personal level. Perhaps at a level that spies, let alone spy chiefs, are not accustomed to sharing. But so long as humans, not machines, are involved in peacemaking, we need to understand peacemakers. You are going to answer rather more personal questions now, because we're trying to understand how you evolved into who you are today.

And with that, the first question is, where were you born?

Asad Durrani: In the city of Rawalpindi. We have a mission hospital here: Holy Family. That's where I was born.

Aggarwal: Okay. And Dulat Saheb?

Dulat: I was born in Sialkot—

Durrani [*teasingly*]: Oops, oops, oops.

Dulat: According to my mother, I was born at home, which means the sessions judge's bungalow in Sialkot.

Aggarwal: Wow, on the other side.

Durrani: *Kya baat hai* [Bravo].

Aggarwal: Durrani Saheb, who was in your family when you were born?

Durrani: I was the firstborn, so just my mother and my father. My father was in service, posted in Rawalpindi, so there was no other family.

Aggarwal: What service was he in?

Durrani: The prison department. He was a junior official in Rawalpindi jail.

Aggarwal: Who came after you were born?

Durrani: I had two brothers and two sisters. None of them went into the military. Both sisters got married and have their own homes. One brother is in the United States, in the marketing business. The other has a technical background. He was in the refrigeration business and is now retired.

Aggarwal: Dulat Saheb, who was in your family when you were born?

Dulat: I had an older brother, born of my father's first wife, an Englishwoman, who unfortunately died in childbirth. He spent his first seven years in England, being raised by his grandmother before he travelled home to India. I was born five years later. He was my half-brother, but for us, he was simply my older brother.

I have a younger sister from the same mother as me. It was the three of us. In the early years, our brother used to really lord it over us because he was so much older, but he looked after us too; he was more than a brother. Sadly, he died young.

Aggarwal: I want to return to something you mentioned. Was your father a sessions judge?

Dulat: When I was born, yes.

Aggarwal: So he was in government service then?

Dulat: Yes. He was from the old civil service. He started as an assistant commissioner or whatever it is. But then he gravitated to the judicial side. He retired as a high court judge.

My father was a somewhat feudalistic but essentially a simple person. And he always had sympathy for the underdog. In some ways, I've always tried to emulate him. The way in which I approach Kashmir and Kashmiris probably has something to do with what I saw him do.

Aggarwal: How would you describe your childhood? Durrani Saheb, why don't you go first?

Durrani: It's such a long time back, so what I'm telling you is really based on flashes of memory. One remembers strange observations. There must have been more important ones, but I've forgotten.

I'm sure I was very young, maybe about two—I remember that outside our house, there was a railway line. Much later, I came back to that same area and said, 'Let me see if that railway line is still there. Our house was close by.' And it was. That memory is confirmed.

One of my fondest memories is of walking to my first school, in Sheikhupura. It was a coeducation school, which was quite normal even in those days. I would cross the jail gardens and a few roads, and enjoyed that walk very much. I mentioned something about that walk in *The Spy Chronicles*, how we used to take a sip of water from a bania's shop.[15] I had a very small circle of friends then—hardly more than two or three at a time. When my brothers and sisters came, the circle became even smaller. I do not know why, but I always loved to be alone. Take a lonely walk, sit all by yourself and reflect. This is strange. Like I said, there must have been something wrong with me.

After all, what business did a child of six or seven have to start questioning the existence of God? It's something I've mentioned in my book *Honour Among Spies*.[16] Why did I come to the conclusion that there was no God? I don't know. Probably I thought that with so much going wrong, there could not be an all-merciful supreme being. I also do not remember when or why I started believing that there must be a God.

Those types of questions *may* describe to you what a curious, confused mind one had.

Aggarwal: Wow. Thank you for sharing that. Dulat Saheb, how would you describe your childhood?

Dulat: Until recently, I never realized that General Saheb and I were born about the same time—I am a couple of months older than him. My childhood was split by the Partition. I have only vague memories about the pre-Partition time, maybe some stories heard from parents and grandparents. That was the first part of childhood.

Both my grandfathers died when I was young. I do remember a bit about my maternal grandfather. He used to live in Lahore. He was not well at the end. I remember him sitting in a chair with some sweets next to him. He used to offer me some so I would sit near him and talk to him. [*Smiles.*]

The second part of my childhood begins in Delhi after Partition. Everything was new. My brother was in college already. When he was home, he used to push me around. Here I only did *lafanga-baazi* [naughtiness]. My friends were mostly the servants' children, people who were around.

My father said, 'This boy is going to get spoiled here by his mother. He should be sent to boarding school.' so, I was packed off. That's another part of my childhood. I was a little kid when I was sent to boarding school—just ten. There are some people who say that they weren't homesick. I think it's a lot of crap. I think you do miss home. It's not the happiest place to be, but at the end of the day, you learn a lot.

In those days, almost immediately after Partition, these schools were dominated by the goras [white people] and the Anglo-Indians. We got pushed around. There was a lot of bullying.

So it was, in a sense, survival of the fittest. You learned to be on your own and fend for yourself. It was a great education. I don't pretend that I enjoyed it—no! I began to enjoy things once I got to college. Suddenly from school to college, you had grown up, and it gave you so much more freedom. That's the way I look back at things.

Aggarwal: How did you both do in school?

Durrani: Very well. I was always amongst the first four or five in almost every subject. There was only one exception, which

I've mentioned.[17] My favourite subject was mathematics. At some stage, I did miserably in a midterm test. That taught me early in life not to be overconfident or to take things for granted. I may have done that again, but except for those one or two incidents, I did quite well in my classes.

Aggarwal: Dulat Saheb, how did you do in school?

Dulat: I was a very average student. We were a class of twenty-six, and my father was quite satisfied if I was halfway. If I was in the first ten, then wow—that was great. I might have won a prize here or there, but I was a very average student.

In those days, although my father took studies and academics very seriously, the idea of the boarding school—or the public school as it was called—was to give the child a rounded personality. You had to play every game in school. You ran the marathon, you participated in athletics. You played hockey, football, cricket. Cricket was my favourite game, so I used to look forward to the cricket season. Interestingly, boxing was also compulsory in school, whereas hockey and riding, apart from physical training, were necessary in the police.

Aggarwal: What activities were you both involved with?

Durrani: In those days, in our schools or localities, one always played one sport or the other, either early in the morning before classes or after school in the mohalla [neighbourhood]. So, sports was one of my favourite activities. Unlike Mr Dulat, I never became a top-class player, but I was always somewhere in a team.

The other activity that I was very fond of was cycling. With a cycle under me, there was no place even in a city like Lahore that was too far. I would cycle from Lahore to Gujranwala.[18]

As far as other activities were concerned, I was not a bookworm, but very curious. I was always going to the library, getting hold of an odd book and reading it. Maybe it was because of my father—he read a lot. He was fond of Urdu literature and could quote many poets.

Aggarwal: Dulat Saheb, what activities were you involved in?

Dulat: Everything was compulsory, so all sports, and besides that, debating and declamation. We had to speak extempore. It was only a two-and-a-half-minute thing, but we had to go on stage and speak on a subject that they would give you a few minutes earlier. Again, it was a question of confidence-building more than anything else.

You had no spare time in school. It was a full schedule. You did what you were supposed to do. That's why, when I got to college, I felt such freedom.

2. Adolescence

Neil Krishan Aggarwal: How do you remember your teenage years? How do you reflect upon the time from when you were roughly thirteen to eighteen years old?

Asad Durrani: I was outgoing in the sense that I was curious. One went over whenever there was an event, or when we were playing against each other or when there was a circus in town. Always being inquisitive, going to places. I may not have enjoyed being in a crowd so much, but looking at things was my passion.

I also enjoyed going to bookshops to buy books and magazines.

I think I had a very strange characteristic, which I did not know could be a psychological problem. If people were standing on one side, I tended to go to the other side. Perhaps I didn't want to be part of a crowd. Perhaps I wanted to be seen as different, taken notice of; I also wanted a different perspective: 'Let's take a look at this another way.' In *Pakistan Adrift*[19] I described the time I went for selection to the Inter-Services Selection Board in Kohat. Ayub Khan had taken over, so there was military rule.[20] We were asked, 'Who do you think are more important for the country—the politicians or the military?' The stock answer was military [*laughing*]. And I said, 'Politicians.' It shows that being part of the minority, of the opposition, coming up with a different view, was part of my psyche.

Aggarwal: Dulat Saheb, how do you remember your teenage years?

Dulat: It's split into two because you start growing up in school—I was sixteen when I finished school. But I was still growing up when I joined college. There was nothing very much different between school and college as far as growing up was concerned.

My first thought when I got to college was, 'Where are the girls?' [*smiling*]. But we did get an opportunity in school. When we reached senior school, we used to have these things called 'socials' with the main girls' school in Simla [now Shimla], about three hours away. Everyone was quite shy at these things, but at least you had a chance to interact with girls despite being in a boys' school. When I got to college, I started to seriously look for girls. It's a part of growing up.

That's why I say it was split into two. You know how kids grow up and what happens to a boy at eleven, twelve, thirteen or fourteen. Those things happen, even in school. It's not anything different.

Aggarwal: You're absolutely right. Attraction and curiosity are a part of normal human development, especially during adolescence.

Dulat: Yeah, yeah.

Aggarwal: What college did you attend?

Dulat: I graduated from school in 1956. I got a second division in school, which was considered a great thing back then. St. Stephen's College was the big thing in Delhi, and you could join it if you came from a decent school or a decent family.

Since most of the boys leaving school with me were going to St. Stephen's College, my mother felt that I should also go there. But my father said, 'What rubbish!' There were two parts to that 'rubbish'. One, he was certain that Delhi University was not half as good as Punjab University, though he had been educated in Government College, Lahore. Chandigarh had just been formed, and it had a Government College. My father said, 'You'll join college there.' I was the first or the second batch there.

The other part—and this was his wisdom—is that he said, 'He's done six years in boarding, where he had to learn to live on his own. Now, he must also learn what home is all about.' My father was posted in Chandigarh then.

My father never spoke very much, and mine was a very formal relationship with my father. In those days, most people had formal relationships, you know. It took some guts to even stand before my father. So, when he said, 'You'll go to Government College there,' that was it. I came home.

Aggarwal: Durrani Saheb, what college did you attend?

Durrani: Ultimately, I ended up in Government College, Lahore. Whatever happened before that describes how I was hardly ever going to stick to a particular line. My father said, 'You're a good student. You should become a civil servant.' I said, 'No, sir. I will be an engineer.' I had the right merit, so I joined the Government College—now Faisalabad, but at that time Lyallpur—in pre-engineering.

I did very well and got a first class, which was not bad. And so, my father said, 'Now, you're going to go to the engineering college?' I said, 'No! I'd like to become a scientist.' [*Laughs.*] Many people in the family had gone to Government College, Lahore, and their role model used to be the famous physicist Dr Chaudhry.[21] I wanted to follow in his footsteps.

I took up subjects that were not going to bring me many laurels. I gave up mathematics. I wanted to study chemistry.

By the time I finished with Government College, Lahore, I said, 'No, I'm not interested in this any more. I would rather go to the military.' Because Ayub Khan had taken over, I said, 'I'll follow this line. Something good might happen to me. I might not be the head honcho of the country, but this is a good field to explore.' So, after graduation, even though I was admitted in the department of Chemical Technology, in Punjab University, a very good institute, I joined the army.

Aggarwal: So your aspiration at the time professionally was to become a scientist, and then to join the military after Ayub Khan came to power?

Durrani: Initially, it was not. I was trying to explore what would be to my liking. Being a scientist or a mathematician meant that one was in the business of exploration.

Ultimately, after going through all this, I thought, 'These things are interesting, but the field I would like to explore is the military.' At that time, I didn't realize it, but I had selected a career that offered me almost everything. I was outdoors, studies continued, a little bit of social mixing, if not with the crowd, then at least the man-management part, where you get to know the soldiers. All these things did interest me greatly. While I was in the Academy, my instructor realized, 'This man has a technical bent of mind. He is good at map reading and mathematics.' So he suggested, 'Some of the good cadets might opt for infantry, but I think in your case you would do well if you became a gunner.' I joined artillery.

Over time, I kept drifting with whatever I thought was more interesting, a little more challenging, a little more into the unknown. So that's what happened.

Aggarwal: Dulat Saheb, what kind of professional aspirations did you have at the time you were in college?

Dulat [*smiling*]: You know, I had no aspirations when I joined college except to enjoy myself and play cricket. Aspirations grow over time.

I've maybe given you the impression that I was not serious about my studies. But I worked pretty hard and topped the college in history honours. I did quite well.

By the time I was graduating—1960 or '61—a lot of people our age who were looking for jobs were going to Calcutta [now Kolkata] and joining the corporate world there. I thought to myself, 'That seems a good life. Why should I not follow suit and go to Calcutta to get a job and lead a good cushy life there?'

But my father would not hear of it. His view was, '*Je naukri karni hai, phir naukri sarkar di karni hai*' ['If you are going to work, then work for the government']. It was as simple as that. So I was not left with too many options. I had to appear for the [civil service] competition. That's what I started preparing for.

So I did a master's in history at Chandigarh University and played a lot of cricket. Unfortunately, nobody really enjoys working and studying hard. I took it quite easy.

I passed the entrance exam. I didn't qualify for the top two—foreign service and the IAS [Indian Administrative Services]. I could take the police service or the central services like my father—that means income tax, customs, railways, all that. My brother had been in the revenue service, and my father was quite clear about what I should do: 'The police is an honourable service. Take it.' So I did.

Aggarwal: The ages from thirteen to the early twenties are a critical time of moral development. We think about

56 COVERT

adolescence and early adulthood as when people develop their sense of right and wrong. It can come from family, friends, books or other sources. How did you both ultimately come to your own conclusions about your moral compass?

Durrani: I'm sure it was a mixture of it all. My parents and other family had values, a moral compass. We talked about what was right and wrong. I may have picked up something from there. Looking at friends or society, one must have also started questioning, 'Is this the only way to judge right and wrong?' And ultimately, one comes to one's own conclusions. 'If I think this is right, and I'm convinced it is, then from now on, this will be the course that I follow.' That may explain how I was changing tracks all the time. Ultimately, I went to a place where right and wrong was less important than to follow the cadre. [*Laughs.*]

What's much more important for me is that over time, one frames a belief of what is morally correct and what is despicable. Sometimes you must compromise or take a back seat or raise your voice. But ultimately, the ends must be in line with one's beliefs.

That was the only constant in my life. Otherwise, the path that I took was not a straight line. It was going right, left, in the middle; learning, trying to survive, sometimes being reckless. I'm lucky that with all the experimentation I did, the things I did to prove I was different, a non-conformist—all ultimately worked well for me. My spirit has always been a little rebellious; in the military too they would say, 'Why must you always rebel?' Probably here the most important thing is that after I decided this was what I wanted to do, I also said,

'I'm not going to submit to the norms of the institution all the time.' It's a very long haul, so going against my own beliefs would not be a good idea. Right till today, if I think that there is something worth doing, then I go ahead and do it, whatever the consequences.

Aggarwal: Dulat Saheb, how would you say that you developed your sense of right and wrong and your moral compass?

Dulat: Two places: school and home. In both places, I learned almost the same thing, except that in school it was said in a more British way. At home, it was said more simply. But the message was the same: there are things that are right and there are things that are wrong.

My father was an extraordinary human being—and he had an amazing quality. He understood human frailty. He was very forgiving. He understood it is human nature to make mistakes. My mother caught me drinking when I was still in college. She was very upset about it. My father said, 'Well, what's happened? Did he have a hangover?'

The basics I learned in school. For example, if you've done something wrong, you own up. Don't try and dodge it. Honesty and integrity were the great feelings, both in school and at home. Anything else could take a back seat, but you couldn't be lying, you couldn't be thieving.

These things were not taught in lectures, you know. My father didn't believe in talk. Instead, he set such a fine example that you could not but follow him.

3. Professional Experiences in Adulthood

Neil Krishan Aggarwal: Please tell me about your first job. How did you obtain it and what skills do you think you acquired from it?

Asad Durrani: I went into the military. That was my first job. I don't think I ever regretted it. Let me say what I enjoyed. Some of it was the outdoors. You are not cut off from your basic passion, which is reading. Man-management was a subject that fascinated me. The soldiers look to you to provide them not only with guidance, but to treat them fairly, without prejudice.

It is a very versatile career in which besides soldiering, one may get a diplomatic assignment; one learns to lecture as there are instructional assignments. I got these assignments, in one form or the other, in almost all ranks. The job gave me satisfaction, and ultimately, despite whatever may have happened, I came to the right career.

Aggarwal: Dulat Saheb, what was your first job? How did you obtain it and what skills do you think you acquired from it?

Dulat: I joined the [Indian] Police Service not by choice but by accident. I couldn't make it to the better services.

Having joined the Police Service, where I learned the most, what I enjoyed most was the training, without a doubt. It was like a continuation of school, except that it was a different kind of training. You had to play hockey—it was a compulsory game for the police. You had to ride and you had to be on PT [physical training] and parade every morning at 5.30 or whenever it was.

But I enjoyed it all. I learned a lot. Most of all, it taught you about camaraderie, like in school. And about competition, though more seriously now that you were in service.

After training I was very keen to go to the Punjab since that's where I had grown up. But I was allotted Rajasthan, and it turned out to be exceptionally good. Different people, great atmosphere. I did my one-year practical police training in Jaipur. Then I put in a stint at a subdivision adjoining Jaipur.

Then I was off to Delhi to join the Intelligence Bureau without knowing what intelligence really was. All I knew was that I wanted to get to Delhi, and this was a way to get to Delhi. I joined the Police Service, and I'm proud of it; but I didn't learn much police work—I was there for a very short while. Then I was off to Delhi and I never went back. As such, my career began in intelligence.

Aggarwal: Did you have a mentor who looked out for your success in your first posts? Durrani Saheb, you mentioned the military. Dulat Saheb, you mentioned the police; we'll get to intelligence in just a moment.

Durrani: Are you asking me?

Aggarwal: I am asking both of you.

Dulat [*laughing*]: I would say that I was fortunate to have a superintendent of police with whom I trained: J.P. Singha, who belonged to a prominent family of Lahore. He was a wonderful human being. He encouraged me in every way to do practically everything that I wanted.

While I was still under training, there was rioting in Jaipur. There was firing and people were killed so a commission was set up. Someone complained that, during the rioting, I had slapped him. Singha Saheb said, 'Your career is just beginning. You should stay out of the city, so that there are no other complaints.' So yes—he was a wonderful person to work under. He didn't train me that well, but he knew the right thing to do and he saw to it that we did not get into any mess that could ruin our careers.

In the IB, I could say my mentor was M.K. Narayanan, with whom I first shared a room. I am grateful to him for sending me to Kashmir.

Aggarwal: Durrani Saheb, did you have a mentor in the military who looked out for your success?

Durrani: If by 'mentor', you mean someone sitting somewhere in headquarters and helping your career along—I did not have a mentor. One's unit commander or colleague, if one is in the right place, can do it. But I've always abhorred this practice as it is so unfair to those who don't have a mentor. In my case, right through my career, the best help I got was that I usually had good bosses.

Once or twice, it became a problem. Since I was doing very well in a particular unit, my commanding officer would refuse to send me on career courses or staff assignments which would have helped me. Back then, I had no idea an intelligence course could lead to serving as a staff officer at headquarters, and not just on an intelligence assignment. The commanding officer usually said, 'No, no, you're very useful. Stay here. You stay in my unit.'

I would apply for anything that came. Any language course, even service with the commando force—whatever.

One day—the latest opportunity was a German language course—he got fed up and said, 'Since you're not going to give up, go!'

Oh, that was such a windfall for me! Of the two hundred officers who volunteered, I was one of the six selected. This goose laid many a golden egg for me. I went on to do the German General Staff Course, later became a defence attaché and post-retirement, the ambassador to Germany.

So, mentor in that sense, no. If someone was happy with my work, he may have given me a good report.

Let me digress a little because Mr Dulat has talked about his hockey and cricket so many times. We played these in school and the mohalla. But I did better in the games I learnt after joining the army: squash and basketball.

The military provided me with means to pursue my passion, if not as an explorer then at least as a hiker. At times, I was officially asked if I was willing to go for a hike, let's say in the Northern Areas. I always volunteered, and some of my subordinates were always ready to join me. This also became a collateral benefit of joining the service. Essentially, since I enjoyed my work, all my assignments bore fruit for me.

Aggarwal: I'm going to ask you both now to think about your transition from your first posts into intelligence. Dulat Saheb, what are the skills you think you gained from the IPS that prepared you for a career in intelligence? And Durrani Saheb, what are the skills you think you gained from the military that prepared you for a career in intelligence?

Durrani [*laughing*]: My answer is very simple. I landed there by accident. I have admitted that.

Aggarwal: I saw that in *The Spy Chronicles*. No sir, I'm not going to let you go so easily. In *The Spy Chronicles*, you told the story of how you got into intelligence.[22]

Durrani: Yes.

Aggarwal: But what I want to hear is how your skills and background in the military helped you for that career in intelligence.

Durrani: My initial inhibitions were misplaced. This was not about cloak and dagger or spooking and backbiting. It was an honourable mission: carrying out assessments of threats, which in my case were always external. Unlike Mr Dulat, I had no IB-like experience.

And so, one got involved, full steam. It was only three-and-a-half years altogether, heading the Army Intelligence and heading the ISI. It was my skills as an army professional that helped, as I had to be able to assess the enemy's military capabilities, what he can bring against you.

Higher level intelligence assignments involve one in social activities. There, too, the military background was helpful, as I was comfortable meeting people—peers, people abroad, people who might matter, sometimes civilian counterparts. All of it was useful.

I had been a defence attaché, so I had diplomatic experience. If an ambassador came with unreasonable demands, instead of quarrelling, I knew how to listen and how to send him back happy but empty-handed!

Even the outdoor experience prepares you to go out in certain areas and visit your tentacles [operatives] far away. Not so much abroad, because I never had much time for foreign yatras, but within the country, going to remote areas like Baluchistan. This was all very helpful. It all happened because of the skills I acquired or the things that I liked doing during my earlier military career.

Aggarwal: Dulat Saheb, what do you think are the skills that you gained from your training in the IPS that prepared you for your career in intelligence?

Dulat: Actually, my response is identical to General Saheb's. I landed up by accident. I did not know what intelligence work was about when I came to Delhi and joined the Intelligence Bureau. I thought I might have a career at headquarters in the years to come; but for the time being it was just learning the ropes.

Back then, at least in India, things were in the classical mould. You were allotted a subject and you worked to understand all about it. Now I see instead a lot of one-upmanship—there was much less back then.

I can tell you that my first couple of years were not very happy. It was like wanting to run away from boarding school—but I had been especially selected and brought there. I thought, 'If I leave, I'll go back with no reputation at all. I can't afford to do that.' I had to go on.

I was there another two years—normally you were kept in headquarters for three years to understand the whole business. I was fortunate that I did four years there. Then I began to understand things better: I worked with more people; I saw more of it.

Then, of course, comes the role of postings. I'm talking about the Intelligence Bureau because the opportunity to head the RAW came much later, only in the last two years of my career.

There are things that happen at times—accidents, as General Saheb said, which frame a career. When I think back, if I had not been sent to Kashmir in '87–'88, I don't think I would have had much of a career. It would have been like anybody else's, an ordinary career. But Kashmir changed its course. I spent a lot of time there. Kashmir has now become a sort of obsession with me. Even today, I try and keep myself abreast of what is happening.

Aggarwal: My next question to you is about how your original careers informed your outlook on intelligence. I'm going to ask you a two-part question. The first part is that in intelligence, what would you say are the skills that you developed as intelligence officers? The second part is that what would you say are the skills that you developed as intelligence chiefs? Durrani Saheb, would you like to go first?

Durrani: In my case, what probably helped me was that right from my childhood I was always curious, always reasoning; so my analytical faculties were developed.

These analytical skills helped. During my time, in the first Gulf War of 1991, when the Americans came to evict the Iraqis from their occupation of Kuwait, our assessment of the combat potential of the Republican Guard was much better than the CIA's. It may be because the CIA follow a political aim, not a professional one, so they exaggerated the danger from Iraq. My team did a good job. It prepared the outlines of the American plan of action, and that was what happened. The Republican Guard just wanted to go back; there were no WMDs [weapons of mass destruction].

Next, the instinct to not accept any statement on its face value. A long time ago, I had come to the conclusion that official versions always economize on the truth because that is their compulsion. So, without any clues, on 2 May 2011, it was my assessment, sitting far away in Abu Dhabi, that the Osama bin Laden raid could not have been carried out by the Americans without our help. Maybe I had an underlying desire to convey that we were not incompetent and had denied our role for political reasons. Over time, many things confirmed it. Now, I don't even have to prove that. Go to Abbottabad, and everyone in that locality will tell you that twenty-four hours before the raid, the roads were closed. So, we were on board. As we say, we were in on the strike.

The military is not in the business of going deep into matters; we look at the facts and come out with something tangible. But I was in the habit of discovering the original sin. My military colleagues used to mock me and say, 'Whatever theme is given to you, you try and philosophize it. You are a brigade commander. You should talk about the operational doctrine and not the doctrinal philosophy.' In the intelligence job, this habit was immensely helpful because one wanted to look a little deeper beyond what was apparent. Mr Dulat knows that what is presented to you on a plate is usually not all there is. It may not even be correct. You must look at the background to come to your own conclusions. And though inexperienced in this discipline, I think at times that this faculty, this propensity of mine, proved very useful.

Aggarwal: Dulat Saheb, what would you say are the skills that you developed as an intelligence officer and then as an intelligence chief?

Dulat: As an intelligence officer, let me first make a point. I know General Saheb has mentioned this. There is a commonality here between the ISI and the IB. The ISI in Pakistan is all manned by the army, and the IB in India is all manned by police officers. So there was a homogeneity there, and a camaraderie that 'we're all officers'.

As far as the learning goes, we learned on the job and we would do various jobs. So you're learning all the time, you're acquiring experience.

I was posted in Bhopal, and from Bhopal to Srinagar. Bhopal was the first time that I interacted with Muslims. In the Punjab where I had grown up after Partition, there were no Muslims except for a little pocket in Malerkotla. We never met Muslims in school, college or anywhere. So, Muslims were a curiosity to me until I got to Bhopal. Bhopal is 30 per cent or more Muslim. There, we made a lot of Muslim friends. We're still friends. So, it was a very good education for me before I went to Srinagar, because Kashmir was 95 to 97 per cent Muslim. Having seen the Musalman in Bhopal, it was easier to understand the Musalman in Kashmir. The rest of intelligence you learn on the job.

I had thirty years in the Bureau. If I might be allowed a moment of immodesty, I would say that I was not an unpopular guy in the IB. I could have very comfortably stepped into the chief's shoes. As luck would have it, I had a batchmate who was a spot senior to me. He became the DIB [Director of the Intelligence Bureau], and I would have retired as number two. But luck favoured me, and I was asked if I would head the RAW.

Now being chief in the RAW was a different ballgame altogether. To start with, I faced hostility, which I understood because, for them, I was an outsider. It took about four to six months for people to get used to me. All the time there was an apprehension in the organization that 'this guy is going to bring the IB into the RAW'. But I resisted that temptation. It was a good test of leadership qualities. Could I swing it?

Aggarwal: Can you say more about those leadership qualities? What were the skills that you think helped you navigate that turbulent period?

Dulat: I decided to take the more difficult path rather than the easy way out—that established leadership. The easiest way out would have been to get myself a staff officer and another couple of colleagues from the IB and put them into important spots. I did nothing of the sort.

The RAW is not as homogeneous as the IB is. It has people from all the services. I was told that there were some troublemakers there. I said, 'Let me first deal with the troublemakers. We'll start from there.'

I certainly enjoyed my seventeen-month stint as chief, which coincided with General Saheb's. I only wish that I'd had another year, because I was really beginning to enjoy myself. Then it all ended. Now, of course, they have a minimum of three years for chief, but in those days, you retired when your time came.

I was to retire on 31 December 2000. A week before that, I was told that I was to join the PMO [Prime Minister's Office]. It was a big surprise. I enjoyed those three-and-a-half years in Vajpayee's PMO with [then Indian National Security Advisor] Brajesh Mishra. So I had five-and-a-half years to watch Vajpayee very closely. That is why, Neil, when I wrote my first book, with Kashmir all stuffed in my head, HarperCollins said, 'We'll call it *Kashmir: The Vajpayee Years.*'

So with time, luck has favoured me and has taken us to where we are now—Track II, peacebuilding, thinking that we can do things, to do something as audacious as write a book with General Saheb. In all of this, chemistry is very important. If the General and I did not gel, if I didn't have the respect I've had for him since day one, it would not have been possible.

Our backgrounds and even thought processes might have been different, but we understood things. We understood each other. When he spoke of Afghanistan, I knew he was the last word. I would not challenge him. And he gave way to me when we spoke of Kashmir. Not only that, he very kindly said, 'You are an intelligence officer. I'm basically a military man.' So I did have that advantage of having served in intelligence for many years.

Aggarwal: What obstacles did you both encounter in intelligence work?

Durrani: First, let me go back to your previous question. I might miss answering it later on: the key qualities of an intelligence chief.

Aggarwal: Please, go ahead.

Durrani: In India people rise from the ranks through merit and take over IB or RAW. In our case, a person can be appointed to such posts at the pleasure of the chief executive of the country or the army. So, we do not always follow the criteria of who would make a good ISI chief.

But my experience was the same as Dulat Saheb's. If you act based on the opinions presented to you by your subordinates, play safe and don't make your own assessments, then you are not likely to be a great chief. After getting the inputs of your subordinates, you should make your own briefs, and chart your own course—and take responsibility for it, regardless of success or failure. Then it is quite likely that if you are not sacked you will go down in history as having made a difference.

Thinking within the establishment, police officers are usually cut out to be better intelligence hands than military men, because a policeman lives with the people, he deals with the people, his instincts have been groomed in a manner that he understands the people. The military is isolated from the general public.

As I said, if you are going to be dependent on your subordinates to give you guidance, you're no good. But now that the job has come to you, use your instincts and give it your best shot. I could have marked time. Frankly, I went there as an interim head of the ISI: 'Yeah, keep the seat warm until we find someone else.' But that year and a half was such an enriching experience.

And the blessing is that after you have retired, you keep meeting people like Mr Dulat, again accidentally. Because one continued on that track which one could easily have left. In time, one saw there was some merit in whatever destiny handed one.

One had to go against conventional wisdom, tradition and laid-down norms which make one stop oneself. We're stuck. I've said that very often. We're stuck because we do not think that people are going to think out of the box. One says, 'Someday we will.'

That is what you probably wanted from your last question to me—what advice one would give. If you think that something different needs be done, then do it. This is your chance. One doesn't get this chance very often.

Aggarwal: One hears at times about maintaining double lives, running other officers or feeling isolated from other people in intelligence work. Without revealing any sort of national security secrets, which of these did you experience and how did you deal with them?

Durrani: Very normally in my case. I again got lucky. Once the job came to me, my family—my wife and children—decided, 'Now you have this job, we will give you all the time so you can concentrate on it.' So, I was running only one life, and that was my professional life. Nothing else came in the way. Everything else was being taken care of by the rest of the family. I did not have to live two lives.

Aggarwal: Dulat Saheb?

Dulat: You know, this question of double lives and triple lives goes along with the job in some ways. Not everything that you know or do is known by others. I was determined to keep my private and personal life quite distinct from my official life, and I did manage to do this from the start. When I came home, I left the office behind.

My wife was very supportive in this. I'll give you an example. All of us who have been in these jobs go through at least a couple of difficult times or crises. That happened at the end of 1999 when we had the hijacking of IC 814. It was one long week of a lot of stress because nobody knew how this whole thing would end. But when it ended on 31 December and the hostages were brought home, I went home and told my wife, 'Let's sit by the fireside. I need a cognac. Let's just sit down and have a drink.' We sat down together, had a drink and brought in the new year. She didn't ask a thing.

It still keeps coming back to haunt you. This is a part of that life. Not everything goes right. Not everything goes correct. But you do it to the best of your ability.

I mentioned the RAW earlier. I thoroughly enjoyed myself. I made good friends also. But what people in the RAW thought of me, you have to ask them. I don't have an honest answer about that. In fact, in my career at the time, maybe I thought that I was neither fish nor fowl. I never completed my career in the IB. In the RAW, I was an outsider. Like General Saheb, I decided, 'I'm alone in this game right now. Suddenly from having the full support of an organization, I've come to a place where I'm on my own.' And I said, 'I will deal with it on my own.' Good, bad, indifferent, whatever it was, I never sought anybody's help.

I made it quite clear to my colleagues in the IB when they told me 'You're one of us,' that though I still felt like one of them, now I was not an IB man—I headed the RAW and it came first for me. This is a question [of loyalties] I was asked many times. I was the first one to have served in both organizations.

Even now, I am asked, 'Which is the better organization?' They are both very fine organizations. The IB is more homogeneous. It's solid—it's been around for more than a hundred years. The RAW is comparatively new. But officer to officer, man to man, it is as good as the IB.

All I can say is that it is not a bad career. It is not a bad life. And yet, when I left the government in 2004, I had the option to stay on, but I thought, it's time to leave. One of the things about government that never went down well with me was the suffocating restrictions around you.

Durrani: Mr Dulat is a very lucky man. I wish I could do that: leaving the office behind and coming home to family. For that year and a half, whenever I got home, my office came home with me [*smiles*]. Maybe I could not handle things as efficiently. Or maybe it was because of the multidimensional nature of the job. You have the military, you have the civil, you have Afghanistan, you have all those things, whatever was happening. The saving grace was that not once in that year and a half did my family complain, 'You're not giving us enough time.'

I once asked my German counterpart, 'You go home over the weekend. Your headquarters are in Munich. Does anyone bother you?' He said, never. Here it was unthinkable to not get a call in the middle of the night, over the weekend, all the time. That's why I say that I envy people who can lead a professional life as well as a family life while having their job. I could not do it.

4. The Transition to Peacemaking

Neil Krishan Aggarwal: I'm going to ask you both now to think about your current roles as peacemakers. What incident or motivation pushed you to consider peacemaking and why? You've both given such detailed histories of working in intelligence and thinking about threat assessments.

Psychologically, it is very interesting to ponder what impulse or motivation reflects a transition into peacemaking.

Asad Durrani: It's a universal phenomenon. Retired military officers, after having dealt with guns all their lives, ask if there is anything else they can do. And then, peacemaking was a more difficult art to learn and practice.

And the second was again accidental. Soon after my ambassadorship in Germany, both India and Pakistan came up with what I consider to be a perfect peacemaking formula, the composite dialogue. I started studying it, and I said, 'Well, if peace has to be made, this is the path forward.'

In 2010, I was in Norway for the Oslo Dialogue. I was called because that year Afghanistan was the subject *schwerpunkt* [main emphasis] at that time. That taught me something more about the subject. But as I said to the leading peacemakers of the world, 'I appreciate your spirit, but what is the result?' Everyone conceded that they have made no headway. They may have succeeded in some smaller, remote places, but in the main arenas they have had not. [*Smiles.*] Maybe that's all I should say right now.

Aggarwal: Dulat Saheb?

A.S. Dulat: I could answer that in one word: Kashmir. I go back to my posting there, '88 to '90. That was a little less than two years. The last six months were terrible, and I was quite happy to get the hell out.

But I realized that the answer to Kashmir can only come through engagement, dialogue and peacemaking. It will not come through the barrel of the gun. You cannot ride a high horse and still hope to succeed in peacemaking.

That is why, when I came back to headquarters, one or two of my seniors felt that I was the best guy to go back and spark engagement with the Kashmiris. I was sort of handpicked to start talking to the Kashmiris. Somebody must have felt that this guy was (a) contemporary, because he had just gotten out of that mess and (b) he seems to have the right kind of empathy for engagement. Because it was not an easy time. Our kind of engagement has an element of trickery, and you try to keep it as straight as possible. I believe in that.

Today, we have a more muscular policy in Kashmir. Quite possibly, it's working fine, but I still believe that engagement is the best way. That is what led me to thinking of peacebuilding. Again, it was purely accident that I went to Pakistan. Salman Haider, a former foreign secretary, was putting together a Track II in Lahore. He said to me, *'Lahore chaloge?'* ['Will you go to Lahore?'] I replied, *'Kyon nahin chalunga?'* ['Why wouldn't I go?']

Aggarwal: What skills would you say that you both had to learn in this transition as peacemakers?

Durrani: Patience. Listen to the others. Don't push them. It's an incremental process—there's a chapter 'Take What You Can Get' in *The Spy Chronicles* —go piecemeal instead of going, 'We want all or nothing' and then ending up with nothing. That ought to be the approach. If it has not happened in the past seventy years, then it may happen in the next seventy.

Perseverance. You can't get out or give up. That is something that I have learned from my colleague Mr Dulat's patience. You can't say, 'I don't think that there will be any progress.' He would say, 'There will be. Yes, over time, it will come.'

As of now, especially after one considers all the past years, I would say that I've been proven right. Things are getting from bad to worse. The status quo is being recreated at another level with even more negatives. Even so, there's one thing that you cannot afford to do, and that is *to give up*.

Aggarwal: Dulat Saheb, what are some of the skills that you've had to learn in this transition to peacemaking?

Dulat: Empathy is very necessary. The other person's point of view is as important as one's own. We can keep airing our own points of view, but unless we're willing to listen, engagement is quite meaningless.

This is the problem I found when we first started on this Track II journey. There were too many types of people involved in the same sort of job. The most troublesome were the diplomats on both sides. Their self-righteousness at times was unbearable, though General Saheb sometimes differed with me.

What happened subsequently was that one of our sponsors decided that there should be a military-to-military dialogue. I'm told that it went quite well. And from there began the spooks' dialogue, which I thought was a good dialogue because I think we talk much more openly and honestly. We didn't always agree—sometimes there were disagreements, even nasty ones. But we spoke much more honestly. I think that's more important than deciding who is right or wrong all the time These 'ifs' and 'buts' are not the right way to go about it.

Aggarwal: Did the skills and instincts that you developed in intelligence work ever get in the way of transitioning into peacemaking?

Durrani: Oh yes, it did.

Aggarwal: How so?

Durrani: It's not about making wish lists or hoping that something will happen. You carry out an assessment, and in that, you put yourself into someone else's shoes. You realize that peace is not going to be easy, not because the process isn't good, but sometimes the absence of peace helps an adversary.

In the last twenty years, because I was concentrating on the western side—Afghanistan and Iran—I came to the conclusion that the Americans may not want to succeed in Afghanistan. If a little *khat-pat* [strife] goes on, it suits them. It gives them a role. So, they are not interested, and they will scuttle any peace process or dialogue that is not theirs.

And on the eastern front, if I were sitting in Mr Doval's [Ajit Doval, National Security Advisor to the Prime Minister of India] shoes, I would say, 'All right. We can live with the present situation. It harms us less than it harms Pakistan.' Now this is my assessment: He'll think, 'What if we settle certain matters, or at least come to certain arrangements? We probably would lose more. The Kashmiris will be happy. The Pakistanis will probably open a bottle of champagne bottle.' So, India might not take the risk of encouraging a change whose dynamics it may not be able to control.

This is the skill of getting into the enemy's shoes to be able to think like him. I would then say, 'Oh God, this peace process you want to work on is a big problem. The other side does not want it.' So I lose hope in our peacemaking.

Aggarwal: Dulat Saheb, did the skills and instincts that you developed from intelligence work ever get in the way of peacemaking?

Dulat: Not at all. I thought it was an asset. You knew, at times, more than what the others knew. So, it was an interesting game, provided that you came upfront and accepted what was what. I do believe intelligence officers tend to have better knowledge than a lot of other people. Often the rules and government do not permit you to go back to old files. But there are also files of the mind. Many times, when I was discussing a matter, I would suddenly recall something from the past. It helped.

The question really is—the guts of the problem, Neil— *Aapki niyat kya hai? Aap karna kya chah rahe hain?* [What is your intention? What do you want to do?] Is this all just a façade? I mean, it's common sense that neighbours need to live amicably in peace and harmony, if not as friends. I think the India–Pakistan relationship is one of the easiest relationships to manage if people on both sides are honest and, I might add, have the capability of carrying people along.

The other thing that comes to my mind when it comes to peacemaking is the Prime Minister under whom I worked towards the end, for those five-and-a-half years: [Atal Bihari] Vajpayee Saheb. He believed in peace. He inspired us. He was the one who put the bus to Lahore and started this whole process at one level. He was a man of peace. He was a crafty politician, but he still believed that this level of confrontation with Pakistan needed to end.

All these things helped. You asked us so many questions that I guess you'll figure out, what do these guys actually have in their hearts? How much of it is lies and how much of it is the truth?

Aggarwal: What advice would you give to diplomats, military personnel and intelligence officers who wish to engage in peacemaking and make the transition as you both have?

Durrani [*laughing*]: Dulat Saheb first. *Jao Dulat Saheb* [Go, Dulat Saheb].

Dulat [*laughing*]: *Jo hukam karo* [Whatever you wish]. I don't think I'm in a position to advise anyone on these matters. It should come to you naturally. That's why I mentioned the chemistry: trust, faith, belief. I think these are truly essential. And over and above that—empathy. This whole business of we being bigger than someone else, or somebody else not being able to match up—no, that won't help matters.

In peacemaking, like in any business, there are believers and non-believers, and it's not confined just to spooks or the military. I felt that generals talking to each other is a great idea, because nobody understands the cost of war more than a soldier does. I don't believe there would be any general mad enough to want war. It's all very well and good to sit in your drawing room and simply talk about peace, but *they* know that war is not an option. I think that this is generally acknowledged and conceded on both sides, so what are the options left? What does common sense say then?

As General Saheb says, let's at least have a stable stalemate. But I'm not a believer in stalemates. I believe that the status quo only helps Pakistan. I think we need to move forward.

Aggarwal: Durrani Saheb, what advice would you give?

Durrani: We continue to disagree because he still remains an incorrigible optimist.

On many points, I would agree: it's a long haul. The peace process is not going to be clinched in one go—we need patience, perseverance; it's a give and take—it's not as if you can get everything and others nothing.

But there's one point on which we will continue to disagree: I think that countries do not make peace out of the goodness of their hearts. They have to be compelled to make peace. So that compulsion is a factor to which people should give a little more thought.

What I'd advise, if you are in a position to do it, is try and raise the cost of war. Sometimes it is raised by strengthening, through the cost of resistance, as the US wants to do in the case of Ukraine by supplying more weapons. They probably assume that once the Ukrainians can defend themselves a little better, then maybe [Russian President Vladimir] Putin will back down. That is one approach.

Another approach is to try and expand the peace lobby among people instead of giving the resistance the means to compel the enemy. The public voice in India, let's say, has a large enough number of people supporting the peace process. Or in Pakistan, one may have to say, 'We have to shed some stereotypes,' and then peace might become more likely.

Dulat: Let me say just one last thing. I agree entirely with General Saheb about peacemakers not getting carried away by this whole peace process. Yes, this India–Pakistan thing doesn't look good these days. Nothing is going to happen in a hurry. In fact, it's not looked this bad for a long time.

So, it is a long process. It might be a question of where to go with it. How realistic is this idealistic way of going about it? I know that it's not going to be easy. Can we go forward in a way that we can finally offer Modiji or General Bajwa a Nobel Peace Prize?

Aggarwal: Well, I'm going to challenge both of you to think about what can be done in these kinds of difficult circumstances over our next sessions. Dulat Saheb keeps flattering me by asking my opinion about both of you as a psychiatrist. I tell him that this entire process—all the questions I'm asking, the theories from which the questions are drawn, the flow and rapport we share in each session—all come from psychiatry and psychology. But since he wants my assessment of you both, and since you both seem to be genuinely interested in my psychological opinions, perhaps we can talk about a few personal points, if it is all right with you.

Dulat: Finally!

Durrani: I am on board, Neil.

Aggarwal: Let's first talk about some commonalities between both of you. Both of your fathers were in government service. Durrani Saheb, you mentioned that your father was an officer in the prison department. I wonder to what extent that influenced your decision to go into the military. Dulat Saheb, you mentioned that your father was a sessions judge, and I wonder to what extent that influenced your decision to go into the IPS. Both of you were exposed to fathers who worked in law and order. Both of you also seem to be interested in the common psychological theme of discipline. If my hypothesis is correct, then in your personal lives you both seem to be working through a classic question in philosophy and the social sciences, which is the extent to which individuals have freedom or agency in social structures of power. Durrani Saheb mentioned that he chose to join the military whereas Dulat Saheb said that his father made a very strong suggestion that he join the IPS. Whatever might have been your initial impulses, you both continued with, and excelled in, these environments.

There's another psychological theme that emerges from your narratives, which is your ability to navigate camaraderie with competition. You both talked about sports in childhood and adolescence as mandatory activities that gave you a community. The sports that you mentioned, especially cricket and hockey, all allow individuals to excel and make their own marks within a team environment. I am curious about how you balance the desire to stand out from your peers with the sense of belonging you may feel in groups that are organized towards a particular mission, whether it is winning on the athletic field, the battlefield, the field of intelligence.

Recent work in psychology is organizing research into four main domains: personality traits; drives and motivations; skills and abilities; and biographical events that shape who we are.[23] Even though these domains are interconnected, the ways that they are interconnected vary for each human since we are all unique. Let's take each domain individually in terms of how you both described your childhood and adolescence.

One theme that surfaces in terms of biographical events is the comfort with being alone. Durrani Saheb mentioned that one of his first memories as a child is of enjoying his lone walk to school. In adolescence, he described himself as cycling long distances; in the military, he talked about his desire to explore nature and go trekking. One key detail was his compulsion to cross to the other side of the street when he would see crowds. This theme of 'charting one's own course' appears recurrently, whether it is in social situations with friends or professional situations in intelligence. A child who questioned the existence of God grew up to question the institutional norms of the Pakistan Army and to later produce his own assessments as an ISI chief.

Dulat Saheb also narrated long periods when he felt alone. An older brother died when he was young. He went to a boarding school, where its bullying required a 'survival of the fittest' mentality. This ability to survive carried him through his transition into the IPS when he was accused of misbehaving with a civilian in Jaipur. As head of RAW, he went alone to meetings and maintained an acute awareness of being perceived as an outsider who was running his intelligence organization.

This ability to feel confidence in solitude may explain a comfort with going against entrenched institutional values and practices to advance peacemaking.

Your personality traits also come through clearly. Both of you have been *open to new experiences*, whether it is General Durrani delving into books, travel, engineering and science, or Dulat Saheb discovering debating, declamation and girls at a boys' boarding school. You both can be *highly extroverted*, with General Saheb enjoying social events on his terms and Dulat Saheb enjoying team sports throughout his school and professional career. You both are *highly conscientious*, with General Durrani pursuing courses such as German language and man-management in the military and Dulat Saheb topping his college in history, though he may have been underplaying his cognitive gifts out of humility.

The last thing I'll mention relates to your motivations for peace. Here, Dulat Saheb's history as a member of the post-Partition generation is striking. I don't know if he would have been as committed to peace if he had been born in Chennai or Bengaluru; Punjabiyat manifests repeatedly throughout his life. Born in Sialkot, he characterized his childhood as 'split by the Partition' and went to Government College Chandigarh since his father's alma mater in Lahore was unavailable. He wanted to join the Punjab cadre after joining the IPS. I hear a sentiment of loss and nostalgia throughout his childhood and adolescence. Perhaps peacemaking offers him a way to fill this personal void. Cultural themes have not appeared so prominently in General Saheb's narratives, but I imagine that his desire to pursue peace with the goal of avoiding war reflects his exposure to the brutalities of violence as a military man.

We will keep talking about the relationship between your personal and professional lives in future sessions. For now, thank you.

3

Case Studies in How We Become Indians and Pakistanis

By the time you read this book, India and Pakistan will have celebrated seventy-six years of independence from the British Empire. Both countries have developed distinct national identities. But A.S. Dulat and Asad Durrani were born five six years before independence in British India. This raises a fundamental question: How did Dulat come to see himself as Indian and Durrani come to see himself as Pakistani?

Developing cultural, ethnic, national or religious identities is a universal psychological process as humans join social groups. Vamik Volkan, a psychiatrist who has participated in Track II diplomacy, defines *identity* in this way: 'Unlike character and personality, which are observed and perceived by others, identity refers to an individual's inner working model—he or she, not an outsider, senses and experiences it.'[1] Volkan connects individuals to groups through what he calls *large-group identity* as 'the subjective experience of thousands or millions of people who are linked by a persistent sense of sameness while also sharing numerous characteristics with others in foreign groups'.[2]

Once children look beyond their parents to others, that sense of sameness with millions of people begins: 'When the child develops further, through identifications with teachers, religious authorities, peer groups, and community and large-group leaders, he or she identifies with their investment in religion, ethnicity, nationality and so on, and shares in the differentiation of those persons unlike the group and inimical to it.'[3]

Adolescents start to critically explore their large-group identities: 'Under the influence of others in the group (especially his peers), the youth now unconsciously "decides" which aspects of large-group identity will become the fixed and permanent means of connecting him or her with the others in the large group.'[4] Hence, how did Messrs Dulat and Durrani learn about identities from their families in childhood and decide which aspects to keep throughout life?

Large-group identities connect us to some people and disconnect us from others. Partition introduced new physical and psychological borders between Indians and Pakistanis. Volkan describes how physical borders maintain psychological distance between people: 'All people have probably experienced some aspect of the psychological importance of borders whether through customs and immigration controls, geographic borders such as mountains and rivers that separate nations or other territories, or the fences and walls that separate neighboring individuals.'[5] Anyone who has travelled to the Wagah–Attari border has seen the psychological importance of the fence separating India and Pakistan each evening during the flag-lowering ceremony, which the political scientist Sanjay

Chaturvedi describes so beautifully: 'Each side, comprising both the performers and spectators, wearing different costumes (Pakistani Rangers in black uniform, their Indian counterparts in khaki, more veiling among women on the Pakistani or "Muslim" side, and a large number of Sikhs on the Indian side) perform the mirror image of the other's action in order to prove exactly the opposite: difference.'[6] It's a reminder that while Indians and Pakistanis have their own identities, the other always looms. In one of our sessions, Durrani described both countries evocatively as 'two cats with their tails tied together'.

Although large-group identities differ, similar processes underlie their development. Symbols such as flags and portraits, annual events that commemorate group glories or traumas, and ritual practices that affirm who we are and aren't,[7] like the Wagah–Attari flag-lowering ceremony, are factors that maintain large-group identities. Institutions like family units, educational systems, society's organization through different classes and media houses[8] are less visible in everyday life, but they also maintain large-group identities about who we are and aren't. In diplomacy it is essential to understand these identities. Differences in identity can affect negotiation styles, what issues receive attention, social roles and etiquette.[9] Participants from enemy groups may become spokespeople for their large groups, which affects success and failure in negotiations.[10] People may never be able to name every single influence on their identity, but understanding how Track II participants like Dulat and Durrani perceive themselves and each other can improve the chances for peace between India and Pakistan.

1. Identity Formation in Childhood

Neil Krishan Aggarwal: You both are older than your countries. I'm curious as to how your identities have formed and changed throughout life. The questions for this session delve into how your identities formed throughout youth, how they've shifted in adolescence and how they continue to evolve. How we see ourselves as Indians or Pakistanis at one point in life may mean something else at a different point in life. When we talk about peacemaking, then how we see the people across the table can also shift based on our experiences.

The first question is very basic: Where were your parents and grandparents born?

Asad Durrani: My father was born in Gujrat, a city now in Pakistan. My mother in Gurdaspur, now in India. I have no idea where my grandparents were born. I never heard about it or can't recall, but I must assume that they were generally what we call 'Indo-Af-Pak' [Indo-Afghan-Pakistani] or certainly 'Af-Pak'. Maybe some of them were born in northern India since this is the place where people used to circulate after migration.

Aggarwal: Dulat Saheb, where were your parents and grandparents born?

A.S. Dulat: Actually, I can't say, because I don't know. But this much I can say: both my parents were certainly born in the Punjab. When I say Punjab, I mean the undivided Punjab. If I were to make a guess, I would say that my mother might possibly have been born in Lahore or in Jhang. My father—I don't know really. Of course, we belong to Nabha. I don't know much about either of my parents, but it must be Punjab.

That's where we belong. I never thought outside of Punjab, at least not until I got into service because that's where we were born, that's where we grew up, that's where we went to school, college and university. Everything was Punjab. And as I told you before, when I got into the Police Service, I was hoping that I would be allotted Punjab. I was hugely disappointed when I was not.

Aggarwal: Well, you've anticipated my next question, which is how would you describe your birth families' national, ethnic and religious backgrounds? Dulat Saheb, you've mentioned that your family is from Punjab. Would you describe your family in other ways, like in terms of religious background or linguistic background?

Dulat: In terms of linguistic background, we all spoke Punjabi at home. Very rarely did my father speak in English. He only spoke English when he wanted to talk to you very formally. Otherwise, it was always Punjabi.

Now, Punjabi is a language where the dialect changes. I guess it's the same with most languages. But in the Punjab, it changes every thirty kilometres or so. The Punjabi that we speak in south Punjab is a little cruder than what is spoken in the northern part of Punjab, most of which has now gone to Pakistan.

Aggarwal: And you also identify as Punjabi Sikh, right?

Dulat: Yes, we're Punjabi Sikhs. But let me explain that. My mother was Hindu. In those days, there were a lot of inter-caste marriages, and she came from a Hindu family. When I was named Amarjit Singh, it was very clear what I was. [*Laughs.*]

Aggarwal: Durrani Saheb, how would you describe your birth family's national, ethnic and religious background?

Durrani: I think it's much more confusing. I may not have connected the dots even for myself. The heritage is simple. My father came from the Durrani tribes of Afghanistan that migrated here about 150 years ago and trickled down to Punjab. My grandmother was a woman from the Vale [of Kashmir]. The language at home became Punjabi because that's what my grandmother spoke. She might have also spoken Kashmiri, but no one else in the family knew it.

My mother came from the Yusufzai line, but they were all Persian speakers. Even today in that big family, most of them speak Persian. So my mother was very keen that we should speak Persian at home. But my father didn't want to learn a new language, and said Persian would be useless for the children. He refused.

They compromised on Urdu. Ours turned out to be the first household in the greater family in which the parents did not speak in Punjabi with the children. Or, as I have mentioned, Persian. We were the first to speak Urdu at home. Later on, many others caught up with that.

As far as religion was concerned, I don't think that there was any special emphasis on it, or even on people's background. We were your normal Sunni family that practised to some extent, the women more than the men, as usually happens. No one was radically religious or rigid.

It was a relaxed environment at home as far as religion, ethnicity or languages were concerned. We spoke Urdu at home, and when we went out to play in the mohalla, everyone spoke Punjabi. Because of school, in due course English became the third language.

Aggarwal: So even though your mother's side was Yusufzai, they spoke Persian instead of Pashto?

Durrani: For most of the Afghans—even the Durrani clan when they migrated from somewhere west of Kandahar—all the manuscripts at home were in Persian. They were supposed to be Persian speakers. People in our parts would speak Pashto and Punjabi, but just to show that they are more literate they would use Urdu and not Punjabi. My mother's family was a purely Persian-speaking family.

Aggarwal: Durrani Saheb, you were born in pre-Partition British India. How did your family understand its newfound Pakistani identity when you were a child?

Durrani: It was very smooth, as I recall. When India was being divided, both my mother and father were passionate supporters of the Pakistan Movement, so they used to pray for Mohammed Ali Jinnah. I don't know if they were members of the Pakistan Muslim League. Luckily, most of us were in areas that were Muslim majority. There was no question where we would belong. We happily became Pakistanis, lucky to have a country of our own. That was the initial reaction.

Aggarwal: Dulat Saheb, you mentioned in our last session that you were born in Sialkot. How did your family understand its newfound Indian identity when you were a child?

Dulat: My father was in the government, and he understood these things. I think my mother found it more difficult because she was not as well educated. She did go to college, but I don't know if she graduated. She always talked about Lahore, her days there. I would say that it was easier for my father.

Also, he didn't have that kind of attachment. He belonged to this [the Indian] side. We belonged to east Punjab or southern Punjab. Therefore, for my father there was no issue, no problem at all.

Like General Saheb had a relaxed family, so also was ours. In fact, religion never really cropped up at all. I used to wonder about our home. In most families, if you were Hindu, you had a small temple in the house. If you were a Sikh, you had a [Guru] Granth Saheb. We had nothing. It was left to everyone to do what they liked.

Aggarwal: According to psychology, our early identities in childhood are limited to our relationships with our family members. For most of us, our relationships start with our mothers. After that, our fathers. Then, we become aware of other people, such as siblings, in the household. As we get older, we inherit larger identities that connect us to people outside the home. Those identities could be ethnic, religious and nationalistic. Please tell me, to the best that you both can remember, the first time you recall thinking about yourselves as citizens. For Dulat Saheb, when was the first time you thought about yourself as an Indian and why? For Durrani Saheb, when was the first time you thought about yourself as a Pakistani and why?

Dulat: When Partition happened, it was all very confusing, as I was a child. The first time I thought of myself as Indian was when my father took me to a cricket match. Soon after Partition, there was a West Indian team that visited India. There was a test match at Feroz Shah Kotla [Stadium] in Delhi. My father was not much of a sportsman, but he loved watching sports. He took me along.

More than watching the game, I spent time watching our players. I still remember that there used to be a very handsome cricketer in those days on the Indian team, a guy called Dattu Phadkar.[11] When I went towards the Indian dressing room, I saw him all padded up and thought, 'Well, this is the Indian team.' [*Smiles*.] That was the first time I thought of Indians as opposed to West Indians.

Aggarwal: Durrani Saheb, when was the first time you thought of yourself as a Pakistani?

Durrani: It must have been right from the beginning, because I do not recall a change, even though I was technically an Indian the first seven years of my life. People probably said that they were Pashtuns or Punjabis or Muslims. I do not recall that anyone said, 'We're Indians.' There was no problem about the 'others' because at that time, so many of my father's colleagues were Hindus and Sikhs, as were our neighbours and the students in one's class. So Partition did not make us feel there was a drastic change and we must start thinking differently. We did think, 'Well, we have a country, all right.' But it did not mean that a big wall had now been thrown up.

And just to explain the relaxed atmosphere at home or the tolerance at home, people in my family were happily marrying Shias, Qadianis—at that time, one didn't give it a second thought.

Aggarwal: Oh wow! Really?

Durrani: And if someone did marry outside the Islamic religion—though I do not recall if anyone did—there would not be much commotion. It seemed like something quite normal that since you were part of a country, then people would be mixing, working together and intermarriage would take place. This is what I perceived and felt as a school-going kid.

As far as Pakistaniyat was concerned, there was some sort of celebration that now we were free, we had a country of our own.

Aggarwal: And when you said that you had Hindus and Sikhs in your class, was that after Partition as well?

Durrani: That is actually very difficult to say because I do not remember, except for a couple of incidents. I used to walk to my school. It was about three or four kilometres. I usually passed through a huge cultivated area, jumped across a wall—in fact, they had made a place for the children to cross over, which we happily used. The shop where we took the break to have a sip of water, belonged to a Bania, a Hindu. We never gave it a second thought whether to take water from his shop or not. And he never bothered who came along.

In the class, there must have been some Hindus and Sikhs for some time at least; but I do not remember.

Aggarwal: Please tell me the first times you recall thinking about the other country. Did it have a positive or negative connotation for you, and why? For Durrani Saheb, when was the first time you started to think about India as a Pakistani? And for Dulat Saheb, when was the first time you started to think about Pakistan as an Indian?

Durrani: Pretty soon negative things did happen despite the tolerance I described, because the process of Partition was accompanied by migration of people and communal riots. My personal experience started a few months before Partition. I was in Delhi with my family. I have a vague memory of something happening—fires, smoke and curfews. We got back safe and sound though, and I do not recall any ugly incidents. We must have taken a train. But since the migration and the riots were happening, the general feeling was that the other side must be the devil incarnate. So, the first reaction about the new India was negative.

Aggarwal: Dulat Saheb, your first reaction about Pakistan?

Dulat: I don't know. I can't recall it, but yes, my mother used to constantly tell us stories about Lahore and all their Muslim friends. Now this is the irony of Partition: my maternal grandfather was a member of the Unionist Party led by Sikandar Hayat.[12]

My mother would say that all her friends were Muslims, and there were Muslims in the house all the time. But then she would whisper, 'These Muslims are not very reliable,' and I wondered why. Later I realized that she had a chacha [father's younger brother] who was hacked to death in an office in Lahore—that sort of thing stays in the mind.

My father never talked about these things. But I do remember he had a close friend who belonged to Nabha, from where our family came. This friend went to Pakistan, but he and his family used to visit us every year for the first three years after Partition. He would come and stay with us.

Aggarwal: You haven't said it, but I imagine that it was a Muslim family.

Dulat: Yes, of course. They were Muslim.

Aggarwal: What were some of the ways that your families reinforced your national identities? How did they talk about the other country?

Durrani: Just because the two countries separated, all the commonalities of history, of working together and living together did not vanish. Yes, there was anger over some developments. But they would also recall good, decent colleagues, miss great friends who had left, mention a Hindu or Sikh neighbour and his wife's wonderful cooking, and so on.

And for us children, importantly, we could still read and talk about the great Mughal Empire, and Delhi was a city that symbolized greatness for the region, of which all of us could be proud.

After a few years, some exchanges started to take place at the people-to-people level, and not just the official level.

Some sports teams came over. National Olympics took place in Sahiwal when I was a schoolboy. We were happy to see the Indian teams and even cheered for them.

I vividly recall that one of the teams consisted primarily of Sikhs; I think it was the Punjab Police. After the event, they came over to my father who was in charge of Montgomery Jail in Sahiwal. It was famous for hand-woven durrees [cotton carpets]. A Sardarji said, 'Durrani Saheb, could you kindly pack up a few of these for us before we leave? Because, then we will take them as hand baggage. Otherwise, we'll have to pay duty.' Even policemen smuggled home durrees from Montgomery Jail because they were so well known.

This is why I say that Partition did not completely disrupt the relationship or make people change their views about the 'other'. Now ours is a hostile relationship: 'The separated country is the devil, and we have luckily gotten rid of it.'

Aggarwal: Dulat Saheb, what are some of the ways that your family or friends reinforced your national identity in youth and that they talked about the other country? You mentioned a bit about your mother earlier, for example.

Dulat: Neither my mother nor my father talked about nationalism in a hostile sense. I'm glad General Saheb reminded me.

Even as a kid, I followed cricket. I think the Pakistani cricket team first visited India in 1950. The interesting thing is that there were players on opposing sides who had played as one team before Partition. I remember that Abdul Hafeez Kardar was Pakistan's captain,[13] and he had been on the Indian team that went to England in 1946. So there wasn't too much of that nationalist feeling. Yes, everyone cheered when we beat Pakistan, but we didn't want to run down Pakistan. I think these things crept in much later.

———————

2. Identity Formation in Adolescence and Adulthood

Neil Krishan Aggarwal: Let's take you now to a time of life when you are older, which is your adolescence (between the ages of thirteen and eighteen), and when you're entering early adulthood (when you are in school and college). What were some of the ways you would say that your school and college reinforced your national identities and how they talked about the other country?

A.S. Dulat: In our part of Punjab, Muslims were a rarity. So, the identity that we acquired was not shaped by differences, and it was much more Punjabi than 'Indian'. Of course, in school we did learn a lot about India and Pakistan. But at home, it was Punjab, Punjabi, Punjabiyat. That is the identity that one acquired, and possibly that explains how we can still get along so well with our brethren across. It doesn't come as a strain.

Aggarwal: Durrani Saheb, how would you say that your school and college reinforced your national identity and how they talked about the other country?

Asad Durrani: Some of the elements that I talked about earlier continued to weigh heavily on how we looked at the other side. For example, cricket matches would be hotly contested but if the environment was good, people cheered the Indian side. I especially remember an Indian batsman who probably scored a century—I think it was [Vijay] Manjrekar—he was the darling of the crowd.

But the same spirit turned around 180° when you had something bigger going on, such as the developments in Kashmir or the tensions on the borders. Then suddenly, the other side became the devil, and the bonhomie was over.

But whenever that phase was over, you were very keen to talk again: 'Yes, yes, of course, how nice that both of us like cricket or can play good hockey.' In fact, the man that I first heard about when we were playing hockey as children was Dhyan Chand, the Dribbling Wizard.[14]

With such an environment and way of thinking, I don't think we can ever draw a firm line marking a cutoff after which our relationship is changed for good. I'm sure in due course we'll come to the present time which has changed things, because as I said, the general environment influences our thinking a great deal, but not for a long time.

Aggarwal: Well, we are heading in that direction now. You have anticipated my question. In our last session, we talked about your work histories and how you both have gone through different careers before becoming intelligence chiefs. You both then transitioned into peacemaking. What were some of the ways that your work environment reinforced your national identities? Durrani Saheb joined the military after college, and Dulat Saheb was in the IPS before he joined the IB. How did these institutions talk about their national identity and the identity of the other country? Did you start to incorporate some of those elements into your own understandings?

Dulat: You see, that's where the consciousness of identity really begins—once you get into government service. Now you're working for your country, and there is an adversary across the border. Even when I was in college, we had the war with China in 1962 and it aroused one's nationalist fervour. But yes, joining service was the watershed moment.

One point that I forgot to mention, Neil, was the assassination of Mahatma Gandhi soon after Partition. I think that was a huge tragedy for the subcontinent. I still remember the day of his cremation. My father went to attend the cremation in Delhi and took me along. At that time, Delhi was not a very big place. There were not the crowds that you see now. Still, it was a watershed moment. I think the history of the subcontinent might have been a little different if the Mahatma had survived five or seven years more. Like, possibly, if the Quaid [-e-Azam Mohammed Ali Jinnah] had not passed away on the other side. But these are all the ifs and buts of history.

Aggarwal: In our last session, you talked about your scholarly training in history. Could you say more about how you think the history of the subcontinent might have been different if both men were still alive?

Dulat: The Mahatma was a great man. He was a support to Panditji [Jawaharlal Nehru], who was sort of his student. That's why Panditji said, 'The light has gone out of our lives' after the Mahatma was assassinated. The Mahatma was committed to peace between both countries. At one of his prayer meetings, he said, 'Both India and Pakistan are my country. I am not going to take out a passport to go to Pakistan.'

Similarly, the Quaid was also a great man. He was relatively secular in his idea of Pakistan. He was basically a pork-eating, alcohol-drinking Englishman.

Aggarwal: There was his famous speech to the Constituent Assembly on 11 August 1947 when he talked about religion occupying a private role in civic life. He said, 'Today, you might say with justice that Roman Catholics and Protestants do not exist; what exists now is that every man is a citizen, an equal citizen of Great Britain, and they are all members of the Nation. Now I think we should keep that in front of us as our ideal, and you will find that in course of time Hindus would cease to be Hindus, and Muslims would cease to be Muslims, not in the religious sense, because that is the personal faith of each individual, but in the political sense as citizens of the State.'[15]

Dulat: Exactly. It's a very different understanding of national identity for Pakistan than some of the identities that bring it closer to political Islam.

Aggarwal: Durrani Saheb, how would you say that your work environment reinforced your national identity and talk about the other country?

Durrani: There are links that continued, and we have talked about some of them. Right from childhood, where did we get our children's magazines from? It was someplace—Delhi or somewhere—that used to produce *Khilona*[16] [Toy]. The girls used to read *Shama* [Candle-Flame], published in Delhi.

And then, when I joined the college, the best chemistry textbook was written by a Sikh—Singh or Bedi, I can't recall exactly.

Among other things, how passionately we used to watch the cinema from the other side! There was a film craze in Pakistan, and our own film industry was not as popular. So whenever we had the chance, we watched Indian films, whether in a cinema or a private viewing of a smuggled movie.

For all these reasons, we never looked at the other side as very different. But as the political situation developed, with Kashmir and the mobilization of separatism that I have talked about, the sense of difference grew. Also because of bloc politics, over time one realized we had different alignments—Pakistan with the Western bloc and India with the Soviet-led alliance.

These things did affect the distance between both sides. Some people were nostalgic and wanted to visit India for old times' sake, some wanted to buy things like Indian saris and Pakistani rice and so on. Others in Pakistan would get angry and say, 'Under these circumstances, how could you want to visit?' 'Why do you want to subsidize the Indian economy?' So there were people on both sides of opinion.

3. How Indians and Pakistanis See Each Other's Identities

Neil Krishan Aggarwal: Durrani Saheb, are there certain events or heroes that you would say all Pakistanis celebrate, regardless of their ethnic, regional or linguistic differences? If so, what are some that come to mind?

Asad Durrani: It's actually a very long list. For us, if I start with the struggle for independence, one of the first names besides our own Jinnah was Netaji [Subhas Chandra] Bose.[17] He was considered a great man. And because of the Lahore connection, Bhagat Singh[18] was always one of the heroes of our independence.

I don't think I can recall all the writers. I remember Krishan Chander,[19] the Urdu writer, and how popular he was. My personal favourite writer from the other side was Nirad Chaudhuri,[20] the Bengali. Khushwant Singh[21] became a household name here because of his *Train to Pakistan*.

In the present day, probably the two favourite authors on Indo–Pak relations or geopolitical affairs are Arundhati Roy[22] and Pankaj Mishra.[23] People like to read them.

When it comes to sports, Sunil Gavaskar[24] remains the hero for the cricket-loving crowd. There must be others whom I can't recall because I'm not too much into cricket. As I said I was a Dhyan Chand fan. Later on, Balbir Singh[25] was considered the best hockey player of his time. Milkha Singh[26] and [Abdul] Khaliq[27] from our side—their rivalry and friendship made them popular on both sides.

I can also talk about Bollywood. I'm not sure if I can recall all of them or even get the order right. There were many non-Muslim actors who always attracted great audiences [*laughing*]. '*Aaj toh abhi tak iski film lagi hui hai* [This person's film is still showing today]. Let's go and watch it.'

Going back in time: Ashok Kumar, Raj Kapoor, Prem Nath and Dev Anand. Later, Hrithik Roshan became a trendsetter for chiselled-bodied heroes. Balraj Sahni was worshipped by the oppressed in my youth.

Among the actresses: Madhuri Dixit; Rani Mukherjee, who was Musharraf's favourite; and Vidya Balan, a fine actress with eastern looks.

In the Subcontinent, the best hero, villain and female actress have been Amitabh Bachchan, Amrish Puri ('*Mogambo khush hua*' became a street expression) and Smita Patil. All were non-Muslims.

The last part is about politicians. Among Pakistanis, there are the four Indian Prime Ministers [Morarji] Desai,[28] Inder Kumar Gujral, Chandra Shekhar[29] and Vajpayee. And one more, who was never a prime minister but remains a crowd puller, is Mani Shankar Aiyar.[30]

So these are the people who continue to attract the attention and fascination of people in Pakistan.

Aggarwal: Durrani Saheb, you took the conversation in a different direction. I didn't think that you would name Indian events or heroes that Pakistanis admire. I thought you would name Pakistani events or heroes.

Dulat Saheb, in thinking about the reverse perspective, are there certain events, heroes or national figures that you would say Indians celebrate about Pakistan regardless of their ethnic, regional or linguistic differences. If so, what are some that come to mind?

Dulat: Like General Saheb mentioned, the film industry. In the initial stages, the industry came almost entirely from the other side. Many of them were Muslims. Even Hindus like the great Kapoor family were Peshawaris.

Personally, for me, my great cricketing hero was [former Pakistani Prime Minister] Imran [Khan].[31] General Saheb

doesn't like him, but he's my favourite Prime Minister of
Pakistan.

[*Both men laugh.*]

I thought that Imran in his time was very nearly as good
an all-rounder as Kapil Dev.[32] I think the other two great all-
rounders of that time who could compare were Ian Botham[33]
and Richard Hadlee.[34] They would only come third and fourth.

Aggarwal: I want to take you to a topic now that starts to
become contentious. This is where some of the differences
that I've noticed in my travels throughout India and Pakistan
become very clear.

Let's talk about the role of Partition. I don't want to bias
your opinions, but it is my impression that Indians see Partition
as a loss of territory whereas Pakistani see Partition as gaining
a country. I don't mean to speak for every Indian or for every
Pakistani, but I think that this event has been assimilated
differently within the national identities of both countries. The
event has very different meanings across borders. Would you
agree with that assessment?

Dulat: I think your assessment is fairly accurate. Partition made
a huge impact in north India, and particularly in Punjab. The
Punjabi Hindu has not been able to get over the trauma. My
mother, for instance, talked of Lahore with nostalgia in the
early years, but as time passed, she said fewer good things
about it.

And then, this nationalism came to the fore. The '65 war
was a watershed moment as it was fought in Punjab. Both sides
of Punjab.

But it varies with your personal experiences and what your family went through. General Saheb mentioned this relationship between Milkha Singh and Abdul Khaliq. Initially, Milkha was unwilling to go to Lahore because his experience of Partition had been so bad. But Pandit Nehru persuaded him to go and run.

Aggarwal: Durrani Saheb, would you agree with my assessment about Partition?

Durrani: People in Pakistan who came from India are not as nostalgic about places they left behind. I have heard of people in India saying, 'Lahore! There is no place like it!' or remembering their village in Sialkot or Jhelum. I've not seen that in Pakistanis.

But I do know that not just the migrants, but others too, believe that the subcontinent was at its best when it was united—the civilization of the past before the British came. The Ashokan empire and the Afghans and many more who kept the region more or less united. The only rule that is considered foreign is the British. People here feel that before that, Muslim rule was the best era of the Indian civilization. If there is any nostalgia, it's about the architecture in Delhi or Agra, or for the time when Bengal produced the world's finest textiles or that some 25 per cent of the world's GDP at that time was contributed by India.

This is something in the past that people not only remember, but will continue to write about. They think that if we could get over the present environment somehow, we would not only produce great sports teams, but become a strong region that the world would find hard to compete with. It's not only nostalgia, but the dreams and illusions people have. That also arises from having a common past.

Aggarwal: Durrani Saheb, are there certain events by which Pakistanis, regardless of their ethnic, regional or linguistic differences, feel angry or humiliated because of Indians? If so, what would those be?

Durrani: Of course, the 1971 war is certainly one. Nearly everyone would say that the '71 war did huge damage to how our people thought about ourselves, about the leadership or about the army.

But there were also other military engagements (not related to India), such as when Osama bin Laden was taken away. My impression is that the majority of our people feel our sovereignty was violated. It's a different matter that I think we cooperated.

Later, when there were drone attacks because of the Americans' war in the Af–Pak region, our people felt we were helpless against the them, and when people were killed, like the 80 to 100 students in the madrassa at Bajaur,[35] there was real public anger. These events seriously affected the national psyche so people felt, 'Someday, we will have to do something about this.'

Aggarwal: Can you say more about the '71 war in particular? About the perception of what the Pakistani leadership or military used to have of itself and how it changed after the '71 war?

Durrani: Yes. The blame essentially goes to the Pakistani leadership. Hardly anyone talks negatively about [Field Marshal Sam] Manekshaw[36] who was the architect of the victory in East Pakistan. They speak about him positively because he was a fine soldier and because of his very kind remarks about our soldiers conduct after the war. But our own civil and military leadership have been the target of criticism. No one else.

Aggarwal: Dulat Saheb, are there certain events that you would say all Indians regardless of their ethnic, regional or linguistic differences, feel humiliated or angry about, especially when it comes to Pakistan?

Dulat: Not really, but ultimately the matter comes down to terrorism in more recent times. These things can get exaggerated too. Pakistan played a huge role in Kashmir. Pakistan may have been surprised by what happened in Kashmir, as General Saheb says, but they took full advantage of it. Moral, military, political—every kind of support was provided.

It was the same when Punjab went out of control. After Operation Bluestar and then Indira Gandhi's assassination and the anti-Sikh riots, things were turbulent in Punjab; there was talk of Khalistan. Again, Pakistan fished in those troubled waters.

It's about the times. In the 1965 war the battle lines had been fairly drawn—Pakistan was on that side, and India was on this side. Later events blurred those lines and aggravated the thinking on both sides.

Pakistan talks about Kashmir, and we talk about terrorism. Terrorism has troubled us, certainly. We had a tough time right through the '80s and '90s combatting terrorism or insurgency. Now, Punjab is, in a sense, normal for the time being, and I hope it stays that way. Kashmir, too, has settled down in its own way. I don't think it's the best way but time will tell who is right and who is wrong, whether Vajpayee's way was the right way or Modiji's is.

Aggarwal: We all have ethnic, regional and religious affiliations. Dulat Saheb, you mentioned this a bit earlier but I want to press you on this point. Which parts of your background would you say that you feel closest to? I will also ask Durrani Saheb afterwards.

Dulat: I told you—Punjab, Punjabi, Punjabiyat.

Aggarwal: I had a feeling you would say that.

Dulat: There is no doubt in my mind about that. I have travelled all over the country. But Punjab never leaves me. It's in my blood.

Aggarwal: Durrani Saheb, which parts of your background do you feel closest to?

Durrani: In my case, there was no special region or background that determined my identity. It may be because we are a country that has been in flux, so we can't define ourselves in those restricted terms. When I have to introduce myself, I simply say, 'I'm a former soldier. I was once in the military.'

That's all. No Punjabiyat, no Pashtun background, or Baluchi or Sindhi. Nor are there people I admire. I simply say that I'm a former military man.

Dulat [*laughing*]: I wish to respond to that. Neil, I agree with General Saheb. I don't go around introducing myself as a Punjabi.
  [*All three laugh.*]

Dulat: I've often said that I'm a retired sarkari afsar [government official]. And that finishes the conversation [*laughing*].

Aggarwal: Sometimes these affiliations vary depending on the aspect of life we're talking about. Depending on what context you're in, you may identify in a different way. Do you notice that the way you identify is different in a home setting versus in government setting?

Dulat: That's very interesting. Can you explain that a bit?

Aggarwal: Sure. In terms of psychology, our identities can be determined by us not just in terms of how we see ourselves, but also by the people around us. Our locations can also be a factor, such as home or work. In one context, I may be a Hindu or a Punjabi, but in another context, I may be a father or husband. Identities can vary based on how we see ourselves and how other people see us.
  Dulat Saheb, I think you understand this because you mentioned that it's not like you go around saying that you're a Punjabi. You often identify as a retired sarkari afsar, but you also feel closest to Punjab, Punjabi and Punjabiyat. What's

critical when we talk about war and peace is how situations activate certain aspects of our identity. We're going to get to peacemaking in a moment, but what I'm wondering is whether you identify yourselves differently at home versus work, such as when you were in intelligence, for instance.

Dulat: Home is home, and the office is different. It's not easy to do, but throughout service I managed to compartmentalize my life. Ours in some ways is a nastier profession than General Saheb's, so I tried to keep it out of the home as much as possible.

Aggarwal: Durrani Saheb, would you identify yourself differently at home versus at work?

Durrani: Outside home one identified oneself in a context. If it was national, of course, one was a Pakistani. But elsewhere, if asked where I place myself, I might say, 'in the military', where I spent most of my career.

If someone wants to deepen the discussion and explore what else I want to say about myself, and that's incidentally how it happens at home as well, then all I say is, I have had my experiences and made my blunders. They were made for good or bad reasons but within a context. My objective is simple: to tell you what happened. You can go ahead and make new mistakes, do not repeat the ones we've made.

It will always depend on the environment in which you are describing yourself for the discussion.

4. Identity through the Languages of War and Peace

Neil Krishan Aggarwal: I want to go back to the language question. This is a phenomenon that is routinely fascinating between Indians and Pakistanis.

Durrani Saheb, we emailed separately about this, but I'd like you to share your response with Dulat Saheb so we have a level playing field for our session. I will ask Dulat Saheb as well. Durrani Saheb, what are the languages that you feel most comfortable with right now?

Asad Durrani: Oh. That is not a very easy question to answer. It depends on the subject. I suppose that if the three of us got together socially, we would be conversing in Punjabi. Especially if we were at a bar.

If we had to talk about serious subjects—India, Pakistan and so on—then I'm ashamed to admit that my favourite lingua franca would be English. That is the language in which one writes, discusses and lectures.

Urdu is supposed to be my first language but I fumble when talking on these subjects, which is embarrassing. I can't find the right terminology or phraseology in Urdu. So, it's English at that point.

Aggarwal: Dulat Saheb, what are the languages you speak and how do you choose to communicate in them?

Dulat: Like General Saheb said, if it's the three of us, then I would like to discuss everything in Punjabi. I'm most comfortable with it. When I'm with Punjabi friends, we speak Punjabi.

I agree with General Saheb that we've been brought up in a system where we tend to speak in English.

Even so, if I am asked to talk about a subject in public somewhere, I very often break into Hindustani. Embarrassingly, this happened to me once in Chennai with N. Ram of *The Hindu*.[37] I said something in Hindustani, and he stopped me and asked me to repeat it in English as many members of the audience did not understand Hindustani.

Then my Punjabi was tested a few years ago on Punjabi television. There was a guy who wanted to interview me. I asked, 'What will it be? Hindustani?' He said, 'No, Punjabi.' I said, '*Chalo phir, Punjabi ho jaye*' [All right, let it be Punjabi]. I'd never spoken Punjabi on TV, but I did all right. I was quite proud that I could manage it. Since then, I've done four interviews with that gentleman, and spoken in Punjabi in other places too.

But by and large, I agree with General Saheb about the different contexts where we use English, Hindustani or Punjabi—especially Punjabi with friends. I can't say that about family now. Our son speaks Punjabi. My wife can speak in Punjabi but she prefers not to. My daughter knows very little. It's not her fault. Mostly kids imbibe their language not only from their parents but from the other people around them, and we moved around a lot while she was growing up. We spent four years in Nepal also. I'm ashamed to say that I never learned any Nepali. My daughter could speak Nepali in those days.

So we all have different language preferences in the family.

Aggarwal: What language did you speak when you were in intelligence contexts?

Dulat: English.

Durrani: With the ordinary rank-and-file, the language is Urdu. But amongst the officers, if we were discussing certain things very formally, then it may be a mixture of Urdu and English. A briefing would usually be in English.

That is the language we speak in an office. It is the same with our civilian counterparts—they may speak English among themselves, but with their office staff they will speak in Urdu or even in Punjabi or Pashto.

Aggarwal: What language do you use in the Track II peace initiatives?

Dulat: English.

Aggarwal: English?

Dulat: You know, General Saheb and I might have spoken in Punjabi when chatting on the side. But the official language is always English when it comes to formal communication [*smiles*]. Nobody can pretend not to know English. You can pretend not to know Urdu or Hindi or Hindustani or Punjabi or whatever. Since we've all been brought up under the same system as kids, we revert to English.

Aggarwal: Durrani Saheb, has it also been your experience that all the Track II initiatives you've been a part of have been in English?

Durrani: Yes, we speak English as a rule. Occasionally, if everyone was comfortable in Urdu or Hindustani, as I recall in Colombo and Bangkok, someone might switch to Urdu, and it might even encourage responses in Urdu or Hindustani. When we are talking informally outside, it would depend on whom one is talking to. I'd chat with Dulat Saheb in Punjabi. With C.D. Sahay, I would speak in Urdu, though his Urdu is was much better than mine. There were a couple of times when an English or American think tank was sponsor—some of the people who attended had learnt our languages and were keen to talk to us in the vernacular.

So there is no rigid rule, but within the formal Track II talks, rarely would it ever be anything but English.

Aggarwal: In psychology, we believe that languages can access different types of emotions and thoughts. You might know this from your own experiences. For example, when we talk about the mother tongue, we often think in psychoanalytic theory that the language in which the mother has spoken to her child evokes a different type of emotion than a language that one learns later.

Do you think that peacemaking would be different if, for example, people spoke in Punjabi and were able to act in a less formal way?

Durrani: Hmm. Yes. Bilkul [Absolutely].

Aggarwal: I note that you both mentioned any formal conversation must take place in English. This seems to be a curious development. There was a news story recently about how India's Foreign Minister S. Jaishankar refused to speak anything but English to former Prime Minister Nawaz Sharif when Prime Minister Narendra Modi went to Pakistan in 2015.[38] Do you think that peacemaking would look different if people were speaking in Punjabi or in a language connected to a more relaxed social atmosphere?

Durrani: Yes. Because I've had such an experience, I can talk to you very frankly about it.

Aggarwal: Please do.

Durrani: If I'm on friendly terms with anyone, I'd rather speak our own common language, Urdu or Punjabi. If I want to keep the person at a distance, I'll use a different language than he might. If he spoke Urdu, I would reply in English; if he spoke Punjabi, I would use Urdu. That is one way to convey to him that we are not chums; not yet.

But as far as the other side is concerned, I have had an experience that Mr Dulat never did—I met my counterpart. Bajpai, I think, was the name.[39] Oh my God! The man kept talking in Urdu or Hindustani—over lunch or dinner, if not during the formal setting. And I was happy to do that because I felt he was sending me a message that we didn't need to stick to formal communication; we could also speak informally.

So, the language that one selects depends upon a couple of things. If it was a good environment, one would convey to the other side, 'I think we can speak a common language. I think you're quite comfortable with its terminology.' So on peacemaking, yes, I agree, this would be a contributing factor.

Aggarwal: That's fascinating. Dulat Saheb, what do you think?

Dulat: I agree with General Saheb almost entirely. It's not really a difference of opinion, but turning it around: when we speak our own common language, it relaxes the atmosphere. It makes things much more relaxed. I think he'll agree.

I'll give you an example, and it's a very interesting example for you as a psychiatrist. We used to have these Track IIs for

spooks. At the end of the day we used to have what could be
called a happy hour, where we would sit together and have
a drink. Not everyone on our side or the other side used to
drink, but even those who did not drink would join in the
conversation. This was a very friendly, relaxed exchange,
very different from what happened in the conference room.

The sponsors were intrigued. They said, 'These guys are
supposed to be adversaries. How do they get along so well?' So
they asked, 'Do you mind if we also join in?' They discovered
we were mostly speaking Punjabi together.

Aggarwal: In terms of psychology, what's so intriguing about
this example is that there's a direct relationship between the
language of English as the medium where all the cognitive or
ideational activity is occurring, but the language of Punjabi
is the medium where the emotional and social activity is
occurring. There's a clear division of space where one type of
psychological activity occurs in one language and a different
type of psychological activity occurs in a different language.
Then the question is whether the real peacemaking was actually
happening after hours, when everybody was getting along and
getting to know each other in Punjabi, and not in the boardroom
where people were speaking more formally in English.

Dulat: That's right.

Aggarwal: Another reason why it's interesting is if Track II is
an informal way of creating the environment for Track I talks at
the government-to-government level, then perhaps we should
consider creative ways Track II can improve social relations and
promote a relaxed emotional environment, leading to a better
atmosphere for Track I.

Dulat: I think, here, we may be getting too far ahead. I don't know how far Track II really helps Track I. It helps the sponsors to get people on both sides talking. But yes, we've got to understand each other better, get more comfortable with each other. We've got to make it easier.

Track I is much more formal, diplomats rarely speak in anything but English. What General Saheb has mentioned is interesting, that there was informality when he and his counterpart met. That's why I have pleaded for institutionalizing chief-to-chief meetings.

5. The Limits of Track II, People-to-People Diplomacy and the Role of Religious Identity

A.S. Dulat: I came away with a feeling that neither side got what they should have in Track II because—and I've always felt this—the Pakistanis are smarter than us. They took something back home whereas I don't think we ever took anything home. Or if we did, it was rarely. There may be some results in a one-to-one, but there was nothing institutional resulting, as it should have been.

Neil Krishan Aggarwal: What do you think Pakistan took away that India did not?

Dulat: The benefits of being institutionally a part of Track II. That's what I'm referring to. There is a method to this crazy madness. The sponsors will come and hear you, listen to you and maybe prepare a report for the people who are higher up. We should also be carrying something back. I don't think that happens. I can say that for ourselves. I have always had the sense that the Pakistanis are possibly smarter than us on this. Not that it matters. Ultimately, it comes to naught.

Aggarwal: Durrani Saheb, do you share that view?

Asad Durrani: I don't think Track II has had much influence on Track I. There is no interest in the corridors of power in New Delhi or Islamabad, people don't ask, 'You've been there— what did you talk about?' or 'Is there anything that you want to tell us?' Even if you volunteer to give a briefing, sometimes they might reluctantly agree to give you a few minutes out of courtesy.

The value of Track II is always overestimated. It helps participants to some extent, depending on what you're looking for. You may be looking for others' views, or for people or for friends. The sponsors who spend a couple of hundred thousand dollars probably cannot spend it any better. They get five or six informed opinions from India and Pakistan, which they would otherwise have to work harder to get.

But the state institutions were not very interested. Once or twice, a couple of colleagues agreed to convey a message. It probably had some little effect as well. So, in that sense, one could say it was useful. If you were in touch with your mother establishment, someone might ask: 'You have been talking to Mr Dulat about certain issues; could you give us a brief?'

Only rarely the wiser ones may admit that this was something they ought to have done, and might listen to advice to do the right thing. In recent times, it probably helped in managing the post-Pulwama complications. Some in Pakistan believed that the two countries were taking a page from *The Spy Chronicles* because there we have talked about mutually agreed responses—'choreographed', if you like. I heard them say: 'It seemed that what you said, was what happened, since both the sides were keen to defuse the issue. And it seems that your point about the Track II back channel has been accepted.' Now whether it was because of us or because it was what any two wise countries would do, I do not know.

But essentially, most of the time our efforts had no effect at all, even on most of the participants of the dialogue, because they go there with their own ideas and come back with the same. They have no intention of changing their mind. Privately, they might even do a bit of chest beating: 'I went there, and there were six Indians. I gave give them a piece of my mind! *Yaad karenge yeh saale* [Those idiots will remember this!]'

The benefits are only to those participants who are prepared to shed their prejudices and at least listen to the other side.

Aggarwal: This is fascinating for several reasons. A major reason is that we've been talking today about identity, and how identity is constituted of different dimensions, like ethnicity, language, region and religion. What I'm trying to understand from both of you is how differences in identity impact the India–Pakistan relationship.

Differences in language do not seem to be an issue as Indians and Pakistanis can communicate perfectly well in whatever language they choose, whether it is English, Urdu, Hindustani or Punjabi. Neither do differences in regionalism, with the two Punjabs or two Kashmirs on both sides of the border acting at various times as a bridge between both countries. Differences in ethnicity do not seem to be an issue—Durrani Saheb, you have talked about how you have Afghan, Kashmiri and Punjabi ancestry, and Dulat Saheb, you also have Punjabi ancestry. Many of the key principles on how differences in identity impose barriers to negotiating peace do not seem to be relevant here.

I don't know if that is because there are no differences at all or because I'm not eliciting important differences accurately. So now, let's turn to religion because we've gone through differences in ethnic, linguistic and regional identities systematically. If we understand what happens at the individual level with both of you, we can then start to think of the social level. You both have described your religious backgrounds in childhood and adolescence. Right now, as adults, what would you say the role of religion is in your daily life?

Durrani: Not much. One leads a normal life per society. One tries not to deliberately violate any religious norms. And whatever other activity one might want to pursue is one's private affair.

Aggarwal: Dulat Saheb, how does religion play out in your everyday life?

Dulat: I agree entirely with General Saheb. In my life or in our lives, it plays a minor role at home. It's not that I'm a disbeliever. I try now to go to the gurudwara every Sunday. I went this evening. I go just to tell the Almighty, 'Forgive me for the sins during the week. I promise to be better next week.' I'm not hugely committed to it.

Aggarwal: Would you say that your family members share your spiritual or religious traditions?

Durrani: My wife and son are more religious than I am. My wife offers her prayers much more regularly. And despite the fact that he has been in Germany for the past thirty years, my son, his wife and children avoid even the couple of liberties I take. I'll take a tipple but he does not. We all avoid pork for the simple reason that there are much better substitutes available. So yes, the family is religious.

Despite this, my wife and family is as relaxed as me on certain things. It's like, 'If some people like to have a drink, what's the big deal?' They are tolerant that way, but within the inner circle of the family I am probably the man who is most *gumrah* [lost]—off the track. Mr Dulat is probably responsible for that.

[*All three laugh.*]

Dulat: Yes sir! I take full responsibility!
[*All three laugh.*]

Dulat: We are an areligious lot, you know. My wife and I are quite similar. The other thing in life one notices, irrespective of your religion, you tend to remember God more when you're in trouble. Khushwant Singh wrote about this extensively. He claimed he was an atheist.

My daughter went through certain times that took her to the gurudwara. It surprised me a little. I told her, when you go, take me along. Our son goes when there is an occasion.

So we're not a very religious family. We did not learn religion at home, and we have not tried to imbibe it in the kids either.

Aggarwal: Durrani Saheb, what role does religion play in your family now? Earlier, you mentioned that as long as somebody was marrying within Islam, it didn't matter much what their particular sect might have been. Would you say that that religion plays a strong role in terms of certain kinds of family celebrations or choices in marriage even now?

Durrani: Yes. The priority is marrying within the religion. One is happy when one's children or grandchildren abide by the minimum norms. Even those of my family who have lived in the United States for a long time would rather look for an Afghan or Egyptian to marry their son or daughter because they practise the same religion. But at the same time, if a child does marry outside, we would not excommunicate the 'culprit'.

I also said on a couple of occasions that since Osman [Durrani's son] lives outside the country, even if he married a good non-Muslim, it should be all right. My wife was a little reluctant. If he had done that, I think we would have gone with it. Religion alone was not going to shock us. But yes, we prefer keeping within the religion.

Some people in our own society are even more rejectionist. They will not go to the next main sect like Shia or Sunni. Sometimes, they will not even get out of their clan mentality. Some Rajputs, for example, would only accept a Rajput boy or a girl within the family fold. Recently, some of our girls have married outside the religion, something unimaginable fifty years ago.

Aggarwal: Do you engage in other kinds of religious activities outside the home? Dulat Saheb, do you engage in activities apart from going to the gurudwara?

Dulat: No, no. I don't engage in religious activity at all. This is just to keep peace of mind. It becomes a thing you do each week. Go to the gurudwara, thank the Lord for His mercy and seek forgiveness for whatever you do wrong.

But like General Saheb mentioned about the children, I think the new generation is quite different. My wife and I married of our own choice but our backgrounds were similar. But the children have not married people with similar backgrounds. They married whomever they wanted to marry and they did it on their own. That's about it.

Aggarwal: Durrani Saheb?

Durrani: It's hardly different. Preferably, if you have married outside the religion, let one of the partners convert. No one in our family ever imagined his daughter marrying into a Jewish family. It was difficult when it happened.

It was in the UK. My brother-in-law was nominally Muslim, and his wife nominally Christian. The children have Muslim names, but a daughter decided to marry a Jew, which meant becoming Jewish. The two 'liberal' parents had to accept it but were very upset. That's why I say that if you decide to marry outside your religion, then agree at the outset what the religion at home will be, at least for the children.

Aggarwal: Do you see religion as a major irritant in ties between Indians and Pakistanis now?

Durrani: I don't think the problem is religion. There would be very few people, I think, even on the Indian side, who would take up an issue on the basis of difference in religion. Now, Hindutva must have changed a couple of things. But even in the days when General Zia[40] promoted Islamic ideology, the problems between us were not because Indians were Hindus or Sikhs. No—it was Kashmir or other unfinished business. Religious otherness was accepted.

We cannot all belong to the same religion. Sometimes the relationship between Muslim and non-Muslim countries is much better than between two Muslim countries. The role of religion in relations between nations gets overplayed. Here people feel that if Muslims were persecuted in India or any other country, bilateral relations would be impacted only to the extent the larger relationship permitted. Chinese treatment of its Muslim community in Xinjiang (the Uyghurs) has had no significant effect on Sino–Pak equation.

Aggarwal: Dulat Saheb, do you agree that religion is not a major irritant between India and Pakistan now?

Dulat: I think it is becoming an irritant. One has to admit that we are doing it more than the Pakistanis. There's also a growing sense of superiority on our side, of 'What is Pakistan? It's a small country. We are superior in every way. What do we have to gain from Pakistan? What is it that Pakistan can give us?'

That is the crux of the problem today. Everything is looked at in terms of what you can get. That's not how diplomacy pushes forward.

In any case, I firmly believe that India and Pakistan now need to move forward. Just diplomacy will not do; action must come from the top if we are to go forward. It's not impossible. It requires the will and, even more, imagination. You've got to think that way; that we're neighbours. Vajpayee once famously said, 'You can choose friends, but you can't choose your neighbours.' And, like it or not, we feel comfortable with Pakistan.

Neil, you know how you sent us that letter written by Einstein to Freud? Freud took two months to reply. Then he said [*laughs*] that war is in human nature. I think the world has changed. Both sides realize that war is not a real option. I think we're agreed on that. So common sense then says, why don't we move forward? The question is *how*. Therein lies the rub.

Even if one agrees with Freud about the inevitability of war—and India and Pakistan have had more than a taste of it—we need to find meaning in life after war.

Aggarwal: Let's dive into the points you just made. I'm going to ask you both about religion in your contemporary societies. The India-born Pakistani poet Fahmeeda Riaz wrote a poem in Urdu when the Babri Masjid was destroyed in 1992. Some of the lines go, *Kaun hai Hindu, kaun nahin hai, Tum bhi karoge fatwe jari* [Who is Hindu, who is not? You'll also issue religious edicts], and *Tum bilkul hum jaise nikle, Hum do qaum nahin the, bhai!* [You turned out just like us. We weren't two nations, brother!]

There is a growing majoritarianism in both countries where people of the numerically dominant religion are challenging the rights of religious minorities. There are conversations about the rise of Hindutva in India, such as an increase in cow-related lynchings, hijab bans and the Ram Mandir issue. Do you see this as related to Indian identity? If so, how?

Durrani: It is more about Hindutva. One can look at this two ways. If it is about the comfort level of the minorities in India—the Sikhs, the Muslims, the Christians—then one has every reason to be unhappy with Hindutva.

If it is about the bilateral relationship, once upon a time I believed that hardline governments can take harder, pro-peace decisions. Then I found out that ideological hardliners would not. In fact, they would take the opposite view.

There is also a third view, which for me is worth exploring when it comes to realpolitik. The world does not run on wishes and desires; it runs on actions taken by society. Therefore, I sometimes say this [Hindutva] may be the best thing that has happened to us. The [Indian National] Congress [party] was getting away with posturing as secularists. They were not. There were many fields where Muslims were disadvantaged. But everyone said, 'What a great country! There is so much diversity and secularism.' Now that façade has been blown to shreds dropped. One takes some consolation from that.

But even more important, another ten to twenty years of Hindutva will ultimately sink India. So one can say that in a couple of decades, we have good news for Pakistan or for the minorities in India.

These are the various ways that you can look realistically at the situation. Dulat Saheb knows that I do not wish this to happen. It has happened often enough; you don't want to add more negativity to an already bad situation. But if you can give an honest assessment how the present situation might lead to certain consequences, that can be useful.

I stumbled upon it about thirty years ago. I said, 'These Congress people are having a good time. They have the best of both worlds. They're doing whatever they want in Kashmir. They can also deprive other people of their seats.' All surveys continued to say that the Muslims were badly treated, but the Congress Party remained smug and happy. Then the BJP came to power, and some perceptions of power were corrected. This is the way one would have to look at the situation, even as peacemakers.

Aggarwal: Dulat Saheb, there are conversations about the rise of Hindutva in India. Do you see this related to Indian identity now?

Dulat: Yes, to some extent it is getting related to Indian identity. I don't agree with everything General Saheb said but it is not necessary for me to contest these things. But I do agree that there is still hope. It's not just the optimist in me. I think that this is the case if one looks at it realistically. It requires, possibly, a hardliner to do the job. Without commenting any more on what he indicated regarding Hindutva, I would just say that Modi could possibly do what Dr Manmohan Singh could not do.

Durrani: Interesting.

Aggarwal [*laughing*]: How do you find it interesting?

Durrani [*laughing*]: Because I am not sure Manmohan Singh had any evil designs for the region. He could not do the good things he wanted to do. If Modi has done the evil things he wanted to do, and if he is going to get away with it, then I would not only be sorry, but I would say, 'It serves India right.'

Aggarwal: There are also conversations about the rise of Islamism in Pakistan. One hears about temple destructions, kidnapped females and forced conversions. Do you see this as related to Pakistani identity? If so, how?

Durrani: True, true. Yes, it's on the rise. We used to say it's just small numbers but it's always been true, and it continues to be so. I have no inhibitions saying that both on the domestic front, in terms of ethnicities or the sectarian relationship, or in terms of our foreign policy thinking, it is getting worse.

Aggarwal: Dulat Saheb, do you share that assessment as well?

Dulat: If General Saheb says it, then who am I to disagree on that front?

[*All three laugh.*]

Dulat: The important thing to note is the point that General Saheb is making without saying it. The minorities in Pakistan are minuscule compared to the minorities in India. Therefore, it's a bigger issue here, always in our consciousness. Where it will go, only time will tell.

Durrani: The consolation is that the rest of the world is no better. People are not getting more tolerant anywhere.

Dulat: Absolutely, but that's hardly any consolation.

Aggarwal: I want to press you on an idea that we have discussed before but in a different context. I want to bring this up again because I now know you both pretty well. There are two common tropes that one tends to hear—that Indians and Pakistanis are the same or that they have nothing in common. If we were all the same, then there wouldn't be a need for peace talks, there wouldn't have been wars and there wouldn't be a border that separates two countries. And if we were so different, then we wouldn't be able to speak on the phone in Punjabi, laugh and joke around with such common reference points such as language, literature and ways of seeing the world. Therefore, there are things that clearly connect us, and it's more than simply having post-colonial experiences.

I want to ask you about this, keeping in mind that you went from actively plotting against each other when you were the heads of your foreign intelligence agencies to now occupying your roles as peacemakers. In your estimations, what makes Indians and Pakistanis similar?

Durrani: Hmm … *Haan ji, Dulat Saheb. Farmaye* [Yes sir, Mr Dulat. Please speak].

Dulat: There is no doubt about it. There are huge similarities, particularly when it comes to Punjab. This has been generally acknowledged on both sides. But India is a much larger country than just the north. The rest doesn't worry so much about Pakistan. Surprising as it might sound, you may find more sympathy for Pakistan in south, west or east India than in the north. It's a big contradiction.

I don't think there is anything definitive. As you know, Neil—since you live abroad and detached from this whole thing—Indians and Pakistanis outside the subcontinent genuinely get along exceptionally well. We share the same language and background.

General Saheb and I have talked about the nostalgia for Lahore. General Saheb said that this gets exaggerated. Maybe, but the point is that people who experienced Lahore still think that it was the most cosmopolitan city in north India at that time.

Why did all our fathers go to Government College, Lahore? There were other colleges also. If you came out of Government College, Lahore, it meant that you belonged to the elite. It was like St. Stephen's College is today, here.

Aggarwal: Durrani Saheb, in your estimation, what makes Indians and Pakistanis similar?

Durrani: The first point has already been mentioned by Mr Dulat. Indians and Pakistanis like to meet and talk about various subjects. Sometimes they have much in common; sometimes they have differences; but they want to talk so they can empathize, understand each other. That is one.

The other is that both see their rivalry in sports as expressing the political divide.

And thirdly, Pakistanis are terribly infatuated with Bollywood, as are the Afghans. On the Indian side, I hear people are very fond of watching our TV dramas. I must ask them why they do that. Sometimes I think that people who watch television at all should get their heads examined. But there it is—we love watching each other's entertainment.

These are the things that I find compatible.

Aggarwal: Now I'm going to ask you to reflect on the differences in a very genuine way. What makes Indians and Pakistanis different in ways that you think are authentic, that cannot be easily swept under the carpet?

Durrani: The interpretation of history is one thing. We tend to not only interpret but study history in different contexts. The curriculum, sometimes even the scholarship. There are very few people who may agree on a version of history that is shared. That is one difference.

The other difference is not easy for me to concede. The Indians' attitudes towards work and seeking knowledge is much more serious than ours.

Aggarwal: Dulat Saheb, what makes Indians and Pakistanis different in your estimation?

Dulat: Unfortunately, one has to admit it is religion. I have delved deeply into Kashmir, though I don't claim that I am an expert. But even there, where Hindus and Muslims lived together for generations, the whole matter is religious. If we deny it, we are only fooling ourselves. That's where it all started. Unfortunately, we've not been able to resolve that.

It's interesting how General Saheb and I agree on most things. But I was a bit surprised when we were talking about Hindutva that he mentioned Netaji and Bhagat Singh. I'm not saying that they were not heroes; they certainly were. But it came after I mentioned the Mahatma's assassination. There are people in our country as well who say that the Mahatma was a disaster. I remember a history professor who said many years ago, '*Shubh nahin tha*' [He wasn't good].

But the world at large now accepts and admires him. The Mahatma was an exceptional human being. Whether, in the end, he did right or wrong—history is still in the process of being written.

Aggarwal: Perhaps this example reflects what Durrani Saheb said about differences in the interpretation of history impacting the national identities of both countries.

Dulat: Yes, yes.

Aggarwal: I also want to point out an inconsistency. I asked you both earlier whether you see religion as an irritant in the India–Pakistan relationship. You both said no, which is very interesting, because you both also acknowledged that Kashmir is a site of contest where the population is mostly Muslim. In that respect, both of you are willing to agree that religion is an irritant. How do we reconcile those two very dissimilar understandings?

Dulat: I am not obsessed with religion. You'd be surprised how many Muslim friends I have, some in Pakistan, including General Saheb. It makes little difference to me whether someone is Muslim or Hindu or Sikh or Christian—we're all the same. But let's face it—the Musalman in India is now having a difficult time.

Durrani: I think one can make a major difference in policy depending on how one looks at a religion and its followers. For example, I suppose there are nearly as many Muslims in India as in Pakistan, so there is no way that we can make Islam the basis of conflict.

In Kashmir, people may be mostly Muslims, but religion is not the only issue. Religious affinity does make a difference, but it's not everything—Bangladesh is Muslim majority too. But since Kashmir is next door, many Pakistanis have a historical connection with it. Also, Kashmir has geopolitical importance for us—water, the borders and so on. All this together makes it an issue. We also have a sense of grievance that we thought Kashmir would come to us. It was promised, the plebiscite was not done and so forth. All this accumulates and creates an impression that it's only about Islam or Muslims, whereas it is about more than that.

Regarding the Kashmiri Pandits, I have never found anyone in Pakistan who says that they should not go back. All people who have been exiled and want to go back—whether it is Kashmiris, Palestinians or even our own people—should have the right to return wherever they once belonged. That is the principle. In the case of Kashmir, the population being Muslim is a small part; the other affiliations are more important.

Dulat: I'd like to add to what General Saheb said. He said very rightly that Pakistan has always felt wiggled out of Kashmir. They feel that it rightfully belonged to them, and they were tricked out of it. When you add Bangladesh and '71 to that, then the grievance only grows.

I'm not referring to General Saheb, but I know of some generals who haven't gotten over '71. General Saheb put it very nicely that it was the failure of their own army or generals or establishment. But there are generals in Pakistan who still feel a need for revenge. They haven't forgotten '71.

Aggarwal: What are the misconceptions you might have had about the other side before encountering them?

Durrani: I don't know if one should call it a misconception. The only one is when you start believing that all Indians are cast in the same mould, and it's the same with all Pakistanis. The views on India vary in different regions of Pakistan, as also of north and south India. It's the same the other way round.

Therefore, there was no such misconception that everyone on the other side was the same and then you meet and find out that they are different. I think people had a fairly good idea as to who on the other side you would work better with, who would sympathize with you, who would support you more than some of your own people do. Anyone with reasonable knowledge would know enough about the other side—there is history, literature, movies, meetings with counterparts in other countries. You were not likely to be surprised when you met an Indian.

When I was Ambassador of Pakistan in Germany, we preferred a Sikh restaurant owner for catering events as he provided good service and charged reasonably. I have narrated in *Pakistan Adrift* how well I was treated at the Indian stall at the Frankfurt Book Fair when they learned who I was.[41]

So no—no surprises at all. You can meet Dulats and you may meet Dovals. Both the Ds I am familiar with. One can surprise you a little more, and the other can disappoint you a little.

Aggarwal: Dulat Saheb, did you have any misconceptions about the other side before encountering them?

Dulat: Not in the least. When I first went in 2010, I was looking forward to it. I didn't have any misconceptions at all. I was looking forward to making friends.

One thing I missed in the Track II conference was that other than the general conducting it, there was nobody from the ISI. I said, 'You've brought me here to Lahore. At least give me an opportunity to meet somebody from the ISI.' He said, 'They don't live in Lahore. You will have to go to Islamabad or 'Pindi, and we can arrange that for you if you want. It will take the whole day.' I said, 'I don't have a visa for so long. My visa expires in a day or a day and a half.'

What comes as a hugely pleasant surprise when you go to Pakistan is the hospitality. We can't match it. It's quite incredible. M.J. Akbar[42] wrote about it when he went for that cricket series—I think it was in 2005. He came back and wrote a piece that said the same thing.

I remember in 2010, during my first visit to Lahore, we expressed a desire for red maltas [oranges], which had become a rarity in our side of Punjab. Lo and behold, before we left, a kind lady gave us a whole bori [sack] of red maltas.

This is how it works. There are so many commonalities. I think misconceptions lie elsewhere. As you said, Partition is one of them.

Aggarwal: Since we've been exploring the possibility of peacemaking and have talked about the differences and similarities between Indians and Pakistanis, what are those aspects of the other side's identity where you feel that common ground can be built? For a foundation to start thinking about joint problem-solving?

Durrani: History is one, obviously. One can build upon our common past. As I said, there is a history of once having been together. There are all sorts of problems within any country, and there were religious conflicts within united India, but it worked out well more often than not. That is just one.

But on the substantial side, there is nothing new. The establishments will not change their mindsets unless they are forced to. At times by circumstances, but most likely when the peace constituency becomes large enough to effectively assert 'Enough is enough.' They don't have to protest on the streets all the time—sustained efforts can make a good number of decision-makers come around. They need to be convinced that they can only be elected if they are supported by the peace lobbies.

Our peace lobbies are not very strong but they can be built up. Perhaps a few people who have a good standing with the public could lead this peace assault.

Aggarwal: Dulat Saheb?

Dulat: I don't think we're going to find the common foundation in a hurry. The situation is only getting worse.

But despite this, we require that foundation of commonality. We may disagree. We may curse and abuse each other. But if peace is ultimately what counts, then some madcap somewhere might decide, 'Okay. I will do it.' I've been saying the same thing over and over with different words, but it's going to come down to personalities. It's not so much issues now, but personalities.

When I think back to Vajpayee's bus to Lahore, those were different times. There was different thinking. Vajpayee had a personal chemistry with Nawaz Sharif. Then it continued with Musharraf. It went much further with Dr Manmohan Singh.

If one looks at it from the Pakistani side fair and square— every Pakistani leader, every Pakistani Prime Minister has talked of peace with India. Whether it's been Nawaz or Imran or now Shahbaz [Sharif], they've talked about peace, whether in Pakistan or when they visited India. We just haven't been able to build that common foundation.

Nawaz Sharif even came here for Modi's swearing-in ceremony in 2014. I thought that was a big moment. Then, for whatever reason, Modi also went to Raiwind in 2015. I don't think these things are meaningless. Something drives you somewhere. Something takes you somewhere.

When Imran was around, I was counting on him. I thought the only way forward was for Imran to come to Delhi. I don't know if Shahbaz wants to come to Delhi or how it would even happen. To rephrase General Saheb, it will happen either when you are pushed to make it happen or something within you says, 'If this is what everyone wants, I will show you how it can be done.'

Aggarwal: When you say that peacemaking is as much about personalities as it is about issues, it is exactly the reason why psychology can be helpful. Psychology and Track II can't solve territorial disputes, water sharing or other conflicts over material resources but it does provide frameworks to understand the personalities of those involved with peacemaking. Let's talk about how your experiences developing large-group identities could be seen as case studies in the personality of peacemakers.

First, the similarities. Dulat Saheb's mother and Durrani Saheb's mother had formative life experiences in the Punjab that now lies across the border after 1947. You both have discussed close family members spending significant amounts of time in territories that now lie in the other country. There is a living familial history of what the other side was like—for Dulat Saheb, it was his mother's Muslim friends. For Durrani Saheb, it was his father's Hindu and Muslim colleagues in government service or the Hindu bania from whose shop he drank water. I wonder whether this personal history leads you both to appreciate your commonalities rather than heighten your differences. You both described close encounters with the violence of Partition—Durrani Saheb recalled riots in Delhi and Dulat Saheb's mother's chacha was killed in Lahore.

It is an open question whether this affects peacemaking in a positive or a negative direction. For instance, what would peacemaking look like between a Pakistani from FATA [Federally Administered Tribal Areas] or Baluchistan and an Indian from Mizoram or Mangalore, with no familial connections to the other side? Would there be less of an emotional axe to grind, and would that absence of commonality also result in an absence of a shared language through which to view the world? Moreover, what would peacemaking look like among a younger generation of government officers who recall Partition solely as a trauma and vilify the other side?

A second similarity is the strong sense of Punjabi identity. For Dulat Saheb, this regional identity of Punjab, Punjabi and Punjabiyat assumes importance over religion, nationalism or other large-group identity markers. Even Durrani Saheb described his fondness for Punjabi, perhaps because he is less able to connect with his Pashtun background which now lies within Afghanistan or his Kashmiri background which now lies within India. Dulat Saheb still travels frequently throughout Indian Punjab, and Durrani Saheb lives in Pakistani Punjab. Your preference for Punjabi during Track II initiatives proves how strong this linguistic and regional identity is for both of you.

A third similarity is that you both describe yourselves as relatively relaxed in religious matters. You both adopt a religiously inclusive attitude towards marriage and describe yourselves as not deeply interested in issues of theology. At the same time, you both adhere to social norms, with Durrani Saheb saying that he performs the minimum practice required in society and Dulat Saheb going to the gurudwara every Sunday. So, while religion is not unimportant, it occupies a social dimension in your lives rather than guiding either of you personally in matters of suffering and salvation. You both agree about the threat of rising religious majoritarianism in both countries. Intriguingly, although you both initially equivocated, you both concluded that the crux of the Kashmir issue lies in the religious demography of the territory.

Nonetheless, there are important differences. Durrani Saheb mentioned the interpretation of history as a foundational disagreement between Indians and Pakistanis, and this seems to be manifested in your personal lives. His family viewed Partition as gaining a country whereas Dulat Saheb's family viewed Partition as a loss. Perhaps one confidence-building measure between both countries could be to agree to openly discuss historical events and adopt a common educational curriculum in order to shift attitudes about the other side, if we are truly serious about building peace lobbies.

The sources of grievance for both countries are also different. Durrani Saheb mentioned the 1971 war and Pakistan's experiences in the Global War on Terror, whereas Dulat Saheb recalled non-state militant actors in Kashmir and Punjab as worsening the India–Pakistan relationship. In our sessions ahead, we will continue to explore how your personal lives are representative of other elite decision-makers in your positions, and how to find ways to build that common foundation for peace. What is plain is that you both view your bureaucratic establishments as entrenching differences rather than overcoming them, so our challenge now is to find ideas that could promote peacemaking.

4

Making Peace Can Be as Hard as War: Why Some Initiatives Succeed and Others Fail

In the last chapter, both spymasters were careful to distinguish between their perceptions of people and governments. A.S. Dulat eulogized Pakistani hospitality but denounced the Government of Pakistan for promoting militancy in Kashmir and Punjab. Asad Durrani affirmed shared historical, linguistic and literary links with Indians but criticized Indian policies in Jammu and Kashmir. If we assume that their experiences are representative of other policymakers in senior positions, then this recognition that people are not the same as their governments may explain why many Indians and Pakistanis get along though their governments do not.

In fact, psychology has developed approaches to understand how elite foreign-policy decision-makers perceive leaders from other countries. Political scientists have imported the concept of the *schema* from psychology, which can be defined as 'a preexisting assumption about the way the world is organized'.[1] International relations experts study how leaders develop worldviews about each other, such as how people process information, draw inferences and create expectations about behaviour.[2] Decoding how others think helps to predict policy choices and suggests reasons for why people pursue some actions and not others.[3] Uncovering these perceptions can be critical; as foreign policy scholars write, 'Perceptions of reality, whether accurate or not, become "reality" in a decision maker's mind, and he or she has no other basis upon which to act; thus these perceptions or images necessarily influence policy.'[4]

Developing assessments of national security based on incomplete information and making predictions about human behaviour is the tradecraft of spy agencies. Asad Durrani has spoken repeatedly of his training in crafting assessments. The nucleus of the ISI is Joint Intelligence X, which prepares intelligence estimates and threat assessments for other ISI branches.[5] Therefore, the importance of analysing information is built into the ISI's very structure. The situation is comparable in India. While RAW spy chiefs have had varying levels of direct access to the Prime Minister throughout history, collecting, analysing and assessing information remains the organization's most important function.[6] Around the world, spy agencies devote huge resources to cultivate informants so as to increase the likelihood that their assessments about political events are valid.

Schemas can be divided into three dimensions that guide foreign policies: (1) the perceived capability of the other country, (2) the perceived threats and opportunities that the other country represents and (3) the perceived national culture of the other actor.[7] Coming up with assessments based on these three dimensions can mean the difference between countries competing and cooperating. The complex psychology of national security essentially boils down to answering a few questions: 'Do the other actor's intentions threaten to reduce my country's current achievement of valued objectives or does the other actor present an opportunity for me to advance and expand my country's interests? If it does represent an opportunity for gain, it can do so in two ways: the other actor can represent a direct opportunity that the observer's country can exploit in a zero-sum sense, or the other actor can represent an opportunity for allied cooperation that benefits both parties in absolute terms.'[8]

In this chapter, Dulat and Durrani offer us unrestricted access into their perceptions about the capabilities, threats, opportunities and cultures of leadership in the foreign policy establishments of India and Pakistan. Neil Krishan Aggarwal starts with open-ended questions so that the men settle into the topic. All three discuss examples of policies where India and Pakistan try to exploit the other country in a zero-sum sense, and where they find opportunities for cooperation to benefit both parties. The discussions expose why making peace can be as hard as making war.

———

1. General Assessments of Each Other's Foreign Policy Establishments

Neil Krishan Aggarwal: In our last series of discussions, we really got a sense of your personal identities and your views about people in the enemy country. What became clear to me was that you both were extremely careful to differentiate your views about the people on the other side, which were warm and cordial, from your views about its government establishment. How representative are your views of the agencies which you led and have worked in? If we understand your establishment's prevailing views about the other side's establishment, we might be able to identify certain barriers to peacemaking. Therefore, the first set of questions is very broad: What are your feelings towards the other country's establishment? And how do you think your country's foreign policy establishment views the other country's establishment?

Asad Durrani: Whenever we give our views, they are our own assessment. It might not be that of the establishment. Others in comparable or compatible positions hold different views, not necessarily in line with the collective wisdom of the establishment. My experience was that regardless of what the establishment staff put together, I made an intelligence assessment independently. If you are the boss, it's your job. Then, you also have to take people along with your view or defend it and argue. That is one.

Regarding views about the other establishment, there is a big difference between how we view the other country and how we view its policies. For example, there is no way that I can have negative views, negative sentiments or negative opinions about a country like India. It is so big. There is a historic connection. I have many friends there. True, we carry historical baggage, but it is the establishment's policy that determines attitudes to it.

Just to give another example: people in Pakistan generally don't hate America as a country; but in terms of attitudes to its policies, I think Pakistan is the second-most hostile country. It may be second, third or fourth—that was a long time ago when somebody was grading the anti-American countries.[9] Surprisingly, Turkey was first and Pakistan was second.

Therefore, my feelings are good towards India. I have friends there. I know that the society is diverse. People are at least as good if not better than our people. But when it comes to policies, of course I have differences. Sometimes they are less; sometimes more, bordering on hostility.

Aggarwal: Dulat Saheb?

A.S. Dulat: Like General Saheb said, I don't see any reason for hostility between India and Pakistan. Sure, from time to time we consider ourselves adversaries. I'll tell you what I think about the other side, about the establishment and about what is happening there, though General Saheb would know much better.

As I've said often, I used to be a fan of Imran Khan and his cricket. I think Pakistan is more unsettled with his departure. If my gut feeling is right, I think Pakistan will have to have elections in the next six months. Otherwise, there will be problems on the street. I think Imran still has a following on the street.

I think our establishment is happier with the new establishment. They were not so happy with Imran for whatever reason; America may be one of them. Our relationship with the United States has improved, going back to Vajpayee's time. It's been improving whereas Pakistan's relationship is not great, although I can never visualize the Pentagon being too far from the military establishment in Pakistan.

Interestingly when General Bajwa, the Chief of Army Staff in Pakistan,[10] had a security conference, he went out of his way to tell the Americans, 'We've always been close. We've always had close ties.'[11] I don't think that statement from the Army Chief went down well with everybody in Pakistan; I've noticed criticism of it, including from some retired army generals. So we're looking at an uncertain Pakistan presently—not a happy situation, either for them or for us.

Durrani: If one goes by statements, then one is on very slippery ground. People make political statements, whether it is the Prime Minister or the Army Chief. If at a given time, they thought anti-American statements were good for their politics, they would even add a bit of bite from their side. Considering the overall situation, I think, Bajwa's statement was not called for. It should not have been made, and it did not go down well at home except among the Western diplomats. But that's what it is.

The politicians and the decision-makers do not always reflect the people's collective sentiment.

Aggarwal: What do you think are the Indian foreign policy establishment's goals and intentions towards Pakistan currently? And what do you think are the Pakistani foreign policy establishment's goals and intentions towards India currently?

Durrani: Time and again, the Indians have given us the message, 'We're going places. We're all right. Not only are we bigger, but our economy is doing much better. We also have a few cards, and we can screw you.' This is the message that we've mostly gotten.

In my period, it was very clear that the message from across was: 'As far as your relationship with India is concerned, we don't think that the equation will improve in favour of Pakistan. So we do not have to try and bail you out if you are in trouble.'

When it comes to the establishment's policies, let me be quite clear: they do not make them out of the goodness of their hearts. They look at the existing policies, history, the environment, and neither side wishes the other success. They want them brought down low and weakened, so that the adversary can't throw its weight about. This is how a country's realpolitik works.

Put simply, when the Indians are in trouble—let's say, because of the relationship with China or because they think that America is again interested in Kashmir—Pakistanis have reason to be a bit pleased.

Similarly, my assessment is that Indians prefer that Pakistan survives—they don't want disintegration of the country, because that has implications—but at the same time they don't want Pakistan to become viable or even strong, where it could take a stand; where it could play games in Kashmir or Punjab that do not suit Indian policies.

Aggarwal: Dulat Saheb?

Dulat: A lot has changed over the last twenty years or so. It's been more than twenty years since I left the agency and eighteen years since I left the government. When Vajpayee took the bus to Lahore, there was a different kind of thinking. He wrote in the visitor's book, 'A strong, stable and prosperous Pakistan is in India's interest.'

Today, I agree with General Saheb that I don't think there is any such thinking here. On the contrary, the thinking is, 'What can Pakistan give us? Put it on the slate. Let's have a look.'

It was quite clear in Imran's time who the leader was. Today, Pakistan is a puzzle. I think we are quite happy with that puzzle.

I was looking to this young Bilawal [Bhutto Zardari] because he is supposedly a bright boy.[12] He said something recently which very clearly showed Pakistan's preference about its own security. All he talked about was China and the strong bond between Pakistan and China. That's well known. He is a bright kid. He is playing it very carefully and cautiously. He didn't want to mention India at all, and I don't expect him to say too much about India in the days to come.

As far as the Prime Minister goes, I don't know if he is in Pakistan or in London or anywhere else. I was told that his Cabinet was in London for five or six days. So there's something not right in Pakistan.

Durrani: I agree that plenty on our side is not in good shape. Many things are not right. But we're talking about establishments and their policies. I don't think that one should take very seriously anything that a foreign minister or a Prime Minister may say at present. The statements are not for the long term. There are plenty of things at home to be sorted out. Assessments of a country's policy during a transition period can be misleading.

Aggarwal: Dulat Saheb, General Saheb has already given us his answer about what he thought the Pakistani foreign establishment's goals and intentions towards India are. What do you think?

Durrani: Generally, the aim of any establishment is to make sure it has enough standing so it figures in the calculations of others.

Considering our relationship, you do not wish the other country to do well enough to gain a decisive advantage over your own side.

Aggarwal: Dulat Saheb, would you agree?

Dulat: General Saheb makes a good point. It's too early in the day for this new government in Pakistan, so we have to wait and watch. My observations may be premature, but it's because the situation there looks murky. It may be because I am sitting far away in a drawing room in Delhi, making my observations. We have to wait and watch.

I'll reiterate that it doesn't look like a very cohesive or clear-sighted government. It will take some time.

Aggarwal: We've talked about what the current policy establishment is thinking. Now, let's move towards more aspirational thinking. What do you think the Indian foreign policy establishment's goals and intentions towards Pakistan should be? Not what they are, but what they should be?

Durrani: Hmm.
　　[*Both men are silent for ten seconds. Dulat starts to laugh.*]

Durrani: Take the lead, Dulat Saheb.

Dulat [*laughing*]: Okay, Sir.
　　[*All three laugh.*]

Dulat: It's an unfair question. Like I said at the outset, I think people on our side are happier with this change. Imran in his last few months was not too popular here. Obviously, he was not the most popular person in Pakistan either. I think everything he did in the last three or four months went wrong for him.

Practically speaking, we prefer this situation. A muddled Pakistan is to our advantage. This is the kind of government we like. We were comfortable with Nawaz Sharif, and this is the other Sharif [a reference to then Prime Minister Shahbaz Sharif]. This being the case, we should take advantage of the time we have with this current government for as long as it lasts.

I think from our point of view this is a good opportunity. We should seize it and try to move forward.

Aggarwal: Durrani Saheb, you can't get away so easily. What do you think the Indian foreign policy establishment's goals and intentions towards Pakistan should be?

Durrani: I don't think I can say what it should be but I know what it is. It was conveyed to us very clearly back in 2004. The environment was very good. Vajpayee was in power. A lot had happened, the whole Kargil thing was behind us and there was a feel-good sentiment all round. That is how we ended up in Delhi under the Pugwash umbrella.[13] On the evening we were hosted by the foreign secretary, his minions made it very clear to us that they were unhappy with what Vajpayee was doing. They said, 'Right now, it may seem we have reconciled to a working relationship with you. But watch out! If there are any incidents like in the past, the policy will be reviewed.'

On another occasion, when a select group of former ambassadors or high commissioners to India were invited by

Sati Lambah,[14] six or seven of them were read the Riot Act by none other than [National Security Advisor Ajit] Doval.[15] He said, 'Even though you're our guests, let me tell you frankly. We would like to have good bilateral relations, but I don't think it's going to be possible.' And he walked away without shaking hands.

These are the messages that have come from India time and again. And I do not blame anyone. Just the way India often perceives the Pakistan Army, we too often talk about South Block and how it views Pakistan. It has no soft corner for peace with Pakistan. They think that if they keep playing tough, Pakistan will have to come round one day.

Aggarwal: On that note, what do you think the Pakistani foreign policy establishment's goals and intentions towards India should be?

Durrani: Under the circumstances, it would be very stupid and foolish for the Pakistani establishment to give the message that it was dying for peace.

Talks take place all the time through back and diplomatic channels—and possibly also by the secret agencies.

But whenever the message from here was 'We have no choice but to talk,' it was sheer nonsense. Indians bloody well know that they have a choice. After all, if we have gone so far without the types of talks Pakistanis suggest, it means we can survive without talking—even without peaceful relations. In fact, that option is more likely than empty talks.

The only good message we can give is, 'We are ready whenever you are. We can talk about anything you like; we can talk about cricket if you don't want to talk about Kashmir, which will take care of itself.'

That is the message that the establishment should be conveying, openly and very clearly, instead of beating about the bush. Though diplomats tend to mince their words, at times the message should be unambiguous.

Aggarwal: Dulat Saheb, what do you think the Pakistani foreign policy establishment's goals and intentions towards India should be?

Dulat: I don't blame the Pakistani establishment for this. Because whoever was in charge—Nawaz Sharif or Imran or Shahbaz Sharif—and I'm waiting for young Bilawal as well—at some point or other the Pakistani leadership has indicated that it would like a good relationship with India.

General Saheb talked about the incident with the ambassadors in 2014 when Doval became NSA. That would not have happened in Dr Manmohan Singh's time. I can't fault Pakistan on the signals it is sending out. The problem is the signals from our side, which I've repeated many times: 'What can Pakistan give us?'

Pakistan generally wants to talk about Kashmir. The view here is that Kashmir is done and dusted; there is nothing to settle in Kashmir. Our main grouse used to be that we wanted to discuss terrorism. Even on that, now the thinking seems to be, 'Okay, if it's still there, we'll deal with it. We don't need to ask Pakistan for help.'

And I would say that the establishment here has been right thus far. How much longer will it be right? Time will tell. History will tell.

Aggarwal: What do you both think is the Indian foreign establishment's attitude towards the region and the rest of the world?

[*Both men are silent for eight seconds.*]

Dulat: Who are you asking?

Aggarwal: Both of you.

[*Both men are silent for five seconds.*]

Dulat: Who did you say was first?

Aggarwal: I'll note for our record that this is the first time in our sessions that neither of you is volunteering to answer. Nor are you asking for clarification. I'm a psychiatrist who does psychotherapy, so I'm quite comfortable with the silence until you are ready to answer.

Perhaps some context for the question would be helpful. In reviewing our transcripts and reading realpolitik theory, what strikes me is how General Saheb views international relations in a very zero-sum way. I've asked you both about how each country's foreign establishment views itself and each other. The next several questions are about how both countries are perceived in terms of their regional and global interests. A few sessions ago, we talked about how Afghanistan has not been an India–Pakistan issue, but that issue has an impact on the calculations both foreign policy establishments make towards other countries in the region. Similarly, we've talked about how Bangladesh has impacted the India–Pakistan relationship in terms of how Pakistanis view Indians after the 1971 war. So, grasping regional dynamics may help us better understand the context of the bilateral relationship itself.

Dulat: Let me take it up first. When the Taliban came back we were confused. What should happen? Where should we be headed? But of late—and I would say in the last six or eight months—our foreign policy has begun to broaden and bloom in the sense that we're reaching out to many more people and many more countries. Our Foreign Minister has been very active. You see him all over the place now. I think there's a lot more confidence in the foreign policy.

That is because when you have the domestic policy in control, you look outwards. As General Saheb said earlier, the new government in Pakistan must be given time, and I agree with that. Here and now, particularly with the last assembly elections a couple of months back,[16] the government has more confidence. The Prime Minister went to Europe recently. We have a good relationship with the United States. On the Ukraine matter, we have remained neutral.

So I don't think anything is really wrong. But I think we need to reach out to China a little more. I'm not a diplomat, but that seems to be common sense.

Aggarwal: General Saheb, what do you think is the Indian foreign establishment's attitude towards the region and the rest of the world?

Durrani: India a very big player. It has room to manoeuvre. It can come up with truly independent policies. Because of its size and standing, India can afford to have a global policy.

In the case of Pakistan, our choices are limited. We can manage our relations with certain countries when there are no critical issues. But when it comes to the region, our policy is essentially dictated either by our relationship with India or how we take care of Afghanistan.

Lastly, since we have now found a good anchor with China, Turkey, Iran and Russia, we can have a pretty effective regional, even extra-regional, policy. It does not mean that they will always provide the kind of succour we need. Even then, it gives us plenty of confidence.

And remember, even when we were reasonably well positioned to play our games in Afghanistan, there was much misconception in India and elsewhere that Pakistan's Afghanistan policy was being influenced by its relationship with India. It was in fact Pakistan that brought India within the fold of the Istanbul process, which was exclusively Afghanistan centric. We knew that if something had to be done in Afghanistan, India better be on board.

So, on 7 November 2011 in the second Istanbul round, India came in. It did not play a very active role since it could see that the Process would not help in advancing its interests. That's the luxury of India having an independent policy—it can choose when to participate.

But within the region, one works out policies the best that one can, either with the help of India or, at times, against India.

Aggarwal: And Dulat Saheb, what do you think the Pakistani foreign establishment's attitude towards the region and the rest of the world is?

Dulat: General Saheb has described it better than any diplomat can. The last sentence hit the nail on the head. Pakistan needs to move forward with India, and if that's not possible, then without India. I think that's the way that Pakistani diplomats and their establishment think. I keep repeating this for the Indian establishment—we have to wait and watch to see what they think.

I read recently that somebody from the Pakistan side said that our trade relations will improve now. If so, great! Any improvement is great. And as one who follows Mani Shankar Aiyar's path of talking all the time, I think that if nothing else, we should talk for the sake of talks, for the engagement.

General Saheb is right that this kind of engagement never ends. There is always somebody talking to someone. But when people don't hear about it, they have doubts. 'What are these two countries up to?' So however small the improvement— whether it's the visa regime in our case, opening up Wagah [border] a little more, getting the high commissioners back to their posts, whatever—these little bits could at least improve the thinking, if not the relationship: 'Yes, we have done this. We are working towards peace.'

Aggarwal: I'm reflecting on what you both said about where the locus of power may be, in terms of the other country's foreign policy establishment. General Saheb said that Pakistan feels South Block controls India's foreign policy. Dulat Saheb mentioned that it seems like the Army controls Pakistan's foreign policy. What do you think the main institutions are in both countries that are developing the foreign policies in particular?

I ask because terms like 'the deep state' or 'the establishment' are so vague and nonspecific that they describe nothing. It's as if foreign policymakers and institutions exist in the air. This lack of specificity hinders analysis of decision-making.

Durrani: This is a misconception that I have tried to address for the last twenty or thirty years, ever since I landed in the corridors of power. The Army may have a big say in foreign policy, but it is often done reluctantly because it was asked to do it.

I remember in the matter of Afghanistan and Kashmir, very often the governments of the day—Benazir Bhutto in the case of Afghanistan and Nawaz Sharif in the case of Kashmir—were asked as Prime Ministers to lead the policy formulation. Both hedged and ultimately asked the Army to take charge as it had more experience.

But even then, most of the time, it has not been the Army alone that called all the shots. Mostly, the Foreign Office was either on board or provided important inputs. Of course, the way these people are, they would not take the blame when something went wrong, and at times the military did exercise its veto. But often they worked together on core security issues. Luckily people like Shahryar Khan[17] and Riaz Muhammad Khan[18] are still around—Dulat Saheb knows most of them—who fondly recall when we were evolving policies together.

The latest coup in Pakistan's foreign policy formulation was the last two decades of Afghanistan. It was led by the Foreign Office. Salman Bashir, then Foreign Secretary and a former High Commissioner to India, got the ISI and the Army

Chiefs—both sensible people—on board. They helped clinch a regional consensus.

Going alone has always been a disaster. Kargil is one example. When it happened, even within the military, there was no consensus. For successful outcomes, no individual or a single organ of the state should decide on such matters.

Aggarwal: Dulat Saheb, what would you say is the centre of foreign policymaking in India?

Dulat: I said a little while ago that now we have a very intelligent, smart, effective and confident Foreign Minister. But are you asking me who calls the shots?

Aggarwal: That's exactly what I'm asking.

Dulat [*smiling*]: Then you know the answer. It's the Prime Minister and the National Security Advisor.

Aggarwal: What's intriguing about your responses is that they show how different types of stakeholders are involved in developing foreign policies in both countries. To ensure the durability of peace talks, these different stakeholders may need to be brought in. In Pakistan, even though the military may not play the lead role, according to General Saheb, it should still have a seat at the table alongside representation from the Foreign Office. In India, having representation from the National Security Advisor alongside representation from the Foreign Office may be more critical than representation from India's military forces. These differences perhaps reflect the separate trajectories that India and Pakistan have taken since Independence and should be respected.

This point seems to be critical because you both have talked about how Track II initiatives tend to be organized with the assumption that institutions are equivalent across both countries. So, for example, you both have talked about the military-to-military Track II, the intelligence chiefs Track II and so on. Perhaps there need to be initiatives that pull people together from across different institutions that truly reflect the actual stakeholders involved in foreign policy decision-making.

2. Recent Examples of Cooperation and Competition between India and Pakistan

Neil Krishan Aggarwal: Over several sessions, we have discussed the inconsistent relations that India and Pakistan seem to have. Let's talk about these issues concretely. That way, we can try to get a handle on where the bilateral relationship is at present. Then in the following sessions, we can talk about where the relationship needs to improve. My examples come from reviewing over a decade's worth of public statements from both countries' Foreign Offices.

First, Pakistan has celebrated Kashmir Solidarity Day every 5 February since 2004. On 14 August in 2021 India started Partition Horrors Remembrance Day with an announcement from Prime Minister Narendra Modi. Both holidays appear to target the other country. What are your views on this? If the intent of these events is to fuel antagonism towards the other country, should they be repealed?

Asad Durrani: That's assuming too much. We celebrate these events only to satisfy a particular domestic group. It's a political requirement. If you don't do it you would be accused of failing a national commitment, for example to Kashmir if one dropped Solidarity Day or assembling on the Chakothi border.

On these occasions, you make the usual speeches but it hardly affects the bilateral relationship. It may be that the relationship is so bad it can't get any worse; but the relationship has never worsened after one of these events.

These celebrations are not targeting the other side. They're merely meant to please your own political constituencies. They're probably pretty useless in producing desired results, like Track IIs are, except for people getting acquainted and learning about the sentiments of the other side. These celebrations are for the birds, and the other side need not take them seriously.

Aggarwal: If that's the case, then it raises other questions. Why did this celebration start in 2004 and not beforehand? What is the constituency that accrued power at that point in time? Specifically, who are the stakeholders that find value in this kind of event?

Durrani: It's a substitute for a real policy. If you find that you can't do anything substantial—you cannot invade India, you cannot send infiltrators, you cannot dent or break down India's standing somewhere else—then you have these days. That's all.

Aggarwal: Dulat Saheb, what is your view on the new event that India started with Partition Horrors Remembrance Day on 14 August 2021, which we all know is Pakistan's Independence Day?

A.S. Dulat: As General Saheb said, these are dates for domestic political constituencies, and don't have any substance. They don't have much meaning except as part of a formula for strengthening Hindutva. But they don't serve a purpose— either the [Kashmir] Solidarity Day over there or the Horrors Remembrance Day here. These are meaningless things.

I agree with General Saheb that these are not going to affect the India–Pakistan relationship. They haven't done it harm, at any rate. Right now, there is no relationship anyway. But if we are to move forward, these won't come in the way, because the power to move is at the top.

That is why I used to always say, and General Saheb didn't agree with me, that something will happen only if Imran visited Delhi. Now Shahbaz must come or find a way to get Modi to Pakistan.

Aggarwal: I'm going to ask you the same question that I asked General Saheb, which is why did India start this event in 2021? What is the domestic political constituency that needs to be appeased that wasn't appeased beforehand?

Dulat: It's not a question of appeasement. This was in 2021— they had the 2022 assembly elections in five states. Events like this are often used for elections. Never before have elections been given such importance as now. This government doesn't want to lose elections.

Aggarwal: Since the Mumbai attacks of 2008, India and Pakistan have not played cricket in each other's territories. Why has cricket become such a contentious issue?

Durrani: Mr Dulat is a great cricket enthusiast. He will tell us. [*Both men laugh.*]

Dulat: It's become or been made a contentious issue because there are so many followers of cricket in both countries. So stop cricket! Why should we play cricket?

The cussedness isn't just with cricket; it goes beyond that. The Indian Premier League (IPL) is hugely popular; it's big money. Pakistani players used to come and play, and were popular too. Some of them lived almost permanently in India. They have gone away now. Common Pakistanis who appeared on TV—they've all disappeared.

Aggarwal: General Saheb, what do you think?

Durrani: I don't know very much. Mr Dulat has summed it up very well. The game is popular, so to hurt your enemy on the sports field, stop playing cricket with him. If you ban kabaddi matches between the two countries, who cares? Thus, cricket has become a political tool.

I remember in Mumbai, there was this chap ... what was his name? Yes, Bal Thackeray. He often threatened to dig up the pitches if the Pakistan cricket team was invited.

But that is not important. The thing is that in our prevailing political environment, some people make sure to remind the public who the enemy is and nip in the bud any activity that might cool down hostility.

Now, that's the sort of thing that only the politicians or the establishment would come up with. Not the ordinary people, not the cricket board, not even the intelligence agencies—we wouldn't even talk about it. This is a purely political instrument to be played at the right time, targeting the right audience.

Aggarwal: Maybe it's because I'm a psychiatrist, and we believe in bringing people together, that this question will sound naïve: But why does the popularity of the sport have anything to do with it becoming a focus for conflict? Why take cricket away?

Dulat: It's not really the focus for conflict. It's a focus for cussedness—we just won't play cricket. We still play hockey sometimes, and it goes unnoticed. We play the Davis Cup in tennis, and it's not improbable that India and Pakistan may have to play each other. So those sports go on.

Aggarwal: This is where I think the inconsistency is. If they already play kabaddi, hockey and tennis in other venues, why has cricket become a particular source of contention for both countries?

Dulat: Money, principle and popularity.

Durrani: That's right. Then there are other problems with bilateral cricket ties: providing security for another country's team for five days; large crowds turn up, and one does not want to add to one's own difficulties.

And if India thinks the Pakistan team might outplay her, it's not a very comfortable prospect. On the other hand, Indians would love to play hockey with Pakistan because at present it can be clobbered whenever we meet.

And then after August 2019, we don't want to give the Kashmiris the impression that we were still exchanging sporting events with India.

It's a big myth that sports and politics can be separated. After the Ukraine invasion, Russian sports teams have been banned from all sports events in the West. Politics does play a role.

Aggarwal: You're exactly right. We have talked about how sports can be a bridge for overcoming political differences, but your assessment is unfortunately very calculated and true. Sports themselves become politicized.

Let's move to another topic that I think is also very politicized. Since the Pulwama attack of 2019, Pakistani actors and musicians have not been able to travel to India for performances. One could defend this move by saying that Pakistanis, who support Kashmir's independence from India, should not expect Indians to provide them with economic opportunities. Others say that the arts provide a bridge for the shared linguistic, literary, musical and performing traditions of both countries that have spanned centuries. What do you both think of this development?

Durrani: It's not a linear way of looking at the relationship. At the worst of times cultural exchanges could continue without ruffling too many feathers. It would not cause people to question, 'Why was an Indian musical group in Pakistan?' But the establishments were paranoid enough to even forbid cultural ties.

Our artists used to go and perform in India, but now they are afraid that even if Indians applauded them, people back home will question, 'Under these circumstances, you want to go and perform in India?' Seeing what's happened over the last two years in Kashmir or if we saw the Chinese and the Indians were not on the best of terms, we would like to be able to tell the Chinese, 'To show solidarity with you, we have decided not to host the Indian teams.'

Aggarwal: So cultural exchanges become a way of signalling the state of international relations to other countries?

Durrani: Oh yes. Although culture is the most important factor that retains links with neighbouring countries. Relations between India and Pakistan cannot be completely severed for one simple reason: our age-old cultural affinities. And then there are the people-to-people contacts. They ensure that we continue to exchange music and other video clips—Indians and Pakistanis send each other media clips of marvellous young Pakistani and Indian singers, for instance.

However, any open display of music in Lahore or Mumbai would be a problem for obvious reasons.

Aggarwal: Dulat Saheb, what is your impression of Pakistani artists no longer being able to travel to India for performances?

Dulat: I think it's unfortunate because it's only cussedness and about a bit of money that somebody might earn. I guess someone thinks, 'Why should Pakistanis be part of Indian cinema?' I'm told that some of the Pakistani actors were pretty good and quite popular not long ago.

If it's not happening, it's like so many other things that are not happening—it's unfortunate. That's all that one can say. Even border crossings are not easy. Getting a visa is not easy.

Aggarwal: And by the same token, Pakistan has not allowed Indian movies to be screened in its theatres. One could defend this move by saying that Pakistan should not provide support for Indian artists when India does not reciprocate. Others say that Indian movies attract more audiences than Pakistani ones, so screening them increases audiences overall, which is good for Pakistan's film industry economically. So banning movies in Pakistan seems to hurt Pakistan's own movie industry.

Dulat: Excuse me. I'd like to say something.

Aggarwal: Please go ahead.

Dulat: Pakistani movies are not as popular as Indian movies, but Pakistani serials are very popular here. They are watched all the time.

Aggarwal: So the question for Pakistan is, why not allow the import of Indian movies? Because even apart from cultural exchanges, there's a clear economic benefit for its own movie industry.

Durrani: You don't have to go to a cinema house to watch the Indian movies. These are available on CDs, which are one of our best products. I was Ambassador in Saudi Arabia when Microsoft reached out to me. Microsoft protested that the unauthorized CDs of their software prepared in Lahore and Karachi were of such high quality that it was affecting their [legal] business.

Besides, copies of Indian films could always be smuggled. Whenever their screening in movie houses is not possible, some people organize the show on private premises. I remember having watched, as a student, films like *Shahjehan*, featuring the Great Saigal,[19] at a friend's place.

But the first to oppose their public display would be the Pakistani film industry, which would suffer revenue losses.

So the policy is also to provide protection to local business. Protectionism is a legitimate tool used by every government.

Our manufacturers protest imports even from friendly China, with good reason, because Chinese products are so cheap. If Pakistani cinema halls started exhibiting Indian films and there were long lines outside, it would not give the right political message.

Aggarwal: I myself remember watching *Mughal-e-Azam* in 2006 to a packed house in Karachi. I saw firsthand just how Indian films were drawing audiences in Pakistan.

Durrani: On *Mughal-e-Azam*, I have a very sad experience to narrate. It was soon after the '71 debacle, and you know what '71 did to Pakistan.

Aggarwal: Yes.

Durrani: We heard that a booster station close to the Pakistani border was going to telecast *Mughal-e-Azam*. So there was a stampede rushing to the shops that sold antennas. It was not a common thing at that time. '*Please, oh ji*, Mughal-e-Azam *dikhai ja rahi hai te antenna chahida hai mainu*' [Please, sir, *Mughal-e-Azam* is being shown and I need an antenna]. I heard that in Lahore, and it sent me into a fit of rage: soon after the Indians helped surgically remove a part of our country, our people were closing down businesses to watch an Indian film. My camera film rolls on the other hand had not been developed because the shop was busy selling dish antennas.

It was a good film, all right.

[*All three laugh.*]

Durrani: I'm now waiting for its coloured version. I believe it's very good.

Aggarwal: At the height of recent tensions, Sushma Swaraj[20] garnered a reputation through her Twitter [now X] handle for allowing medical visas to Pakistanis as a humanitarian gesture. India also participated in a meeting of SAARC [South Asian Association for Regional Cooperation] Health Ministers on COVID-19 that was held in Pakistan in 2020. The question that I have as a psychiatrist, and this is a topic that is quite dear to me, is: Why is medical and scientific diplomacy not institutionalized in both countries when there are common concerns such as climate change, where there could be clear areas of cooperation?

Dulat: Nothing between India and Pakistan gets institutionalized in a hurry. It depends on what suits whoever at what time.

Neil, you made a good point about medical tourism. Health care in India is cheaper than in most of the world, and it should be available to everyone. We get Arabs and Afghans—so why not Pakistanis?

Durrani: Yes, it's true: nothing is institutionalized on any front. And even these projects are not necessarily humanitarian. When the Indian state makes such gestures, we would be deluding ourselves to assume that it was out of goodness of heart. There may be a political angle. Also, another angle like, 'Look at this poor country.' They expect political dividends, so the aim would be to rub it in: 'This country (Pakistan) cannot even treat its own people in need.'

It still is helpful. When people were going for treatment to Indian hospitals, it had some positive fallout in Pakistan.

Aggarwal: Like what?

Durrani: Let me give you another instance when the two countries had embarked upon a range of people-to-people contacts. Sushma Swaraj, a brilliant BJP politician, though her end was not very pleasant, did great service to her country when she visited Pakistan as part of an Indian delegation during the Vajpayee period. Her mastery of the Urdu language and poetry was better than most of our parliamentarians.

Aggarwal: Oh wow. Are you saying that her linguistic skills were better than most of the politicians in Pakistan you've encountered?

Durrani: Except for some people who come from our Urdu-speaking areas like Karachi, hardly anyone could match the way she spoke Urdu or quoted some of the poets. Absolutely marvellous. But let me quickly add that the famous Laloo [Prasad Yadav] from Bihar who came on a solo visit did a much better job with his rustic antics, and, in fact, created a political constituency in Pakistan. And, by the way, our own Fazlur Rehman did it better than everyone else. The so-called 'hawk' on a visit to Deoband bowled over the Indian strategic community with his 'wicked-wicked' ways.

Aggarwal: Wow.

Durrani: Yes.

Aggarwal: So this is a good area, then, to consider for improving India–Pakistan relations, if you both think that there is scope for medical humanitarianism or medical tourism. Is it possible that India could initiate a new type of visa for this purpose, which would ease travel for anybody, whether it's a Pakistani, Afghan or anyone else? This kind of visa regime could then help to build peacemaking gestures through people-to-people contacts.

Dulat: None of these things is happening because the visa regime, if it exists at all, is so tight. I don't see it opening up in a hurry for anything.

If it has happened in the past, it will again happen when somebody is in dire need or in a crisis. Somebody may then say, 'Okay, why can't we do this?' Like when we sent wheat from Pakistan to Afghanistan. Why can't this be institutionalized? Why can't Pakistan allow wheat to travel through to Afghanistan? These are questions which keep coming up.

On our side, what keeps coming up—and please understand this, Neil—is the perception that we don't need anything from Pakistan. What can Pakistan give us? Pakistan is a bankrupt country. It's living on loans from Saudi Arabia, from UN banks, from the Americans, this and that.

Unless this whole perception is somehow broken, I don't see any forward movement, really. I'm an optimist but here I agree with General Saheb that I don't think it will happen.

Track II or Track III or whatever—a lot has changed since Modi came to power eight years ago. There was a time when Ajit Doval as National Security Advisor might have been quite happy to visit Lahore. General Saheb knows that; I have suggested it also. But now the situation is quite different. I think it's a different Ajit Doval too.

Aggarwal: General Saheb, you were about to say something.

Durrani: Actually, I agree with him. It's true. That is the feeling there as well, which leads to the question: 'What would India gain by having better relations with Pakistan?' Another couple of billion dollars in trade: peanuts, when compared to the near-hundred billion with another 'unfriendly' country like China.

And to expect that for the sake of that small money or for that small gesture, India would make critical compromises, let's say, on Kashmir would be unrealistic. India's thinking was more likely to be: 'If any development benefits Pakistan, even if it is less than India, we must prevent it. We can afford to forgo those gains, while the loss would hurt Pakistan.' I don't think this type of thinking should be called Machiavellian or Kautilyan. This is a very real calculation that takes place.

For example, once upon a time in Siachen when we were looking at the costs of maintaining troops, someone from my community at that time—and I'm talking about thirty-five or forty years ago—said, 'A roti for a Pakistani soldier on Siachen costs forty rupees. But for India, it might be many times more. So let the bloody chaps pay more for their chapattis.'

Now sometimes, people in Pakistan may believe that Siachen was helpful. People were being trained in high altitude warfare, and India was suffering more because of the logistics. But in the meantime, the Indian logistical situation has improved.

This was just to illustrate how people in the establishments might argue, and therefore it becomes understandable why providing any relief to Pakistan might be anathema to South Block. They may well argue that if it was done, the Kashmiris might get ideas and the dynamic of the improved situation may not go in India's South Block's favour. That's the reason India prefers continuing with the status quo; even though Mr Dulat has often said that it was more helpful to Pakistan—maybe in the long run, but not in present times.

We have supported the Kashmiris time and again. But in August 2019, Mr Dulat's favourite Pakistani Prime Minister Imran Khan merely renamed a road and drew another map. The message from some of our common friends from Kashmir on the Indian side was: 'We knew your limitations, but this time around you have underwhelmed even yourselves; what do you think we should expect from you now?'

If they are still hanging in, it's because of Modi and Doval who are not giving them any choice. Otherwise, if I were sitting there, I would say, 'Look at these Pakistanis. Almost every time when something happened, they never came up even to their own modest capabilities.' This is a theme that can be discussed ad infinitum, but it also explains how the establishments look at the process of peacemaking.

When I met my counterpart back in '91, the initiative was from the Foreign Office. We had nothing against it. I went along, and after that, if there was no progress, it was because of political decisions taken in Delhi and Islamabad. It may have been a good initiative, but why follow up if India didn't, or if it didn't suit Pakistan as much as India?

Aggarwal: Let's talk about another topic that has received a lot of attention. Why do you think both establishments in India and Pakistan agreed to opening the Kartarpur Corridor? Why was this particular site chosen? Why have other religious sites not been made available for religious tourism?

[*Both men are silent for several seconds.*]

Durrani: This has been on the cards for many years. It probably started with Nawaz Sharif. It's just across the border—you can see it. It's a holy place for the Sikhs, and all we had to do was to provide them with a corridor, and earn tremendous goodwill from a neighbouring community. I think the first man who thought about bringing the neighbouring communities together was Gujral with his concept of sub-regionalization.

Even then, it took long, but its time did come and those at the helm understandably took credit—Imran, Bajwa or whoever else—and I don't mind if they got it.

Whether the euphoria was dampened by COVID, or if it is India's policy that has broken the momentum and deflated the good will, I cannot say. But the fact is that every time you start doing something good—like the bus between the two parts of Kashmir, this corridor, or Vajpayee's bus initiative—something or the other *must* come in the way, because that is how the relationship has been programmed.

Aggarwal: Programmed by whom? If you're going to use the analogy of a program, then let's stick with it. By whom, and how does one think about changing the software of that program?

Durrani [*laughing*]: IT [information technology] is India's great strength.
[*All three laugh.*]

Durrani [*laughing*]: I think you'll need to get the right response from Hyderabad or Bangalore that claim to be India's equivalent of the Silicon Valley—though being far away from the scene of running battles, they are possibly more relaxed about the bilateral relations.

Aggarwal: Dulat Saheb, why the Kartarpur Corridor in particular? Why not include other sites? Looking at some of the politicians' comments and official statements from India, there hasn't been a very positive reception. Sometimes there has even been criticism when Indian politicians have visited the Kartarpur Corridor.

Dulat: Like General Saheb said, this is something that has been a long time in the making. I didn't realize that it was Nawaz Sharif. Well done! He deserves credit for it.

Like we talked about with medical tourism, I think that religious tourism also has a chance. It has an opportunity if it is properly managed on both sides.

The Sikhs are considered a neutral party. There are also Hindu temples in Pakistan, and if passages could be built across and people could visit these Hindu temples, it may just provide an opening. Just like there are plenty of people in Pakistan who would like to come to Ajmer Sharif. Unfortunately, visas are not available.

So this is a possible area for peacemaking. If it's a question of targeting or programming, then it's not a bad area to target because there are very few people who would say that they don't believe in any God. I think religious tourism offers an opportunity if somebody were to work on it. I keep mentioning Bilawal—maybe young Bilawal could think about this.

There's an area on that side between Rajasthan and Sindh where there are a lot of Rajputs. They belong to Bilawal's political party. Their marriages also go from one side to the other. One has to look for opportunities like that.

Because it is Rajasthan and Sindh, it goes unnoticed. But if it were to happen in the Punjab, there would be a hue and cry about it. Even though the more natural relationship is from Punjab to Punjab. There's a lot of irony there.

General Saheb made a remark about IT and going to Bangalore or whatever it is. But the India–Pakistan relationship is basically a north Indian problem. People in Bengal or Tamil Nadu or Kerala or even Maharashtra are more sympathetic to Pakistan than people in the north.

Aggarwal: Dulat Saheb, you had mentioned something earlier today that I am going to touch on right now. For the past two years, Pakistani politicians have suggested resuming trade links with India. These suggestions have been met with domestic opposition. How do you both read this cycle of proposal, rejection, proposal, rejection?

Dulat: I would put it very simply, and I'm sorry to butt in before General Saheb, because I prefer to hear him first.

It's like this. Whatever is happening is chicken feed, really. It's too little, too late. I'll give you an example. Basit Saheb had just arrived in Delhi as High Commissioner.[21] I happened to meet him a party hosted by his deputy. This was during Dr Manmohan Singh's time. Elections had not been held, and the BJP had not yet come to power.

I said, 'Basit Saheb, I hope you've brought us some good news.' He said, 'Yes, I have. You're going to hear of it very, very soon.' So I understood what he was talking about; it was that MFN [Most Favoured Nation economic status] thing which gets stuck every time. But I think somebody advised him, 'Don't be silly, this is not the time to do it. There's going to be a change of government very soon.' The BJP was coming to power. It's much better to wait for the new rulers.

It didn't happen, and it has never happened. So timing is of the essence. You get an opportunity, then do it! Don't miss it! Ours is a relationship where you must not miss any opportunity. It's the easiest relationship, jinxed by distrust.

Sorry, Sir. I butted in.

Durrani: The first head of the SAARC Chamber of Commerce was Inam-ul-Haq, about twenty-five years ago. Whenever we asked him, 'Who would benefit more from trading together: India or Pakistan?' he always said, 'Pakistan would benefit more from this arrangement.' This might not have been the case because of the imbalance in the two economies but he firmly believed it. In that case, one felt, 'If both of us were going to benefit from it, wouldn't someone from the other side try and scuttle it?'

The concept has had its highs and lows before crashing on the subcontinental rocks. I do not know what all came in the way, but in the overall environment, such feel-good projects were not likely to fly.

Dulat: Is that where we are?

Durrani: Yes.

Aggarwal: In 2003, India and Pakistan agreed to a ceasefire along the Line of Control [LOC]. That held for years until violations increased. The ceasefire was reinstituted in 2021.

What do you make of the timing of the ceasefire? Why did it not happen sooner? And why not forever?

Durrani: Nothing is forever. So it was not likely they'd say that this was forever [*laughing*]. It goes on as long as both the sides find it necessary: for example, we do not have to have any reason to violate the ceasefire, or we have some other problems right now, so why heat up another front. After the post-August 2019 turmoil, keeping the LOC quiet was understandably in India's interest.

And usually whenever casualties take place, civilians suffer more casualties on both sides than the two militaries; Pakistan *does* not only think about people on its side but also about the civilians on the other side. That is our claim, that's our locus standi. People on either side must believe that we feel for them.

In the case of India, I can always quote Yashwant Sinha, a former BJP bigwig, that India, having lost the hearts and minds of the Kashmiris due to its muscular policy, can now only try to keep the territory.

Somehow or the other, the situation has worked out in favour of keeping the ceasefire. Because neither side was going to gain by its violation.

The larger principle, of course, is that an agreement is possible only if it is of mutual interests. If the two countries were interested in targeting certain groups, whether in India or in Pakistan, they might be willing to jointly hunt them down— they may even exchange intelligence on the common threat.

Aggarwal: Dulat Saheb?

Dulat: You mentioned the 2003 ceasefire; that was Vajpayee's time. Now when the ceasefire happened, being an optimist or a peacenik, I was quite excited. I even wrote a piece that it should open many more doors. But it has opened nothing, really. What is encouraging is that both sides can see that the ceasefire has held, and there haven't been too many transgressions on either side.

Why nothing more has happened is not for me to explain. On one of the Zoom shows from over there Mushahid Hussain[22] said that India wanted the ceasefire because of the pressure from China. Now right or wrong, it just shows the mindset on both sides. Even when something good happens, you don't want to give credit to the other side or to yourself. That is the real tragedy.

Since then, I have begun to realize that if no progress followed, nothing further will happen in the near future.

There's just one little thing that I want to say without needling General Saheb. He keeps coming back to Kashmir, and I've kept quiet. But let me put it like this: Sir, *Kashmir de vich, tusi baazi bahut saal pehle haar gaye si* [Sir, you lost the game in Kashmir many years ago]. The Kashmiris lost faith in Pakistan after 9/11 when Musharraf joined the war against terror.

I agree with him about the abrogation in 2019. I can understand how not only the Kashmiris, but Pakistanis felt. But the Kashmiris felt let down that Pakistan had gone about responding wrongly. Now, I don't think Pakistan—and I'm putting it very bluntly—has a role in Kashmir unless there is huge blundering from our side. Like in the past, at times we invite Pakistan back into Kashmir.

You're looking grim, Neil [*smiling*].

Aggarwal: I'm just listening to you. I'm wondering what General Saheb is thinking.

Dulat [*laughing*]: General Saheb will not disagree with me. He may not like what I'm saying but he won't disagree with me.

Durrani [*laughing*]: It's nothing new. I've made my pitch. All I can say is that I'm grateful for small mercies. If the ceasefire is holding on, then I'm grateful for this and happy for the Kashmiris.

But if anyone thinks this will become a role model or pioneer project for anything more, well, that's not going to happen. People decided the ceasefire was useful for their own reasons—advantages, disadvantages, casualties, and so on and so forth.

If you don't want to observe a ceasefire, then there are ways in which it can be violated. Trust me, once people are deployed in places like the Line of Control, it is unrealistic to assume that they'll abide by it for years. At times, they may even start firing to break the monotony. We've been lucky so far.

Dulat: When we were doing our book together, General Saheb made this point that Kashmir could be the bridge between India and Pakistan. I agree with him.

But we're a bit outdated. The reality is different today. I didn't admit it for a long time but now I do. I have become more of a realist now and just try to be optimistic.

Aggarwal: Part of my training as a psychiatrist is to try to listen for inconsistencies that people perhaps do not intend but which are nonetheless revealed during a conversation. Here's one inconsistency: If you say that post-2019 Pakistan doesn't have a role in Kashmir any longer, then how can Kashmir become a bridge between India and Pakistan?

Dulat: I didn't say 2019. I went back to 9/11, to 2001. Even earlier, once the Kashmiris realized the futility of the gun. Apart from the money or arms coming from Pakistan, the Kashmiris were not gaining anything. Even the political setup managed by Pakistan, the Hurriyat Conference, was in disarray. So it's been going downhill.

But General Saheb often quotes my statement that 'the status quo suits Pakistan'. And it is in that context that I agree with General Saheb that Kashmir could be a bridge. It should be a bridge because—and here is the optimist in me—I do not go along with the narrative that Kashmir is done and dusted now that Article 370 is gone. I still do not believe that the status quo suits us.

Aggarwal: Because?

Durrani: Regarding bridge building, this is a very old lesson from people who are involved with studying disputes. When a problem seems to be intractable, when neither side can give up enough to find a solution, whether it is Ukraine, Afghanistan or Kashmir—then instead of insisting 'You do this, and I will do that,' a stage is reached where the antagonists might try and work together—at least on this thorny issue

There's an old saying on the subcontinent that if you ask a monkey to divide the cheese between two cats, the monkey will take most or all of it. If the American monkey is asked to mediate, with India agreeing in the belief that the two are strategic allies, neither of us would get much.

And that is the consideration that some armchair strategists would have in all these places with intractable conflict. Henry Kissinger talked about making Ukraine the bridge. We know see what happened two hundred years ago when the Russian and British Empires agreed to declare Afghanistan to be a buffer between the two.

In the case of Kashmir, since there is no apparent solution that is going to satisfy the three sides—the Kashmiris, the Indians and the Pakistanis—we can start building up with buses, trade and more. At least bring relations to a manageable level. It's the only thing that will bring us to a place where we can progress. If not, all we'll do is talk about various aspects of the relationship like agreeing on a ceasefire and then violating it, not doing trade even if it benefits us. That's why we call Kashmir the core of the contention.

Aggarwal: A stray Indian missile landed in Pakistan in March 2022. If there were ever a reason for the security situation in both countries to explode, that might have been it. Pakistan called for a joint investigation, to which India did not assent. Why did the matter not escalate?

Durrani: That's a subject that I've dealt with for a long time. Take the example of a colonel on the Cuban side during the Bay of Pigs crisis. He saw some movement and—hats off to him—he decided that if anyone took drastic action, it might lead to a nuclear exchange. So he didn't report it. God knows how he had that vision, that wisdom.

In our case, I think we just got lucky because I don't think there was any visionary colonel keeping watch. The Indian missile was a dud; it did not carry a warhead. So don't tell me that it was accidentally fired. It was fired to test our response system—how alert were the Pakistanis—and to ensure that it landed where there would be no damage unless it hit someone on the head.

The lucky part was that someone on the Pakistani side was sleeping at the wheel. Under normal circumstances, once one detected the missile in flight, whether it was armed or not, the standard operating procedure is that you press the red button. Since that chap was probably not awake, a nuclear catastrophe was averted.

It is quite possible that someone else could have panicked. Post facto he could have said, 'Although the missile has landed, let me just show how alert I was. Here is a small tactical nuclear weapon that I'll fire. Or a conventional weapon.' And that would have been a live one.

In Cuba, it was because of a sane colonel; in the subcontinent it was the hand of God.

Aggarwal: So in your estimation, it's pure luck.

Durrani: I think the mischief on the Indian side was by design. There is enough built-in safety in these weapons systems such that it can be destroyed in case of unintended launch.

In that case the first thing that one thinks of is to destroy it. One factor is casualties if it lands. The other is that the Pakistanis would get hold of it and reverse engineer it. So, you destroy it if it has gone astray. If you cannot bring it back— normally, you can't because it is not remote controlled—then you destroy it.

Aggarwal: So, it's your assessment that the Indians did it deliberately.

Durrani: Yes; I've already said it.

Aggarwal: On humanitarian grounds, India and Pakistan routinely repatriate prisoners, people who stray into the other territory along the border and fishermen. Why are these considered humanitarian issues but not other issues? One could include other issues under the humanitarian rubric. For example, there are families that have been separated since Partition that could meet for reunions. Or medical diplomacy to promote common interests like combatting infectious diseases. What is unique to prisoners, people straying into territory along the border and fishermen, that Indians and Pakistanis seem to agree that there should be mutual exchanges?

Durrani: Because these people are harmless. They go fishing and may drift into troubled waters. Not many were likely to take a fishing boat in a vast ocean to go spooking. That's one reason.

The other is that even in the case of spies, you don't kill them. You arrest them, interrogate them, milk them dry of information but keep them alive to trade for any of yours caught by the other side. Hanging of spies is rare and completely useless, even counterproductive. First, they're an asset for bargaining; second, if you hang one, the next catch would rather take arsenic than surrender to you. We have been hanging on to Kulbhushan [Jadhav][23] for years, and since he's a high-profile man, I'm sure one day we will get four or five of ours back.

As for these people on the borders, whether they are fishermen or rangers or smugglers, they have a better relationship with each other than our bilateral relations. They exchange sweets; ask their counterparts, 'Next time when you come smuggling, please get me a couple of crates of aam [mango], rolls of kapde [cloth] or some saris for my wife.' The two countries can learn the art of coexistence from them.

If we want to learn about keeping a relationship, I think we could learn from dacoits. These people have a code. They know what the red lines are, what will benefit them and keep the business going.

Aggarwal: Dulat Saheb, do you have anything to add about why Indians and Pakistanis can repatriate prisoners, people straying to the other territory along the border and fisherman but not cooperate in other areas?

Dulat: Though we consider ourselves adversaries, when it's something serious, then we are reasonable. For example, do you remember when that Balakot thing happened in 2019, and Wing Commander Abhinandan fell on the other side? Imran Khan was kind enough to return him in two days.

If there is a red line, it is war—no sane person wants a war. The generals, least of all: only someone who has fought knows what war really is. I'm not surprised to hear that the ceasefire was at the initiative of the DGMOs [Director General Military Operations], to whatever extent that is true.

We always hear this Western-driven narrative that South Asia is the 'last dangerous place on earth' because both India and Pakistan are nuclear countries. They say, 'Who knows? There may be a madman on either side who will press the

button.' But I don't think anybody seriously thinks along those
lines. It's mostly posturing: 'We can do what we can do,' and
'We can do it better than you.' That kind of thing.

In one of our sessions, you mentioned Mumbai. When the
26/11 attacks happened in 2008, it was a terrible time, really.
Dr Manmohan Singh was under enormous stress. We also
talked about the attack on Parliament in 2001, but Mumbai
was more serious. Better sense and better conscience prevailed.

People thought that the Congress under Dr Manmohan
Singh would suffer politically. But the Congress came back to
power in 2009 without any problem.

Aggarwal: In 2016, the Indian Coast Guard and Pakistan
Maritime Security Agency signed a memorandum of
understanding to extend their diplomatic cooperation in
exchanging information regarding apprehended vessels,
marine pollution, natural disasters and calamities, combating
smuggling, illicit trafficking in narcotics, piracy and
coordination in search, rescue and return sea passage. Each one
of those functions is a law-and-order function. Why can India
and Pakistan collaborate on sea but not on land?

Durrani: I think that the law of the seas is just one reason. Both
sides have to respect it.

Secondly, it's easier on the sea. You can recognize each
other's vessels. On land, you do not know. Everything gets
mixed up. The man who was probably the biggest believer
in peacemaking between the two countries was the Indian
Admiral [Laxminarayan] Ramdas.[24] He once suggested joint
patrolling along the LOC. I said: 'Sir, for Heaven's sake, the
area has no resemblance to the Indian Ocean. Here, if you ask

me to carry out a joint patrol with the Indian side, I will mislead them instead of cooperating with them.' It's so easy to do on the Line of Control.

On the high seas, it is easier to observe each other and act accordingly—to ensure that no one is going to take you for a ride or deceive you. On land, you're not even sure how to make it happen.

Aggarwal: There are several assumptions in your answer that I'd like to extract for my understanding. One is that the law of the seas seems to be inviolable, in the sense that we have talked in previous sessions about how Indians and Pakistanis have differences in the interpretation of history when it comes to their bilateral relationship, but most dramatically when it comes to Kashmir. However, when it comes to the law of the seas there's no difference in interpretation in terms of what member states are obligated to do. Is that correct? Is that why maritime cooperation is easier?

Durrani: Mr Dulat, Sir?

Dulat [*laughing*]: I agree with the General Saheb. I think also that things on the sea remain vaguer. So, it's not so much a question of right and wrong. It's easier to cooperate. Whenever there's been a war, the navies should take credit for whatever they do, and there is no doubt that they play their roles.

But the real fight happens on the ground, like General Saheb said. I keep repeating this but the '65 war was fought in Punjab. I can tell you that Ambala was bombed, and it is just about thirty kilometres from Chandigarh, my hometown. So we saw what war meant.

I think it's easier on the sea. Interestingly, General Saheb alluded to our former navy chief who used to talk about joint patrolling. We had more peaceniks in the Navy than in the Army.

Aggarwal: We've gone through several examples of cases where India and Pakistan agree to cooperate, and others where they do not. So what can we learn from this? For example, when it comes to cricket, the performing arts, trade—they have not. When it comes to medicine, the Kartarpur Corridor and religious tourism, the Line of Control, repatriating vulnerable peoples or maritime security—there is cooperation.

I picked these topics by going through the past ten years' statements of cooperation by the Indian and Pakistani Ministries of External Affairs. I think that our conversation illustrates the current state of affairs. Can either of you give us a sense of the broad principles on which both countries decide to cooperate and not cooperate in certain areas?

[*Both men laugh.*]

Dulat: Basically, I see it as one-upmanship. Where things will go unnoticed, like on the high sea or on the coast, then it's easier to cooperate. Things that are most conspicuous, and therefore become political, are most difficult to cooperate on. If a Pakistani High Commissioner landed in Delhi tomorrow, it would become very big news. It could become a political issue too. That's the way I see it.

Durrani: I agree. It's easier to cooperate with things under the radar.

Aggarwal: Since we've spent so much time talking about the establishments today and policymaking—and the two of you have interacted with people from the other side—what types of thinking in the other side's foreign policy establishment come in the way of cooperation with your country? Could those types of thinking be identified and dispelled, such as through our work, so that we could help to promote an environment of peace?

Dulat: I look at it like this. If somebody like General Saheb were responsible for making peace with India, we would have a better chance than with a Foreign Secretary of Pakistan. I'm not naming names or anything.

Aggarwal: Sure. As you feel comfortable.

Dulat: I can give you an example. When Modiji first became Prime Minister, he invited all the major heads of government for his swearing-in. The conspicuous absence was Pakistan. I got a call from a couple of Kashmiris who said that Nawaz Sharif should be invited. He might come. Those were early days, and people were willing to listen.

I passed the message on. It was not rejected. The only question I was asked was, 'What if we were to invite him, and he did not come?' My answer to that was, 'No big deal if he doesn't come.' He'd only be letting himself and Pakistan down.

I asked a former, very senior diplomat in Pakistan for his opinion. He said, 'No, no, Don't take a chance! I don't think Nawaz would come.' I said okay.

Then, of course, I asked General Saheb what he thought. His answer was typical of him: 'I see no reason for him not to go.' If he were invited, then he would go. That's what happened. And that's what happens when you've got your head screwed on right.

Having watched Track II—diplomats are not the easiest people to talk to. They think that it is part of their business to oppose things rather than find solutions. Again, I'm not casting aspersions on particular individuals or even a particular category of people but that's the way it happens. I've seen diplomats squabbling about the 'ifs' and 'buts' and 'hows' and 'whens'. When the military dialogues started, General Saheb came up with the idea of spooks' dialogues. They went off quite well. We talked frankly.

Aggarwal: Durrani Saheb?

Durrani: That about sums it up. If you want peace, you will not come up with excuses. If the Indians were to say that in Pakistan, it's the military that calls the shots, then I would respond that 'Your bloody South Block wallas have patented this argument to shy away from the dialogue—our military, whenever in power, has always strived to improve relations with India.' If you have the intention to make peace, you will not let misunderstandings get in the way.

Establishments are clever and have dealt with each other long enough not to misunderstand or misinterpret each other. It's the malintent that leads to these disingenuous arguments.

The episode that Mr Dulat mentioned about inviting Nawaz Sharif—that diplomat may not have wanted Nawaz Sharif to go. Otherwise, he wouldn't simply decide on his own. With the slightest knowledge about Nawaz Sharif, one would be sure that he would take every opportunity to reach out to Delhi. So would many others. There are others who would drag their feet and not go. But in his case, it was clear he would go running.

So, making an assessment based on your likes and dislikes is the norm.

Dulat [*smiling*]: Neil, I don't think it's always the song. It's sometimes the singer.

Aggarwal: You're right. That's why I think psychology has a role to play, because we're talking about individuals and personalities when it comes to war and peace.

Dulat [*laughing*]: You're more than a physician. You're a magician.

5

An Honest Assessment of Future Peacemaking

No topic of conversation triggered more disagreements among us than future steps towards peacemaking. The charitable interpretation is that disagreements show people feel so secure with each other that they speak plainly. A more cynical interpretation could conclude that such disagreements embody fundamental differences on how to advance the bilateral relationship.

These disagreements cannot be attributed to any lack of preparation. A.S. Dulat and Asad Durrani have participated in official and unofficial negotiations for nearly two decades. Neil Krishan Aggarwal has mediated thousands of interactions in psychotherapy where conflict is defused by acknowledging negative emotions and shifting a group's focus to collaborative problem-solving. When moderating these sessions, too, he followed best practices in applying psychology to international relations, such as generating hypotheses about the barriers that stall the discussions, inviting feedback and bringing underlying assumptions charged with strong emotions into conscious awareness.[1]

One clue that proposing concrete steps towards peacemaking would be a contentious topic came during a text exchange on our Spychiatrists WhatsApp group. The day before our last set of conversations, Aggarwal sent the following text: 'I have taken a stab at tomorrow's questions. Please have a look and see what you think.' The text did not differ from prior formats, in that he organized the process and content of each session. However, he included this additional message: 'I would not want our work to end on a pessimistic note. I hope we can find some solutions. The questions are moulded with that in mind.' After reviewing the questions, Durrani responded, 'We can certainly discuss the points raised in your questions. This is not the first time that peacemaking in the subcontinent is being discussed. The real issue to be discussed is why hasn't it worked—and if there is a way to overcome those stumbling blocks.' Never before had Aggarwal tried to influence the course of discussions, in this case by wanting what Durrani would later describe as 'a happy ending'. And never before had Dulat or Durrani expressed approval or disapproval of the questions they were sent before each session to prepare themselves.

Psychology's theory of *transference* can help us situate these interpersonal dynamics. Introduced by Sigmund Freud in his works on how to conduct psychoanalysis, the term transference has evolved as multiple theorists have contributed to its understanding. One contemporary definition of transference comes from the psychologists Kenneth Levy and J. Wesley Scala, who write, 'We define transference as a tendency in which representational aspects of important and formative relationships (such as with parents and siblings) can be both consciously experienced and/or unconsciously ascribed to other relationships.'[2] Aggarwal called Durrani to discuss the text messages and questions for the final session:

Neil Krishan Aggarwal: I hope I didn't offend you with my text message. I realize that I may have stacked the deck conversationally in hoping for a positive resolution.

Asad Durrani: Not at all.

Aggarwal: I know that you have participated in multiple peace initiatives and dialogues in the past. I'm wondering whether you have been frustrated with their pace or lack of progress, and whether I should interpret your message in that light.

Durrani: No, not at all. One has learned not to be starry-eyed and come up with wish lists.

Aggarwal: Could you tell me where you learned that?

Durrani: It could be my training. First in the army, then in intelligence.

Aggarwal: Do you think there could have been any influence from your parents or siblings at all?

Durrani: I don't think so. My parents were conservative, but I recall nothing special. I was older than my siblings, so I don't think they influenced me. It probably comes from when I was six or seven years old. I mentioned to you before, and in *Honour Among Spies*, about how I started questioning the existence of God and began doing things my way. I think I was born with this scepticism. I learned how to draw my own conclusions based on an assessment of the facts.

Aggarwal: Do you think your viewpoint is reflective of the military or intelligence establishments you've served in?

Durrani: No. My viewpoint has been in the minority. Normally, when people say something like, '*Inshallah*, so-and-so will happen,' then I stop at '*Inshallah*.' I want a rational basis.

Based on this exchange, we began to discuss whether the three of us were reenacting interpersonal roles from the past within our group. A.S. Dulat became the champion for peace, as he has described throughout this book and in other venues.[3] Aggarwal has also written for scientific audiences about his desire for peace between both countries and the need to analyse all viewpoints towards a resolution that will satisfy the maximum number of stakeholders.[4] Durrani took a more realist position, as he described in Chapter Two. Analysing how people relate to each other in small groups can help understand how individuals learn to relate to others in their families, communities and workplaces.[5] In therapy, a psychiatrist strives to understand how he or she relates to others to better frame conversations.[6] Based on this principle, we decided to eliminate our original questions and begin where Durrani recommended.

1. Why Peacemaking Repeatedly Fails between India and Pakistan

Neil Krishan Aggarwal: This is the last set of conversations for our book. Durrani Saheb sent a comment on WhatsApp yesterday that frames where we should begin. Let's start with his incisive challenge. Why has peacemaking not worked in the past?

Asad Durrani: Because of the price of peace. It demands certain compromises to be made. If you want to negotiate an agreement with anyone, even for the management of a conflict, let alone its resolution—there is a price to be paid. You have to make compromises. If one side believes that the price for peace is higher than for conflict, then it chooses conflict. It refuses to compromise.

Maybe I should also ask my friend to comment on this.

Aggarwal: What do you think?

A.S. Dulat [*laughing*]: I never disagree with my friend. But I look at this a little differently. As I said before, it's the singer, not the song. It requires somebody to think differently, to be different, or at least pretend to be different.

I keep coming back to Vajpayee's bus to Lahore. Now that was a special thing. Dr Manmohan Singh also took a bus across, down in Srinagar. That's thinking differently. You must have this burning desire: 'We have to do something.'

Are you paying a price or gaining a price? Ultimately, the cost of war is much more than the cost of peace.

But right now, I agree with General Saheb: nothing will happen. I'm not optimistic. There are many reasons. The government has changed in Pakistan; we don't know yet how good it is. It needs to settle down and stabilize. People here are happier with this government than with the last. The question is whether it wants to work for peace, and if it will have the support of the military and the people—it's a complex matter.

Here, of course, things have changed since Vajpayee's time, particularly in the last eight years of Modiji. These people are realistic and want things on a plate. 'If you have something to offer us, let's have a look. What have they got for us?' That's not the best way to look for peace but that's how it is.

Aggarwal: Durrani Saheb noted that the price of peace can be sometimes higher than the price of conflict. He didn't say 'the price of war'. But Dulat Saheb, you have mentioned war several times. That's a very interesting difference.

Dulat: Then I take my words back. I thought he implied war. Maybe I misheard or misunderstood.

I agree with him. That's how people here look at it: 'Why are we wasting our time? You guys can't even do what you offer. You can't deliver.'

Our man here, Prime Minister Modi, can deliver if he wants to—this guy is ruling the roost. Vajpayee delivered even though he was heading a coalition of some twenty-two parties.

But I take back my words. Sometimes the price of conflict may be cheaper, and that's the way people in our establishment think.

Durrani: Vajpayee's example is a very good one to explain how peace is derailed. He brought the bus after we had gone nuclear. His initiative was scuttled because of the foolishness of Kargil. Ironically the person who had scuttled it before—Pervez Musharraf—went to Agra.

Ultimately, the two sides came together in Islamabad in 2004. They agreed there must be a design for action within the larger framework of the Composite Dialogue. I was surprised when they said, 'We will run the bus in Kashmir.' I considered it a big breakthrough.

But when the buses started moving, obstacles cropped up. That is where one should look at the role of the spoilers or scuttlers. Some of them are genuinely against mending fences; some are merely sceptics; a third group will scuttle things to harm the other side, like, 'If Pakistan is suffering more, let them.'

A variety of reasons could come in the way. Nuclearization of the subcontinent brought one bus to Lahore. The pro status quo forces in Delhi ensured that the buses would not cross the LOC for too long. They are detractors of the process who nip it in the bud, and they are pretty powerful.

Aggarwal: Who are some of the scuttlers and spoilers?

Durrani: There are many. Firstly, there are some non-state actors who may be sponsored by a state—even an extra-regional one—which doesn't want peace. They sabotage the process through acts like Mumbai, Pathankot or attacks on Parliament—some of them may well be false flag operations.

Secondly, there are state organs like the South Block that has traditionally been hawkish. Tavleen Singh[7] once described this institution as programmed to hate Pakistan. It ensured that the government in Delhi would refuse to respond to Musharraf's four-point proposals.

Then, organizations like the RSS in India or the JI [Jamaat-e-Islami] in Pakistan could exert political or public pressure on their respective governments.

Finally, the US is against peace in regions like ours or the Middle East because then it can't play one country against the other, and its military industry loses contracts.

That brings me to my key point: any bloody fool can start a war and also ensure that it continues, even if it is bound to fail—like the Americans in Afghanistan for twenty years. To establish or restore peace, every major actor must be on board because any one of them can throw a spanner in the works.

This is why there was no peace between India and Pakistan despite some very good efforts. The Composite Dialogue was the best structured one. The architect was Indian Prime Minister I.K. Gujral, but even that crashed on the subcontinental rocks. I will try and say a few more words to reinforce my previous argument.

Aggarwal: You can say them now if you like.

Durrani: It was 1997 when the initiative was taken by Gujral. Nawaz Sharif responded positively. They had two excellent foreign secretaries to work out that formula—Salman Haidar[8] on the Indian side and Shamshad Ahmad[9] on ours. Salman Haider was simply brilliant. I suppose most of the ideas were his or Gujral's.

The design logic of the Composite Dialogue was: Since we get stuck every time we talk about nearly intractable issues like

Kashmir, why not start with the 'low-hanging fruits'—the less contentious issues. We'll move incrementally and deliberately. Even if we don't resolve any issues, we can at least create an environment in which the three stakeholders—the Pakistanis, the Indians, the Kashmiris—are more comfortable. Then we can take on the more complex issues like Kashmir. The concept led to the formation of eight different tracks; Kashmir and security were to be addressed by the foreign secretaries because they were so important. Since the foreign secretaries meet so seldom, these issues were put on a separate slow track. Because if the pace was to be set by the progress on Kashmir, nothing would move. Movement on less critical matters—visas, culture, economic stuff—should, however, be possible. That would encourage us to start negotiating thornier issues. Meanwhile, it would send the right signals to the poor Kashmiris that efforts were on to resolve their plight.

The 2004 conference in Islamabad was very helpful. Vajpayee came and signed the famous agreement.[10] He was followed by the Indian foreign minister. I was present when they announced the decision to run buses between the two parts of Kashmir. It was a message to the Kashmiris that while the two nations were addressing minor issues, Kashmir was foremost on their minds.

Soon thereafter when this project too jammed in its tracks, one asked oneself: What were these forces that toppled a robust construct that had withstood the buffets of Kargil and more, and was now the bedrock of the India–Pakistan peace process?

One concluded that if changing the status quo might benefit Pakistan more than India, it would be subverted. Their argument would be: 'If the process merely brings us $2 billion trade with Pakistan, then it is not worth all the compromises we would have to make on Kashmir, and it will give the Kashmiris and Pakistanis confidence to bargain for more.'

To be fair, some from Pakistan also dislike such a process. They argue that by putting Kashmir on the slower track, India might get peace and stability in the region, and would then have no compelling reason to address our core issue.

Another big initiative was taken by Manmohan Singh and Yousuf Raza Gilani, when they agreed to create a joint anti-terror mechanism. That formula very capably and courageously addressed the problem of terrorism. Again, many bureaucrats on both sides were opposed to it, because the framework provided for sharing of intelligence and joint investigations on matters of mutual concern—and more critically, giving the other side access to what they considered their sovereign domain.

The officialdom wants to prove its loyalty to their country, it was making sure nothing harms its interests. The result is you remain stuck where you were. I'm only talking about the situation before Modi came, because after Modi, the nature of the ballgame has changed.

Aggarwal: Dulat Saheb, do you have any reflections on what Durrani Saheb just said?

Dulat: No, General Saheb is always right. If peace is left to the bureaucrats, then it is not going to happen.

When we talk about the low-hanging fruits, unless the problem of Kashmir is settled in everybody's minds, we will not move forward. That can only happen when people at the top decide, 'Okay, this is a big issue.' Everything in Kashmir is the way the current government wants it, so why can't we settle on that? It would also give the Kashmiris some respite.

Something has changed in Kashmir. Earlier, it was the separatists who held that dialogue between India and Pakistan was necessary. Now the mainstream Kashmiri leadership is saying it because it gives Kashmiris hope that they will not always be at the receiving end.

When the ceasefire took place, I thought it was the first good thing in a long time. The ceasefire is still holding. True, as General Saheb says, there are people ready to scuttle it. We have not moved beyond the ceasefire as we should have logically done. Why has it not happened? It hasn't happened because people don't think it's necessary.

We heard at the time that Pakistan is reconciled to the abrogation of Article 370. My argument to move forward is, if the Kashmiri is reconciled to the abrogation, so should Pakistan. As Musharraf used to say, 'Whatever is acceptable to Kashmir and Kashmiris will be acceptable to Pakistan.'

But the point is: Is it acceptable to Kashmir? It depends on point of view—there are three sides to this triangle. It would be a positive development if Pakistan was reconciled to it, since it makes it easier for the Kashmiris to then move on.

I think, by and large, the Kashmiris are reconciled to it. But we're not out of the mud just yet. We're still stuck in Kashmir.

Aggarwal: Dulat Saheb, you gave a very provocative interview in which you told Karan Thapar it was your assessment that a Pakistani cell could be operating in Kashmir with some impunity since the perpetrators of murders have not been caught.[11] Whether it's a Pakistani cell or an indigenous Kashmiri cell remains to be seen, but what you're calling attention to is a fundamental challenge here based on the realpolitik rubric that General Saheb has been advancing from the first day of our sessions. The Government of India has been reconciled to the abrogation of Articles 35-A and 370. The Government of Pakistan doesn't assent to that. Prime Minister Shahbaz Sharif said only yesterday that he wants the Government of India to reinstate those articles. It's clear that the Pakistani leadership has no interest in agreeing with the Government of India on this issue.

Dulat Saheb, it has been your recent assessment that the security environment in Kashmir is in its worst phase since 1990. Doesn't that suggest that at least one significant section of Kashmiri society does not agree that the abrogation should be finalized?

Dulat: The Kashmiris are like that. They will not be satisfied, and yet they may be reconciled. It's a peculiar Kashmiri characteristic.

That, to my mind, is not the issue. When I said that there is a Pakistani cell functioning in Srinagar, I didn't mean that they were from the ISI. It could be Lashkar [-e-Tayyaba], it could be Jaish [-e-Mohammad], it could be anybody. These boys are much better trained and more professional than required for whatever they are there to do.

When we last saw militancy erupt in south Kashmir in '89 and '90, it was just boys willing to die for Allah. This time is different, more threatening. They are professionals. We always talked of terrorists as infiltrators—the numbers ranged between 200 and 300; there's a similarity there. But it's happening after a long time. What is the cause? The powers that be need to figure that out.

---

2. Overcoming the Barriers to Peacemaking

Neil Krishan Aggarwal: Durrani Saheb, could you characterize the extent of the spoilers and scuttlers? If we understand that, perhaps it would help us overcome some of those stumbling blocks to peacemaking.

Asad Durrani: I'll talk about a few factors that affected the situation in Kashmir. There were some steps taken by India that contributed to the worsening of the situation. I can't blame the Indians for doing what they think will benefit India rather than for peace or Kashmir's sake. They might even ultimately harm India. But if the cost of changes seems too high in their calculations, a stalemate will continue.

My main criticism is of the leadership on the Pakistani side, whether it is civil or military. It is shocking, but from the start, the governments here—except in very small patches—did not have a Kashmir policy. Nor did they seriously pursue the aim they had spelled out. Politically, it was convenient for certain rulers to talk about the situation or to exploit a development, like in the wake of the uprising in late '89 and early '90.

But to work out a policy and pursue it diligently was just too inconvenient for them—also domestically. And if you ask me, at times they dragged their feet or even had a hands-off policy if they feared or suspected that it would create problems for them with their guardian angels in Washington.

Such regimes would at best ask the military or the intelligence agencies: 'Try to contain the crisis but don't let it grow into something uncomfortable.' This happened many times.

The few times actions were taken, like sending infiltrators in '65 or to Kargil, they were not thought through. They were for personal or political gains and planned so poorly that the outcome was counterproductive. In the process, two things happened. First, if some Kashmiris are still pro-Pakistani, it is only because they think India is the worse devil and once they throw off the Indian yoke, they will next sort out their problems with us.

The second is probably more important for people like me. Like it or not, there are enough people who remain committed to violence. In the absence of a grand strategy, which was for Pakistan to make, they don't know what else to do except for a pinprick here or an explosion there. They will continue to adapt to the circumstances to keep the struggle alive—and they have achieved that. Ultimately if they can bring both sides—especially the Indian side—to a point where they find conflict costs more than the compromises for peace, there might be change for the better. In the absence of anything better, this seems to be reasonable thinking on the part of people who want to do something.

Then there are those like Mr Dulat and myself who keep coming up with formulas and concepts—backchannels and such fancy stuff. These are good suggestions but mostly amount to wish lists that the establishments don't take seriously.

Political leaders make statements because that is what's expected of them. But 'We need peace with India' means nothing unless you can say how that is going to be achieved.

For example, the other day at a security conference, Bajwa said he wanted good relations with India. Political or military leaders don't ever say they don't want good relations with India or America. These statements are for the birds.

The actual issue is about evolving a policy, taking the opposition on board, and then over a long period of time executing it step by step. And if there is a hurdle or roadblock, one can make a so-called strategic pause and resume or adjust the plan as required by the new environment. As we have not done that, it has not been too difficult for the Indians to manage one crisis after the other to their own benefit.

Aggarwal: The way you both describe this, peacemaking becomes an even murkier challenge. On both sides there are factors that the other side may be frustrated with, but it doesn't present any solutions. For example, if we're looking at this from an Indian realpolitik perspective, then why should India negotiate with a Pakistani establishment that doesn't have a coherent policy on Kashmir? If it seems that a broad swathe of society, whether civilian or the military leadership, cannot be brought on board, then even a well-intentioned Indian negotiator may not find a counterpart in Pakistan who can deliver. If we're looking at this from a Pakistani realpolitik perspective, one could say that whenever there have been attempts at negotiations—with the Composite Dialogue, after Agra, after the Mumbai attacks, after the Pulwama attack—India doesn't maintain all the other tracks in the Composite Dialogue, even though Pakistan seems to be willing to relinquish prior claims on Jammu and Kashmir. India doesn't show up as a good negotiating partner.

Durrani: This is what I call rationalization. Since the intent is *not* to do it, you find any excuse or create a justification for not doing it: You cannot talk to Pakistan because the military controls everything; or because some group carried out a 'terrorist' act on behalf of Pakistan. Who cares if the act was stage-managed! Davidsson, a German Jew, has written a voluminous book, *The Betrayal of India*, to prove that the Mumbai 26/11 was a false flag operation.

When Musharraf was in power, he was considered to control everything. There were no violations on the ceasefire line. Even then, the negotiations did not take place. Both sides were not serious about it. Let alone his four points, no one was willing to even take up one point and explore it. It's the bigger policy and the bigger intent that come first. Then, all the pieces can fall into place.

Aggarwal: One of the most valuable lessons from our prior sessions, which seems to be culminating today, is that perhaps people like me who are invested in the idea of peace assume that peace is the ideal state between both countries. You both are calling attention to the fact that actually, peace is not the strategic ideal that governs the relationship between India and Pakistan, and that those of us who do operate with that assumption are mistaken. That peace is perhaps a belief that we want to have but the evidence points to the contrary. Dulat Saheb has mentioned that perhaps this kind of thinking is obsolete or outdated because it's been over twenty years since Kargil and nearly twenty years after Agra. Both countries have changed significantly, so maybe we shouldn't be thinking about peace as an ideal state of affairs between India and Pakistan.

Both of your assessments challenge a core assumption that I've had, which is that both establishments want to find pathways to peace. That's the part that I find disquieting. Durrani Saheb's assessment is fact-based and clear that nothing should lead us to that assumption. If that's the case, how does one move forward to overcome those stumbling blocks?

Durrani: First, we must realize that if it hasn't happened in seventy years despite many good efforts, then there must be something intrinsically wrong or problematic.

Apart from that, one or two things could be built up. Whenever we have gone through these exercises trying to come up with such ideas, the only new thing that one could think of was the idea that we spelled out at the end of *The Spy Chronicles*, lauded by the very high-level group that discussed it at its launch. It was of establishing a backchannel. Some other steps could be taken and some structures created. Everything worth its while has been thought about and talked about.

But if still there has been no positive movement on the Indo–Pak front, then perhaps we should consider ways of cajoling or coaxing the leadership to do something. One suggestion is to increase the price of conflict. It could be an uprising like what happened after '89. If we had had confidence in ourselves, we could have sparked one when Modi abrogated 370. That is one way—a kinetic approach—to exploit a bad situation in pursuit of a good cause, of making peace.

Another way is to build up the peace lobbies on both sides, which are currently not very strong. People, especially at the grassroots level, are no hawks. Most of them dream about a better future. Try and mobilize them. Try and take them to a stage where politicians will have no choice but to pay heed to their desires. That may turn the corner.

These are the things I can suggest. But to say that there may be an *amritdhara* [river of nectar], a recipe to cure the problems, and that leaders from both sides can be made to drink from it—that won't happen, because to them it is like Khomeini's 'cup of poison'. People like us won't ignore the difficulties or problems just to make the ending a little more optimistic. We will point out to our respective sides not only where they have gone wrong, but also where they have deliberately sabotaged certain processes.

Aggarwal: Dulat Saheb, do you have any reflections?

Dulat: I entirely agree with General Saheb in all he said. I don't think Pakistan has a Kashmir policy. I don't think people in Pakistan are too bothered about Kashmir, and I've pointed this out to him.

The one person who I think involved himself quite reasonably was Musharraf. I agree with General Saheb that those four points are redundant, and not even one would be acceptable here. But when Musharraf came up with that formula, the Kashmiris started to like it. They thought, 'If this is the way out, it's fantastic. We are for it.' And I'm talking about the separatists. At that time, the mainstream was a little cynical but the separatists said, 'This is the best formula.'

It may be wishful thinking or my optimism but, based on inputs from people there, I certainly felt that we had a window of opportunity in 2006 or 2007. There's no point looking back and lamenting that, but the point is Musharraf did apply himself on Kashmir, whether his ideas were right or wrong, or if Pakistan would accept them. But that's about the closest that we have come on settling Kashmir.

On this question of peace to which we keep returning, I think we actually are at peace. There's no war. It's like General Saheb describes it: it's a stalemate; it is stable; it holds the ceasefire. One could argue that we could leave it at that, at the status quo. So long as people on the border don't have to suffer, at least. Then, gradually, let Kashmir evolve itself, and hopefully both sides will support it.

Aggarwal: You both have talked about Musharraf's four-point policy at various times in our project. But what can both governments realistically do at this point, given that each side claims the entirety of pre-Partition territory? If you both think that Musharraf's four-point formula is a realistic plan, then how does sub-governance and autonomy work when Indian-administered Kashmir has become a union territory after 2019 and Pakistan-administered Kashmir is centrally governed? What would the other point of joint supervision and management look like, given that the status of Jammu and Kashmir within both countries has changed so much? To go back to Musharraf's four-point formula now almost seems outdated.

Dulat: Let me take you a little further back because you've mentioned autonomy and self-rule. Different people have different names for this.

When Narsimha Rao was Prime Minister,[13] he was very keen. He realized that six years of Governor's Rule was more than enough. Kashmir needed an elected government. His own dreams didn't bear fruit, but the National Conference did come back to power. Before the election, he had said that if what the Kashmiris really want is autonomy, then the sky is the limit.

Now, autonomy is over. Finished. It's a word that should not be uttered any longer in Kashmir. Like the status quo between India and Pakistan, there is a status quo in Kashmir. When both sides sit down to talk and realize the reality on the ground, perhaps we can come to some agreement that okay, this is it.

Obviously, then in all fairness, there must be something for Pakistan. Whenever we near a settlement, they have said, 'There should be something for us.' Now, too, they want that something. So, in our Parliament the government made a commitment to give back Kashmir statehood. If India and Pakistan were to talk sensibly, then whenever statehood was revived, Pakistan could claim credit for it.

Aggarwal: Let's play that argument out. Pakistan already rejected the idea that Jammu and Kashmir had acceded to India, even when it had statehood before 2019. So if they accepted that it might regain statehood, wouldn't that be seen as a step backwards and viewed negatively?

Dulat: That is one of the main demands from Pakistan at this point of time. The other matter that everyone has conceded is that Article 370 is sub judice. What the Kashmiri mainstream has been saying is, 'You're committed to restoring statehood. Please do so.' And the response has been, 'Yes, we are committed but we'll do it when it suits us.'

Durrani: There are a few things that people do not realize. And that is regardless of all of the arguments that we can come up with. Let's assume that for sixty or seventy years, India seemed to persuade Kashmiris, using a mix of soft and hard power, that they were better off with it. That contentment was never sustained, and Kashmiris repeatedly resumed their movement for autonomy. If the Kashmiris on either side had at any stage reconciled to Indian sovereignty, there was very little Pakistan could have done about it. Similarly, if the people of Kashmir were to decide that they were fed up with both countries and would like to have an independent homeland, neither country could, in the long run, deny them their freedom.

They would continue their struggle for independence, and we would not be able to convince them that since the UNSC [United Nations Security Council] resolutions did not provide for the so-called third option, they better opt for India or for Pakistan.

That has not happened. Thirty, forty years ago, India might have persuaded Kashmiris that their future lay with them. That did not happen either, which led me to believe that many or most of them would rather have a free Kashmir. They can then work out the nature of their relationships with the rest of the world.

Instead of going on talking about our respective national interests, we'd better start looking at what Kashmiris want. However, I don't think our two countries would agree on any common approach. India will do what it wants its own way. Pakistan will have to work out a strategy on how to live with an independent Kashmir. But before that we have to work out how to help them achieve independence. And then, how to live with it.

This would not only be more practical but the sensible way to address the problem.

Aggarwal: So is the assessment that you just gave related to your prior comments about Kashmir being a bridge between

India and Pakistan? That instead of working only for their own countries' interests, they jointly work towards the interest of Kashmiris?

Durrani: UN resolutions are there to provide a locus standi, and there are excellent arguments to support them. The best that I've ever come across are given by the International Council of Jurists based in Switzerland, in their booklet *Human Rights in Kashmir* published in 1996.

They started by looking at the dispute only from the legal angle but then decided to look at the issue in a broader context, and concluded that the Kashmiris have a right to self-determination. Pakistanis and Indians have no locus standi, and no act of theirs can deny the Kashmiris their legitimate right.

But we also know that regardless of the soundness of any arguments, they were not helpful, except in discussions. On the ground, it will not matter. What matters is how we manage or order the ground situation in our interest or against the interest of the other side—or in the interest of the Kashmiris.

Elementary, my dear Watson.

Aggarwal: I hear Durrani Saheb taking a different perspective from where *The Spy Chronicles* ended. In that book, Aditya Sinha asked you both to come up with a roadmap. What I hear from Durrani Saheb is something like, 'No—let's watch and see what happens in Kashmir on the ground first. Then each side will determine its own policies based on security considerations.' That is a different perspective on the bilateral relationship—or the trilateral relationship, if you include Kashmir—from where you were in 2018 with *The Spy Chronicles*. Is that an accurate assessment?

Durrani: Yes, to an extent. Whatever we concluded in '47, '48 or '71 is not written in stone. Or when we were finishing that book. We still believed—Mr Dulat more than me—that we could work out a roadmap to address this bone of contention. And my take was, 'Sir, if it can be done, then let's work out how to move forward.' The way to achieve this has been spelled out in *The Spy Chronicles*.

We talked about different ways of approaching it. Mr Dulat believes in certain steps, and I said that maybe a more structured approach would help. Up to that time, one still believed that it was possible.

Since then, Mr Dulat has conceded many times that his optimism has dampened. On my part, I never thought that I was a pessimist; I have always considered myself a realist, and that has also changed. Back then the abrogation of 370 had not happened; Modi had not shown his cards; and Hindutva had not taken India so firmly in its grip.

All these back channels and confidence-building measures only help if both sides are sincere about peace. Otherwise, the CBMs [confidence-building measures] can be used as deception. You win time to prepare yourself better for the next round.

Since so much changed, I suggest that now, it is up to us—especially the Pakistanis and the Kashmiris, working together or separately—to ensure that any design, in which the Kashmir problem is not resolved to the satisfaction of the three parties, does not succeed.

So essentially, we are talking about scuttling all efforts that do not serve the interest of the Kashmiris.

Aggarwal: Dulat Saheb, do you have any reflections?

Dulat: There are various ways of looking at this. Shakespeare once talked about a tide in the affairs of men. I think we've missed that tide many times.

What General Saheb suggested realistically is not such a bad idea. Let us wait and watch how Kashmir plays out in the next six months or a year. And then everyone will understand better where they stand.

But this idea that both of us are suggesting will disappoint the Kashmiris because what gives them hope is not necessarily that India and Pakistan are resolving anything but that Indians and Pakistanis are keeping Kashmiris engaged in all they do.

Aggarwal: Why is that level of Kashmiri engagement so important? Why not resolution?

Durrani: I suppose that whenever we talk about Kashmiris, Mr Dulat can describe their sentiments, aspirations and character much better. But to my mind, this is a people that is proud of their past. Their Kashmiriyat takes precedence over any nationalism or religion.

These people will continue to fight until their grievances are addressed. We have got to the present point because of how the Kashmiris responded to Indian and Pakistani policies. If they had pinned their hopes on us, they have been disappointed because we have not delivered. If the Indians and people like Modi ride roughshod over them, then the consequences of militancy are not because of any acts of ours, but how the Kashmiris themselves have acted, at times across the religious divide.

Maybe our two countries are so dumb that they have no idea that disingenuously playing certain cards—the sectarian with the Shiites in Kargil, or the religious with the Pandits in the South, would not deceive the people of Jammu and Kashmir.

Aggarwal: Today it's an unspoken assumption that when we talk about peace or peace building, we inevitably come back to Kashmir. We don't talk about any of the other tracks. In your assessments, does this mean that the centrality of Kashmir has been accepted on both sides? For Pakistanis, that has been the core contention. I don't hear Dulat Saheb mentioning any of the other tracks like confidence-building measures through restoring communications, trade, transportation links or anything about water-sharing, Siachen or Sir Creek. It's just Kashmir today. Is it safe to assume that?

Dulat: Neil, don't get me wrong. I mention Kashmir because Pakistan will not stop mentioning it. When the new Pakistani Prime Minister Shahbaz Sharif talks about Kashmir and says that the situation there is not acceptable, then I'm sorry to say I don't think he knows what he is talking about.

Let's put Kashmir on the back burner—this is something that Pakistani Prime Minister Imran Khan had once suggested. This is what suits India. The first baby steps that we could take would be to restore visas and bring back High Commissioners. We don't have a High Commissioner in Islamabad and Pakistan doesn't have a High Commissioner here.

In every way, what we are projecting is that Pakistan doesn't matter. It is Pakistan which pulled out its High Commissioner after the abrogation to make a point. Surely, we can start talking again once the two foreign ministers and the two foreign secretaries talk, if people at the top are agreeable to it. I think that's a good sign.

I'm told that you can't get an Indian visa in Islamabad. Here, a few visas are given but very selectively. So the people-to-people contacts that General Saheb mentioned have reached their lowest point. Pakistan kindly opened the Kartarpur Corridor, but no one knows when it is open and when it is closed. You can go there but still not make it in.

Some time back, the minister for trade in Pakistan said, 'We must have trade with India. It's more important to us than to India. We must break the logjam.' But it doesn't happen.

Let the new government in Pakistan apply themselves to this question of India, and then we can decide. I think young Bilawal should do that. From what one hears, he has a goodish mind. Then, reach out to somebody here. It's a question of not just ringing the bell but somebody hearing it.

I used to say that the best way to break this logjam is for Imran to come to Delhi and have lunch with Modiji in Hyderabad House. Now there is a new setup in Pakistan. But it doesn't matter which setup you have.

I think you need to think this out. I don't blame either side but I feel India thinks, 'What can Pakistan give us?' And Pakistan—without applying itself or realizing anything—says, 'This is not acceptable.' What is it that is not acceptable? Do you understand what you're saying when you say that something is not acceptable? You say that the situation in Kashmir is not acceptable but you don't know what the situation in Kashmir is.

So, Neil, I think you're looking for a way out.

[*Both men start to laugh.*]

I think you should be able to find a way out. Take a mix of what General Saheb and I have said, concoct a witches' brew and make something of it.

Aggarwal: Part of the problem in being a psychiatrist and spending my life managing conflicts is that I can see both sides. It would be easier if I were entirely sympathetic to a hawkish Indian perspective or to the Pakistani perspective. But like you both, I have gone to India, Pakistan and Jammu and Kashmir. I have spent significant amounts of time with people there. I have read across multiple perspectives to understand what is at stake for parties that position themselves as diametrically opposed to each other. In that respect, I don't think that there is any way out.

That's been the biggest lesson in writing this book. When I moderate our sessions, speak with you both on the phone and reflect on my transcriptions of our words, I realize that there is no way out, but there's also no alternative.

Dulat: Yes, that's right.

Aggarwal: That's also the tragedy of the situation. Dulat Saheb, you've talked about grand gestures, such as Imran Khan or Shahbaz Sharif going to Delhi to have lunch with Modiji. I wonder if the grandest gesture instead would be for India to announce elections in Jammu and Kashmir. Or for India to announce statehood for Jammu and Kashmir.

So much of the thinking that you've described, Dulat Saheb, rests on the assumption of taking the post-2019 situation in Jammu and Kashmir as settled, and I don't see Pakistani sentiment agreeing with that, based on what General Saheb has said and what one reads in the Pakistani media. I think the Indian side has to make a gesture of goodwill, given the disproportionate amount of power that India wields in Jammu and Kashmir, and say something like, 'We're going to create an opening.' I don't think either of you would disagree with that.

But I don't think that's enough anymore. If I were to speak from a realpolitik Pakistani foreign policy establishment perspective, I imagine that they would look at the announcement of statehood and think that Kashmiris already had statehood even before 2019, so why would this be a concession to them? They may see it as a step forward in a relative sense but still a step backward in an absolute sense compared to where relations were before 2019.

This is the issue that I see.

Dulat: That's exactly it. The challenge, to go back to Shakespeare, is how to create hope where there is no hope.

I think I was trying to communicate something similar to your last idea. It would be wishful thinking, but if Delhi were to announce restoration of statehood and simultaneous elections, these would be developments that Pakistan could take credit for, whether Pakistan understands it or not. Of course, we would not give Pakistan credit.

It's a question of what one can make out of the current situation. In the past, as General Durrani will recall, we used to have a lot of discussions about the separatists. When the separatists started moving forward in talks in the early 2000s, I said that we have an opening there. Pakistan is holding them back; if it were to cooperate a little and encourage them to move forward, then maybe we could resolve this matter.

Now, when I said this, a lot of people said, 'You're being too clever by half.' I was not being clever. I was telling them the reality of the ground situation. That time is gone. That's why I was talking about the tide in the affairs of men. That tide has gone.

But today, if Delhi were to announce the restoration of statehood and simultaneous elections with a level playing field, then at least Kashmiris would have a government of their own, whether it was good, bad or wretched. The Kashmiris have criticized various leaders at various times, but one of the lessons that they have learned since 2019 is that your own government, however bad, is better than being run by somebody.

Durrani: The best approach or formula that we may accept one day as the only practical way to move forward is one that has already happened in some parts of the world. It is what Gujral referred to as sub-regionalization. Wise man that he was, he did not spell it out clearly, but having seen developments in Europe and followed the concept of the European Union, I think what he meant was that instead of an overarching agreement between India and Pakistan, let the adjacent subregions of the two countries bring together their respective populations that had so much in common with each other, and thus detoxify the venomous relationship between India and Pakistan.

For example, in the European Union, Austria and Bavaria are neighbours who understand each other. They handle their local issues without having to look to the centres of power in Brussels or Berlin. So those relations become more important. You allow the neighbouring regions to interact with each other. The borders become irrelevant.

We experimented with something like this briefly with the two Punjabs movement, in which the chief ministers hoped people could play kabaddi, do a bit of duty-free trade (I wouldn't call it smuggling) and work on projects like Kartarpur.

The Punjabis, the Sindhis, the Bengalis, the Kashmiris from both sides could work together without changing either side's political models or nature of the borders. A stage might arrive where you don't even think about United Nations resolutions or Article 370s, and are simply comfortable with the people next door. The Bavarians often told Berlin or Bonn: 'We are all Germans but we can empathize much better with the Swiss or the Austrians, than the Rheinlanders or the Prussians.'

They reached this arrangement after 200 years of acrimony, so if we too want to take another 130 years, that's perfectly all right. But this seems to be the way to go. It will not be dependent upon policies in Delhi or Islamabad, on people like Doval or some other people here, or on those no-good doers who are always good for throwing spanners but never raise a little finger to get things moving on ground.

That's the way, if you want a pleasant-sounding ending for the book, which is more practical too. This can be done, and will probably happen, because ultimately power lies with the people and not with the centres of state.

Aggarwal: But the centre still determines visa access and who can meet where. At the time of the two Punjabs exchange, the visa regimes were more liberal. Under the current dispensation when the visa regimes are more restrictive, for the two Punjabs this can only happen at Kartarpur. It can be done with the diaspora in countries like Canada, the UK or the US. But then, those communities are not in India and Pakistan.

Dulat: Yes. That's true.

Aggarwal: There is also a challenge to Durrani Saheb's idea of building peace lobbies to put pressure on politicians on both sides: that if they felt their political positions endangered, they would act to bring peace. But what one learns from studies of political psychology is that international relations or foreign policies very rarely impact voting behaviour unless there is an acute threat or a mass conscription into war, like the demonstrations in the US against the draft during the Vietnam War. However, India and Pakistan have chronic, low-intensity conflict which does not directly affect most people; most of the people on both sides of the border don't see their loved ones maimed or killed. In the absence of intense experiences, it's unlikely peace lobbies will be strong enough to exert pressure on politicians to change their calculus.

Dulat: I wouldn't say that there is no peace lobby, but it has weakened in India over time. Let me put it bluntly: after Dr Manmohan Singh's time.

Durrani: Peace lobbies were building up. I don't know what checked their growth. Was it Modi's arrival? Or coronavirus? There are groups like SAFMA [South Asian Free Media Association] and even the ex-servicemen had created bi-national groups to work towards peace. These people were coming together to promote peace, but something has gone wrong, and I can't put my finger on what it is.

Otherwise, over time, like Clausewitz's theory of expanding torrents, these small streams would have joined together to form a peace-tsunami. And there would have been no way the decision-makers could have ignored the gathering storm.

One has not heard about peace lobbies lately. Some peace activists like Gautam Navlakha have been put behind bars—not that this is going to stop him from doing what he wants to do. But these kinds of heavy-handed acts discourage others—though not for long.

Aggarwal: I wonder whether we should end the book here. It's not what we intended.

Dulat: The point is for us to talk honestly.

Aggarwal: Yes.

Dulat: One comes to the sad conclusion that there doesn't seem to be a silver lining. We have to wait it out.

We started this whole discussion on day one with Track II. Track II is still functional. They do meet—there was a meeting recently. There is going to be another one in soon. So those efforts are continuing, and they are good efforts. At least they provide something for people on both sides to carry back home.

That's why I said before that when you're together for three days, a lot of conversations take place outside the meeting room—*The Spy Chronicles* tried to develop this idea.

Track II—and I attended one not long ago in Muscat—is held in the most cordial atmosphere. They are good people. They talk sense. Surprising as it may sound, somebody even suggested having a meeting in Goa.

Aggarwal: You both have been rather ambivalent about Track II. It seems that even though it brings people together and allows for new ideas to emerge outside of the box, it doesn't seem to change much in terms of actual foreign policy establishment thinking.

Dulat: No, it can't. Let's face it: the real thing is Track I—bringing the two singers on board.

Durrani: We have spoken enough about tracks—one, two or six. They have their place but ultimately, it's the state track that one likes to influence. Peace marchers coming in large numbers, carrying white flags, or with Kalashnikovs.

If you ask me, it must happen because both the states are stupid. Haven't we heard and read enough, for example, from Barbara Tuchman[14] when she talks about the March of Folly? She starts from the early Greek times. All governments have acted unwisely. Some of them did manage to take care of their own people better than the others. Otherwise, when it comes to the bigger picture, they hardly ever acted for the greater good.

And that's why one says whenever something happens like the abrogation of 370 or what happened at the end of '89, let people mobilize themselves. People have to be encouraged. Sometimes they will take up the gun—that will happen. That's the only way to put some sanity in the heads of the decision-makers.

A psychiatrist would understand that probably much better than others.

---

3. A Befitting Ending: No One Gets What They Want, and We've All Got to Live with It

Neil Krishan Aggarwal: Our group process has reached a very different place from where we began. It's more pessimistic;

it's darker. But it's also accurate. It's the culmination of all the times that we have met.

I think I was misguided in assuming that there could be a positive ending that is refreshing and optimistic. General Saheb put me in my place with his WhatsApp message. I've made my peace with that now because neither of you are saying that there isn't a chance for peace—it's just not going to happen at the government-to-government level. If there's going to be peace, it has to be people-driven. It's unfortunate that at this point in history, the people of India and Pakistan are not motivated enough to act in that direction.

It doesn't mean that peace won't happen. It just means that peace won't happen now.

Dulat: Hold on for a moment, Neil. You're beginning to disappoint us. We've done our bit. We've spoken as honestly as we can.

I mentioned earlier about the witches' brew. I'm sure you have read *Macbeth*: This is what you are. This is what you're going to be. And this is what you could be. That's what you need to make people understand.

Aggarwal: I hear that as a difference between the two of you. This seems to reflect the eternal optimist in you, Dulat Saheb.

Dulat: I know that you want to see a positive ending. But we'd be lying to ourselves and to each other if we didn't recognize that a lot has changed in the past four years, since *The Spy Chronicles*. It's a different world in here.

You've got to figure out a way. That's what psychiatrists are good at.

Aggarwal: I have multiple ways. I just don't know how realistic they are.

Dulat [*laughing*]: We've been realistic enough. Your way must be the ultimate way.

Aggarwal: Throughout our sessions, I've refrained from sharing my personal background. Readers are going to be more intrigued by your backgrounds and motivations than mine because I'm not a public figure as the two of you are.

Since this is not psychotherapy, and the rules of therapist non-disclosure do not apply, I will share my motivations for pursuing this work. Like Dulat Saheb, I grew up in a post-Partition family hearing about the splendours of Lahore and Peshawar. I have this ardent desire to see both countries come together and have people-to-people exchanges. I want access to these ancestral areas. I grew up essentially grieving the loss of a cosmopolitan, multilingual, multireligious lifestyle my grandparents described, which was never truly mine. That's what we call the intergenerational transmission of trauma.

You might remember that several sessions ago, I asked you both about your professional trajectories and how you got into intelligence work. As I ponder my own formation, I became a psychiatrist and social scientist partly because I was working through the loss and grief of so many post-Partition families in my community, how that led to whole families migrating, and how, effectively, distant governments manifest their cruel presence in the everyday lives of ordinary people. If a patient comes to my office, my natural impulse as a physician is not to say, 'Your situation is bleak. It is hopeless and nothing will change for the better.' Our training is to find solutions and try to inspire hope. Maybe that's misguided here because—

Dulat: Let me stop you here. What you're saying is perfectly right, but the solution has to come from you. You're explaining yourself, and I think that is the best ending for this book. You must have the last word. People have heard the two of us enough. They know what we think and what we're all about. But your last word is what will count in this project.

Durrani: I agree. As far as hope is concerned, it must never be killed. *Duniya bar umeed qaim ast* [The world stands on hope]. That's a very old saying in our part of the world. But at the same time, you do not build hopes and then let them get dashed, because that becomes even more dangerous. Be realistic on certain things—all the stumbling blocks, the possible ways forward, what can change the situation for the better. But I agree with Mr Dulat. Have the last word. Say that the situation may look bad but some things offer a silver lining.

Aggarwal: Here is what I propose. I go back to the psychology of intractable conflicts. I'll explain some general points so we have a common understanding, and then think about how we can apply this to India and Pakistan.

Psychologists see all intractable conflicts as sharing certain characteristics:[15] (1) they last at least one generation and result in accumulated hostility, (2) they result in physical violence, (3) they are perceived as irresolvable with zero-sum outcomes, and (4) they require vast economic, military and technological investments to manage. People learn to live with anxiety, fear, hatred and stress in the hopes of winning the conflict, or at least not losing it. Societies cope by constructing collective memories that are not necessarily based on an objective facts but on interpretations that suit their interests. These memories justify the conflict, praise the nation, delegitimize opponents and centre on victimhood. Such narratives help people cope with their negative emotions. The narratives justify violence against the enemy. They endow people with a sense of superiority and foster unity. They also prepare people for more violence. These narratives are shared widely in educational materials like textbooks and in cultural materials like books, films, music and monuments.

We know this to be true: as Durrani Saheb mentioned before, one area of disagreement between Indians and Pakistanis is their rival interpretations of history.

Conflict resolution—the political process through which parties eliminate the incompatibility of their goals and interests, and establish a new situation of compatibility—is also psychological:[16] negotiators and governments must change their beliefs. They must commit to collaboration. They must bring constituents along. They also have to stop vilifying opponents. Reconciliation is the process by which most members of society change narratives about themselves, their former adversary and the relationship between both groups.

Again, Durrani Saheb is showing us his psychological depth by delinking peacemaking from conflict resolution between states and emphasizing reconciliation on a people-to-people level.

So how do we do this? History teaches us that we must do this in the following ways:[17]

Each society must change its goals: Establishing institutions and mechanisms for formal conflict resolution signals to all parties that leaders aren't going to keep pursuing goals in a zero-sum way that causes conflicts with others. Instead, people must find common goals. After World War II, the leaders of France and Germany ended centuries of conflict by envisioning the political and economic union of Europe, with Franco–German reconciliation as its pillar. That could happen in India and Pakistan as well.

Each society must change its beliefs about the adversary: Rather than delegitimize enemies, each side must recognize that other side has a common humanity, with people who possess a range of different views.

Each society must change its beliefs about itself: Members of society have to grapple with their direct responsibility for causing and prolonging conflict. Each side must recognize the suffering of the former adversary rather than claim a monopoly on victimhood.

Those are the theories. Now for some practice. Let's go back to the Composite Dialogue framework since you both seemed to endorse it. Does it have legal force?

Durrani: It was never legally binding. Even the Simla Accord, signed by two Prime Ministers, could not be invoked in a court of law. The Composite Dialogue was merely a sound framework, which the two countries could follow if they liked.

Dulat: That is the case with everything between us!

Aggarwal: Of all the tracks in the Composite Dialogue, I would start with initiatives that require the least psychological changes. I'd start in two areas where both sides could claim victories.

First, combating drug trafficking jointly requires no change in psychological perceptions. While it requires cross-border cooperation among counter-narcotics agencies, both governments have experience in putting aside differences in the largest interest of common humanitarian concerns. Sadly, both Punjabs are struggling with increases in opiate addiction. Sponsoring conferences for academics and health practitioners in SAARC member countries would be a way to exchange medical and public health information. This could convert counter-narcotics operations into a multilateral initiative with strong international support. The main issue here is just granting a limited number of visas.

Second, religious tourism offers the most scope for people-to-people contacts where both countries could claim victories without requiring any psychological changes. Let's start with what the Government of Pakistan can do. As recently as November 2021, Pakistani leaders across the political spectrum wished Pakistani Hindus a Happy Diwali.[18] Excluding the religious political parties in Pakistan, there seems to be a clear effort to recognize Pakistani Hindus and not conflate them with all Indians.

We know there are political angles to their statements, but let's give these leaders the benefit of the doubt. They can promote the image of Pakistan as a protector of minority rights, by permitting religious visas to Indians for established Hindu pilgrimage sites. For example, the Hinglaj Mata temple in Balochistan has long attracted Sindhi and Rajput Hindus. The Odero Lal temple in Sindh, a shrine to Lord Jhulelal, would interest Sindhi Hindus. I would start there. It's a win for the Government of India, especially under the BJP, for it can claim it is batting for the rights of Hindus, domestically and abroad.

If the Government of Pakistan is truly interested in projecting an image of defending Kashmiri rights across religious the divide, it could score a coup by renovating the Sharada Peeth temple complex in the Neelum Valley, which has cultural, historical and religious significance for Kashmiri Pandits. The tried and tested Srinagar–Muzaffarabad bus route can be reinstated. This kind of initiative functions on two tracks: officially with the bureaucracy in Kashmir, and people-to-people exchanges.

Such initiatives promote the kind of sub-regionalization that Durrani Saheb has lauded.

For its part, the Government of India could promote religious tourism as well. The BJP government has already indicated its interest in catering to minorities in Pakistan through bills such as CAA–NRC. Therefore, allowing Pakistani Hindus and Sikhs to travel to Indian pilgrimage sites would be an easy public relations win. The Government of Pakistan could claim a victory as well by showing how it treats its minority populations with trust rather than as suspect populations. Amritsar, Ayodhya, Rishikesh and Varanasi are just some of the cities that have the capacity for large-scale infrastructure.

There are two areas where the Government of India could reach Muslims in Pakistan. First, letting them visit the Chishti-order dargahs in Ajmer and Delhi would be an easy victory, as they are established pilgrimage sites with cultural, historical and religious significance, especially among Sunnis. Second, Pakistani Shiites could be granted visas to participate in Muharram activities in Lucknow, Hyderabad and elsewhere. These efforts would bolster the BJP's credibility and make up for the diplomatic fallout among Muslim-majority countries after its spokesperson was recently accused of blaspheming Prophet Muhammad.

The advantage of these initiatives is that each government can pressure the other in a positive way. For instance, if the Government of Pakistan were to unilaterally announce religious tourism for Hindus and Sikhs alongside a liberalized visa regime, then the Government of India would start to face pressure to do something similar. And vice versa.

All the other tracks in the Composite Dialogue—for example, Sir Creek, Siachen, water sharing and, of course, Jammu and Kashmir—require societies to truly reflect on the psychology of intractable conflict. Changing perceptions of one's own society, the adversary' society, the relationship between both societies, and ultimate goals, wouldn't be realistic at present. So, let's keep to recommendations based on, to return to *Macbeth*, what we are and what we're going to be.

What we *could* be is a topic that we'll continue discussing behind closed doors. We can choose to reveal ourselves when the time is right.

Notes

Introduction

1   Peter Jones, *Track Two Diplomacy in Theory and Practice* (Stanford: Stanford University Press, 2015).

2   Many of the psychological questions are drawn from: Deborah L. Cabaniss, Sabrina Cherry, Carolyn J. Douglas and Anna Schwartz, *Psychodynamic Psychotherapy: A Clinical Manual* (West Sussex: John Wiley & Sons Ltd, 2011).

3   Questions on childhood, adolescent and early adulthood are drawn from: Cabaniss et al., 2011. Questions on occupational history are drawn from: Group for the Advancement of Psychiatry, 'How and Why Clinicians Should Take a Thorough Work History During COVID-19 and Beyond', *Psychiatric Times* (18 May 2020). Questions on the psychology of espionage are drawn from: Ursula Wilder, 'Inside the Mind of the Spy: Agents Struggle in the Shadows', *Brookings* (5 July 2012). https://www.brookings.edu/opinions/inside-the-mind-of-the-spy-agents-struggle-in-the-shadows/; David L. Charney and John A. Irvin, 'The Psychology of Espionage', *The Intelligencer: Journal of U.S. Intelligence Studies* 22, no. 1 (2016): 71–77.

4   Questions on identity come from: American Psychiatric Association, 'Cultural Formulation Interview' (Washington, DC: American Psychiatric Association, 2013); American Psychiatric Association,

'Cultural Formulation Interview Supplementary Module 5: Spirituality, Religion, and Moral Traditions', (Washington, DC: American Psychiatric Association, 2013); Juan E. Mezzich, Giovanni Caracci, Horacio Fabrega, Jr. and Laurence J. Kirmayer, 'Cultural Formulation Guidelines', *Transcultural Psychiatry* 46, no. 3 (2009): 383–405; Vamik D. Volkan, 'Psychological Concepts Useful in the Building of Political Foundations Between Nations: Track II Diplomacy', *Journal of the American Psychoanalytic Association* 35, no. 4 (1987): 903–935.

5   Questions on perceptions of foreign policy establishments come from Richard K. Hermann, James F. Voss, Tonya Y.E. Schooler and Joseph Ciarrochi, 'Images in International Relations: An Experimental Test of Cognitive Schemata', *International Studies Quarterly* 41, no. 3 (1997): 403–433.

1: Life after *The Spy Chronicles*

1   Jawed Naqvi, 'Spy Book Release Spurs Criticism of Repression in Held Kashmir', *Dawn* (24 May 2018).
2   Ibid.
3   Ibid.
4   Ibid.
5   Sushant Singh, 'True Lies and Spies', *Indian Express* (2 June 2018).
6   Praveen Swami, 'The Punjabi-Uncle Way of Peacemaking', *Business Standard* (28 May 2018).
7   Rezaul H. Laskar, 'Review: The Spy Chronicles by A.S. Dulat, Asad Durrani and Aditya Sinha', *Hindustan Times* (8 June 2018).
8   Aisha Saeed, 'Book Review: The Spy Chronicles: RAW, ISI and The Illusion of Peace', *Daily Pakistan* (24 May 2018).
9   Nyla Ali Khan, 'Spy Chronicles: A Review', *Daily Times* (6 June 2018).
10 Imad Zafar, 'How Controversial Is "The Spy Chronicles"?', *Express Tribune* (3 June 2018).
11 'GHQ Summons Former ISI Chief to Explain Stance on Book Co-authored with Ex-RAW Chief', *Dawn* (25 May 2018).
12 Ibid.

. Qadeer Tanoli, 'Former ISI Chief Asad Durrani Placed on ECL', *Express Tribune* (29 May 2018).
14. '"The Spy Chronicles": Nawaz for Credible Panel to Probe Facts', *News International* (26 May 2018).
15. 'Durrani–Dulat Book Violated Military Rules: Pakistan Army', Indo-Asian News Service (26 May 2018).
16. '"If Politicians Co-Authored a Book with Indians, They Would Be Charged with Treason": Rabbani', *Express Tribune* (25 May 2018).
17. 'Ex-RAW Chief Defends Durrani over "Spy Chronicles"', Asian News International (29 May 2018).
18. 'The Spy Chronicles: Defence Ministry Raises Objection on Removal of Durani's Name from ECL', *Express Tribune* (22 February 2019).
19. 'Former ISI Chief Durrani Files Contempt Case for Not Removing His Name from No-Fly List', Publishing India.com (25 June 2019).
20. Malik Asad, 'Govt Has Restored Pension to Former ISI head, LHC Told', *Dawn* (2 October 2020).
21. 'A Q&A with Asad Durrani | Honour Among Spies', Harper Broadcast, HarperCollins Publishers India (2020). https://harpercollins.co.in/honour-among-spies-interview/.
22. 'Asad Durrani Was Affiliated with RAW since 2008: MOD', *News International* (28 June 2018).
23. 'Islamabad High Court Orders Removal of Former ISI Chief Asad Durrani's Name from No-Fly List', Asian News International (4 March 2021).
24. Vamik Volkan, 'Psychoanalysis and Diplomacy: Part I. Individual and Large Group Identity', *Journal of Applied Psychoanalytic Studies* 1, no. 1 (1999): 29–55.
25. In May 1997, Indian Prime Minister Inder Kumar Gujral met his Pakistani counterpart Nawaz Sharif in Male, Maldives. The two agreed on the Composite Dialogue Process (CDP) whereby both countries would discuss all outstanding issues simultaneously. The eight issues were: Peace and Security, including confidence-building measures (CBMs); Jammu and Kashmir; Siachen; Wullar Barrage/Tulbul Navigation Project; Sir Creek; Economic and Commercial Cooperation; Terrorism and Drug Trafficking; and the Promotion of Friendly Exchanges in various fields. The CDP ended with the attacks in Mumbai on 26 November 2008. See Sajjad Padder, 'The

Composite Dialogue between India and Pakistan: Structure, Process and Agency', Working Paper No. 65, Heidelberg Papers in South Asian and Comparative Politics, Heidelberg University, Heidelberg (2012).

26   In an editorial for the *Washington Post*, Former US Secretary of State Henry Kissinger wrote, 'Far too often the Ukrainian issue is posed as a showdown: whether Ukraine joins the East or the West. But if Ukraine is to survive and thrive, it must not be either side's outpost against the other—it should function as a bridge between them.' See Henry A. Kissinger, 'To Settle the Ukraine Crisis, Start at the End', *Washington Post* (5 March 2014). Consistent with the aims of our project, Secretary Kissinger also advocated for the role of psychology in diplomacy, observing that 'Putin is a serious strategist—on the premises of Russian history. Understanding U.S. values and psychology are not his strong suits. Nor has understanding Russian history and psychology been a strong point of U.S. policymakers.'

27   Opposition parties had planned a no-confidence vote against Prime Minister Imran Khan until he advised the President of Pakistan to dissolve the Parliament on 3 April 2022 and called for elections.

28   Asad Durrani later clarified that he headed the ISI when pro-Soviet groups were being neutralized.

29   This is a verse from the poem '*Chhod ke sab din o iman Mir jis ke vaste*' by Mir Taqi Mir (1723–1810).

30   The diplomat Shivshankar Menon was High Commissioner to Pakistan from 2003 to 2006.

31   *The Spy Chronicles* included an anecdote in which A.S. Dulat helped Asad Durrani's son who was travelling in India for business with a Pakistani passport and encountered issues with law enforcement.

32   Asad Durrani clarified that he was referring to an attack on 7 January 2020 when Iran's Islamic Revolutionary Guards Corps took responsibility for firing twenty-two missiles at two bases in Iraq where American troops were stationed. No American casualties were reported. The attack came in response to the American military killing Major General Qassim Suleimani, the spymaster and head of the Revolutionary Guards' influential Quds Force.

33   Asad Durrani is referring to the Baglihar Hydroelectric Power Project to whose construction Pakistan had objected under the Indus Water Treaty. In June 2010, both countries resolved this issue of the Chenab

River's water flows at a meeting of the Permanent Indus Water Commission. See Gargi Parsai, 'India, Pakistan Resolve Baglihar Dam Issue', *Hindu* (1 June 2010).

34   In *The Spy Chronicles*, Asad Durrani attributes the 'neighbour's neighbour' policy to Chanakya (375–283 BC), a political strategist who aided the first Mauryan emperor Chandragupta's military dominance.

35   A.S. Dulat is referring to an Indian Airlines flight that was hijacked from Kathmandu, Nepal, en route to New Delhi, India, on 24 December 1999.

36   Article 370 of the Indian Constitution allowed Jammu and Kashmir to preserve its special status, flag, constitution and administrative apparatus. It was abolished on 31 October 2019.

37   Article 35A of the Indian Constitution defined who could be classified as a 'permanent resident' of Jammu and Kashmir, according to which the state conferred rights such as property ownership.

38   Abhinandan Varthaman (b. 1983) is an Indian Air Force fighter pilot who was apprehended after his plane crossed into Pakistani airspace on 27 February 2019. He returned to India on 1 March 2019 after the Government of Pakistan released him as 'a gesture of peace'.

39   According to the Indira–Sheikh accord signed between the Kashmiri leader Sheikh Abdullah and India Prime Minister Indira Gandhi, Jammu and Kashmir dropped its aspiration for self-determination and became 'a constituent unit' of the Indian union with its own administrative structure under Article 370.

40   Jagmohan Malhotra (1927–2021) was the fifth Governor of Jammu and Kashmir from 1984 to 1989, and then from January to May 1990.

41   A.S. Dulat is referring to an incident in which Indian troops from the Central Reserve Police Force opened fire on Kashmiri civilians on the Gawkadal bridge in Srinagar.

42   Mufti Mohammad Sayeed (1936–2016) was the Chief Minister of Jammu and Kashmir from November 2002 to November 2005 and from March 2015 to January 2016.

43   Ho Chi Minh (1890–1969) was a Vietnamese revolutionary who fought against French–American imperial interests. He was Prime Minister from 1945 to 1955 and President from 1945 to 1969.

44   Former Pakistani President Pervez Musharraf proposed a four-point solution on Jammu and Kashmir: both sides would gradually

withdrawal troops, the territory would have self-governance, there would not be changes to the region's borders, and India and Pakistan would conduct a joint supervision mechanism. See 'Musharraf Offers Kashmir "Solution"', *Guardian* (5 December 2006).

2: The Psychological Foundations of Track II, People-to-People Diplomacy

1   William Davidson and Joseph Montville, 'Foreign Policy According to Freud,' *Foreign Policy*, no. 45 (Winter 1981-82): 145.

2   Ibid., 155.

3   Albert Einstein and Sigmund Freud, *Why War?* [1933], Redding: CAT Publishing Company (1991), 3.

4   Ibid., 5.

5   Ibid., 12.

6   Ibid., 17.

7   Ibid., 19.

8   Vamik Volkan, *Psychoanalysis, International Relations, and Diplomacy: A Sourcebook on Large-Group Psychology* (New York: Routledge, 2018).

9   ——, 'Psychoanalysis and Diplomacy Part I: Individual and Large Group Identity', *Journal of Applied Psychoanalytic Studies* 1, no. 1(1999): 29–30.

10   Mian Tahir Ashraf, M.N.M. Akhir and Javaid Akhtar Salyana, 'Mapping of Track Two Initiatives: A Case of Pakistan–India Conflict (1988–2001)', *Pakistan Journal of Social Sciences* 37, no.1 (2017): 16–29.

11   Muhammad Sajjad Malik, 'Track II Diplomacy and Its Impact on Pakistan India Peace Process', *Strategic Studies* 31, (2011): 108–128.

12   Pervaiz Iqbal Cheema, 'The Contribution of Track II towards India–Pakistan Relations', *South Asia Survey* 13, no. 2 (2006): 211–233.

13   Muhammad Khalique Kamboh, Sadoon Masood, Ghulam Mustafa and Nida Shabbir, 'Mapping of Outsource Diplomatic Initiatives: A Case of Pakistan-India Relations', *Journal of Indian Studies* 7, no. 1 (2021): 93–106.

14   Volkan, *Psychoanalysis* (2018), 5.

15   General Durrani is referring to this passage in *The Spy Chronicles*: 'One change I recall from soon after Partition was the absence of a matka. The shop halfway to school where we often stopped to sip water had a new owner. Unlike his Hindu predecessor, he had no use for the pitcher that contained the elixir of life.' (p. xix).

16   General Durrani is referring to this passage in *Honour Among Spies*: 'At an early age he started doubting the existence of God but changed his mind on Machiavellian grounds: "If there turned out to be a Creator in whom he did not believe, he would be in trouble; but if he retained faith in an Almighty who never existed, it should do him no harm." In due course, however, he did become a believer—again under the spell of some convoluted logic. His thesis ran more or less as follows: "Since man could not possibly fathom the concept of infinity in time and space, there must be a supreme entity who did—and that could only be God." One could bet that this man was destined to be perpetually in trouble.' See Asad Durrani, *Honour Among Spies* (Gurugram: HarperCollins, 2020), 16.

17   General Durrani is referring to this passage in *Honour Among Spies*. It is worth quoting in full since he offers readers a personal psychological assessment: 'While taking a mid-term test in his early school years, he did not do well in one of his favourite subjects, arithmetic. That should have taught him a useful lesson: to guard against overconfidence and not take things for granted. But when it happened ever so often—just when he had convinced himself that he had covered all the flanks and success was inevitable, something grievously went wrong—he started believing in the hidden hand of fate and decided that instead of exercising caution he would simply follow his instincts.' Durrani, *Honour*, 16.

18   As the crow flies, the distance between Lahore and Gujranwala is nearly 97 km.

19   See Asad Durrani, *Pakistan Adrift: Navigating Troubled Waters* (London: Hurst & Company, 2018).

20   Ayub Khan (1907–1974) was a military general who staged a coup d'état in 1958 against Iskandar Mirza and ruled Pakistan until resigning in 1969.

21   General Durrani is referring to Dr Rafi Muhammad Chaudhry (1903–1988), a professor of particle physics at Government College Lahore who helped to establish Pakistan's nuclear research programme.

22   *The Spy Chronicles* includes this recollection from General Durrani:
     'Do you know who cleared me for the posting ultimately? I was a
     senior instructor at the Command and Staff College, for us a prized
     position. When my name came up for the Germany posting, it had
     to be cleared by various agencies. One of them went to my in-laws'
     house in Model Town, Lahore, to ask about me. No one was at home,
     so they went and asked the neighbours' chowkidar, "Yeh kaise log
     hain?" That chap said, "Yeh acchhe log hain." I got the green signal and
     I always say that my neighbours' chowkidar provided the certificate
     that the intelligence agency sought.' See A.S. Dulat, Asad Durrani and
     Aditya Sinha, *The Spy Chronicles: RAW, ISI and the Illusion of Peace*
     (Gurugram: HarperCollins, 2018), 11.

23   Brent W. Roberts and Hee J. Yoon, 'Personality Psychology', *Annual
     Review of Psychology* 73 (2022): 489–516.

3: Case Studies in How We Become Indians and Pakistanis

1   Vamik Volkan, 'Psychoanalysis and Diplomacy: Part I. Individual and
     Large Group Identity', *Journal of Applied Psychoanalytic Studies* 1, no.
     1 (1999a): 31.

2   Ibid., 32.

3   Ibid., 41.

4   Ibid., 42.

5   Volkan, 'Psychoanalysis and Diplomacy Part II: Large-Group Rituals',
     Journal of Applied Psychoanalytic Studies 1, no. 3 (1999b): 223–247.

6   Sanjay Chaturvedi, 'Process of Othering in the Case of India and
     Pakistan', *Tijdschrift voor Economische en Sociale Geografie* 93, no. 2
     (2002): 157.

7   Volkan (1999b).

8   Geert Hofstede, 'Diplomats as Cultural Bridge Builders', in
     Intercultural Communication and Diplomacy, ed. Hannah Slavik Malta
     (DiploFoundation, 2008), 25–38.

9   Wilfred Bolewski, 'Diplomatic Processes and Cultural Variations:
     The Relevance of Culture in Diplomacy', *The Whitehead Journal of
     Diplomacy and International Relations* 9 (2008): 145–160.

10   Volkan (1999a).

11 Dattatraya Phadkar (1925–1985) was an all-rounder who played for India's test cricket team.

12 Starting in 1921, Sikandar Hayat Khan (1892–1942) became one of the leaders of the Punjab Unionist Party which mobilized to protect the interests of Muslim, Sikh and Hindu landowners.

13 Abdul Hafeez Kardar (1925–1996) was the first captain of Pakistan's test cricket team.

14 Major Dhyan Chand (1905–1979) was an Indian field hockey player who earned three Olympic gold medals in 1928, 1932 and 1936.

15 Shahid Javed Burki, *Pakistan: Fifty Years of Nationhood* (Boulder: Westview Press, 1999), p. 26.

16 *Khilona* was an Urdu monthly magazine popular in India and Pakistan that featured stories, poems, cartoons, and a column for young writers. The Dehlvi family owned the corporate house that published the magazine Shama until the 1980s. See Firoz Bakht Ahmed, '"Khilona" Will Always Live', *Deccan Herald* (February 26).

17 Subhas Chandra Bose (1897–1945) was a nationalist leader who was President of the Indian Nationalist Congress from January 1938 to April 1939 and the second leader of the Indian National Army from July 1943 to August 1945. Towards the end of his life, he renounced non-violence as a tactic for India's independence from the British Empire.

18 Bhagat Singh (1907–1931) was an Indian revolutionary who was hanged at the age of twenty-three years at Lahore Central Jail. He was convicted of killing the British police officer John Saunders and the British police constable Channan Singh who chased him after Saunders's murder.

19 Krishan Chander (1914–1977) wrote over a hundred works of fiction spanning multiple genres in Hindi and Urdu.

20 Nirad C. Chaudhuri (1897–1999) was an Indian writer born in Kishoregunj, Mymensingh, East Bengal (now Bangladesh) who settled in England. He is best known for his book *The Autobiography of an Unknown Indian* published in 1951.

21 Khushwant Singh (1915–2014) was an Indian author whose *Train to Pakistan*, possibly his most famous work and widely considered a classic of Partition literature.

22   Arundhati Roy (b. 1961) won the Booker Prize for Fiction in 1997 for her novel *The God of Small Things* and has written political commentaries on a wide range of issues.

23   Pankaj Mishra (b. 1969) is an Indian essayist and novelist.

24   Sunil Gavaskar (b. 1949) was a captain of the Indian cricket team during the 1970s and 1980s and is considered one of the greatest opening batsmen in the history of the sport.

25   Balbir Singh Dosanjh (1924–2020) was an Indian field hockey player who earned three Olympic gold medals in 1948, 1952 and 1956.

26   Milkha Singh (1929–2021) was an Indian sprinter who earned a gold medal at the 1958 British Empire and Commonwealth Games, two gold medals at the 1958 Asian Games in Tokyo, and two gold medals at the 1962 Asian Games in Jakarta.

27   Abdul Khaliq (1933–1988) was a Pakistani sprinter who won gold medals at the 1954 Asian Games in Manila and the 1958 Asian Games in Tokyo.

28   Morarji Desai (1896–1995) was the sixth Prime Minister of India from 24 March 1977 to 28 July 1979. He was awarded Pakistan's highest civilian award, the Nishan-e-Pakistan, in 1988 for working with Pakistan's General Zia-ul-Haq to improve relations between both countries. Notably, he also detested India's RAW, claiming that Indira Gandhi used the agency to spy on domestic opposition leaders. See Simrin Sirur, 'Morarji Desai—The Indian Prime Minister Who Won Pakistan's Highest Civilian Honour', *The Print* (29 February 2020).

29   Chandra Shekhar (1927–2007) was the eighth Prime Minister of India from 10 November 1990 to 21 June 1991.

30   Mani Shankar Aiyar (b. 1941) is an Indian politician who belongs to the Indian National Congress party. He has been a member of both houses in India's Parliament and served as India's first consul-general in Karachi from 1978 to 1982.

31   Imran Ahmed Khan Niazi (b. 1952) served as captain of the Pakistan's cricket team intermittently between 1982 and 1992. He led his team to Pakistan's only Cricket World Cup victory in 1992.

32   Kapil Dev Ramlal Nikhanj (b. 1959) led India's cricket team to World Cup victory in 1983, and has been the youngest captain, at the age of twenty-four, to win the World Cup for any team. He is the only player in history have taken more than 400 wickets and scored more than 5,000 runs in test matches.

33   Ian Terence Botham (b. 1955) was a former English cricketer who held the world record for the most Test wickets from 1986 to 1988.

34   Richard John Hadlee (b. 1951) was a former English cricketer who became the first player to score 1,000 runs and take 100 wickets in the history of one-day international matches.

35   On 30 October 2006 at about 5 a.m., eighty-two people died in a madrasa in Chenagai village in Bajaur agency. The United States initially denied the attack but American analysts pointed out that only the American military had sufficient precision weapons capability to carry out a strike at night.

36   Field Marshal Sam Hormusji Framji Jamshedji Manekshaw (1914–2008) was the Chief of Army Staff of the Indian Army during the 1971 war with Pakistan.

37   Narasimhan Ram (b. 1945) is an Indian journalist who has been the managing director and editor-in-chief of the English-language Indian newspaper, *The Hindu*.

38   The *Hindustan Times* reports: 'Jaishankar met Nawaz Sharif again at Jati Umra in Raiwind on December 25, 2015, when PM Modi stunned the world by landing at Lahore from Kabul while en route to Delhi and also attended the wedding of PM's granddaughter. Apparently, at Raiwind, PM Nawaz Sharif quizzed Jaishankar about why he was speaking to him in English. The now Indian foreign minister replied because he was a foreign head of state to him. It is another matter that Jaishankar has links with Lahore through his maternal side.' See Shishir Gupta, 'PM Sharif's Toxic Language on Malik's Conviction Belies Hopes of Normal Ties', *Hindustan Times* (26 May 2022).

39   G.S. Bajpai was the head of RAW from 1990 to 1991.

40   General Muhammad Zia-ul-Haq (1924–1988) became Pakistan's sixth president after a coup d'état in 1977 and promote the Islamicization of the country's secular laws that were inherited from the British Empire.

41   Asad Durrani writes in *Pakistan Adrift* about his experiences at the Frankfurt Book Fair: 'I had selected a book from an Indian stand, to be paid for and collected by a member of my staff. It was delivered on the last day, with compliments from the Indian publisher and a note saying it was an honour for them that the ambassador of Pakistan had visited their stall' See Asad Durrani, *Pakistan Adrift: Navigating Troubled Waters* (London: Hurst & Co., 2018), 59.

42 Mobasher Jawed Akbar (b. 1951) is a prominent Indian journalist and politician who was India's Minister of State for External Affairs in Narendra Modi's cabinet from 2016 to 2018.

4: Making Peace Can Be as Hard as War: Why Some Initiatives Succeed and Others Fail

1   Robert Axelrod, 'Schema Theory: An Information Processing Model of Perception and Cognition', *American Political Science Review* 67, no. 4 (1973): 1248.
2   Richard K. Hermann, James F. Voss, Tonya Y.E. Schooler and Joseph Ciarrochi, 'Images in International Relations: An Experimental Test of Cognitive Schemata', *International Studies Quarterly* 41, no. 3 (1997): 403–433.
3   Ibid.
4   Michael D. Young and Mark Schafer, 'Is There Method in Our Madness? Ways of Assessing Cognition in International Relations', *Mershon International Studies Review* 42, no. 1 (1998): 79.
5   Hein G. Kiessling, *Faith, Unity, Discipline: The ISI of Pakistan* (Noida: HarperCollins *Publishers* India, 2016).
6   B. Raman, *The Kaoboys of R&AW: Down Memory Lane*, New Delhi: Lancer Publishers & Distributors (2013).
7   Hermann et al. (1997).
8   Ibid., 408.
9   Asad Durrani is referring to The Pew Research Center's Global Attitudes Project from 2008 which polled respondents in Muslim-majority countries about a range of topics, including perceptions of the United States. The full report can be found here: https://www.pewresearch.org/wp-content/uploads/sites/2/2008/09/Pew-2008-Pew-Global-Attitudes-Report-3-September-17-2pm.pdf.
10 General Qamar Javed Bajwa (b. 1960) has been Pakistan's Chief of Army Staff since 29 November 2016.
11 General Bajwa's statement came on 2 April 2022, two days after former Prime Minister Imran Khan accused US President Joseph Biden's administration of conspiring to topple his government. At a forum in Islamabad, General Bajwa said, 'We have a history of long and excellent strategic relationship with the U.S., which remains our

largest export market. Pakistan enjoys a close strategic relationship with China demonstrated by our commitment towards Pakistan China Economic Corridor. We seek to broaden and expand our ties with both the countries without impacting our relationship with the other.' See Khalid Qayum, 'Pakistan Seeks to Expand U.S. Relations, Army Chief Says', *Bloomberg* (2 April 2022).

12 Bilawal Bhutto Zardari (b. 1988) is the Chairman of the Pakistan's Peoples Party and Pakistan's current Foreign Minister. He is the son of late Prime Minister Benazir Bhutto and former President Asif Ali Zardari.

13 Asad Durrani is referring to the Pugwash workshop featuring members of Indian and Pakistani political parties, non-governmental organizations and civil society who interacted in Kathmandu, Nepal, to discuss prospects for peace from 11 to 14 December 2004. See https://pugwash.org/2004/12/15/workshop-on-jammu-and-kashmir-and-the-india-pakistan-dialogue-the-prospects-ahead/.

14 Satinder Lambah (b. 1941) joined the Indian Foreign Service in 1964 and has served as India's Ambassador to Germany (1995–1998), Hungary (1986–1989) and the Russian Federation (1998–2001), among other foreign postings. He was also High Commissioner of India to Pakistan (1992–1995).

15 *The Spy Chronicles* includes this quote from Asad Durrani: 'Six high commissioners had an invitation from the Aspen Centre, Sati Lambah was the moving force. They considered their most substantial meeting was when they called on the NSA. Ajit Doval treated them indifferently, saying: "We are watching you. If something good does not come out of our investigation, and if we find a link between Pathankot and Mumbai and a state structure, there will be consequences." When the meeting finished he did not shake hands with a group that is highly regarded in both countries. Just walked away. The message was conveyed.'

16 A.S. Dulat is referring to the BJP's victories in the 2022 state elections held in Goa, Manipur, Uttarakhand and Uttar Pradesh.

17 Shahryar Khan (b. 1934) is a Pakistani diplomat who became Foreign Secretary in 1990.

18 Riaz Muhammad Khan joined Pakistan's Foreign Service in 1969 and has served as the country's Ambassador to Kazakhstan and Kyrgyzstan (1992–1995), Belgium, Luxembourg and the European Union

(1995–1998), and China (2002–2005). He was also part of Pakistan's back-channel diplomacy with India from 2009 to 2012.

19 Asad Durrani is referring to the Punjabi actor Kundan Lal Saigal (1904–1947), widely considered to be the first superstar of Indian cinema.

20 Sushma Swaraj (1952–2019) was an Indian lawyer and diplomat. She was the Minister of External Affairs during Prime Minister Narendra Modi's first term from 2014 to 2019.

21 Abdul Basit joined the Pakistan Foreign Service in 1982. He was Pakistan High Commissioner to India from 2014 to 2017.

22 Mushahid Hussain (b. 1953) is a Pakistani politician and journalist. He has also been the Chairman of the China–Pakistan Institute in Islamabad.

23 Kulbhushan Jadhav (b. 1970) is an Indian national whom the Government of Pakistan arrested under suspicions of spying for RAW.

24 Admiral Laxminarayan Ramdas (b. 1933) was Chief of Naval Staff of the Indian Navy from December 1990 to September 1993.

Chapter 5. An Honest Assessment of Future Peacemaking

1 Joyce Neu and Vamik Volkan, *Developing a Methodology for Conflict Prevention: The Case of Estonia* (Atlanta: The Carter Center, 1999).

2 Kenneth N. Levy and J. Wesley Scala, 'Transference, Transference Interpretations and Transference-Focused Psychotherapies', *Psychotherapy* 49, no. 3 (2012): 392.

3 A.S. Dulat refers to himself as an 'optimist' twice in *The Spy Chronicles*.

4 Among other publications, see Neil Krishan Aggarwal, 'Exploring Identity, Culture and Suffering with a Kashmiri Sikh Refugee', *Social Science & Medicine* 65, no. 8 (2007): 1654–1665.

5 Rayna D. Markin Cheri Marmarosh, 'Application of Adult Attachment Theory to Group Member Transference and the Group Therapy Process', *Psychotherapy Theory, Research, Practice, Training* 47, no. 1 (2010): 111–121.

6 Jeffrey A. Hayes, Charles J. Gelso and Ann M. Hummel, 'Managing Countertransference', *Psychotherapy* 48, no. 1 (2011): 88-97.

7   Tavleen Singh (b. 1950) is an Indian journalist and a columnist for *The Indian Express*.

8   Salman Haider (b. 1937) was a career diplomat who was India's Foreign Secretary from March 1993 to June 1997.

9   Shamshad Ahmad (b. 1941) was a career diplomat who was Pakistan's Foreign Secretary from February 1997 to February 2000.

10   Asad Durrani is referring to the joint statement of India and Pakistan on 6 January 2004 after both leaders met during the SAARC summit in Islamabad: 'Prime Minister Vajpayee said that in order to take forward and sustain the dialogue process, violence, hostility and terrorism must be prevented. President Musharraf reassured Prime Minister Vajpayee that he will not permit any territory under Pakistan's control to be used to support terrorism in any manner. President Musharraf emphasised that a sustained and productive dialogue addressing all issues would lead to positive results.

'To carry the process of normalisation forward, the President of Pakistan and the Prime Minister of India agreed to commence the process of the composite dialogue in February 2004. The two leaders are confident that the resumption of the composite dialogue will lead to peaceful settlement of all bilateral issues, including Jammu and Kashmir, to the satisfaction of both sides.' See Ministry of External Affairs, 'India–Pakistan Joint Press Statement, Islamabad', Government of India (6 January 20046). https://www.mea.gov.in/Speeches-Statements.htm?dtl/2973/IndiaPakistan_Joint_Press_Statement_Islamabad.

11   Neil Krishan Aggarwal is referring to A.S. Dulat's interview with *The Print*. See The Wire, 'Kashmir's Most Dangerous Terrorism Since 2019 by Professional Srinagar Cell Linked to Pak—A.S. Dulat', YouTube (19 May 2022). https://www.youtube.com/watch?v=soDoKmz1_So.

12   Elias Davidsson, *The Betrayal of India: Revisiting the 26/11 Evidence* (New Delhi: Pharos Media & Publishing, 2017).

13   Pamulaparthi Venkata Narasimha Rao (1921–2004) was India's ninth Prime Minister from 1991 to 1996.

14   Asad Durrani is referring to the American historian Barbara Tuchman (1912–1989) and her book *The March of Folly: From Troy to Vietnam*.

15   The ideas of this paragraph are summarized from Daniel Bar-Tal, 'Sociopsychological Foundations of Intractable Conflicts', *American Behavioral Scientist* 50, no. 11 (2007): 1430–1453.

16   The ideas of this paragraph are summarized from Daniel Bar-
     Tal, 'From Intractable Conflict through Conflict Resolution to
     Reconciliation: Psychological Analysis', *Political Psychology* 21, no. 2
     (2000): 351–365.
17   Some of the ideas in the next three paragraphs come from Bar-Tal,
     'From Intractable Conflict through Conflict'.
18   The following statements are sourced from PTI, 'Pakistan PM Imran
     Khan, Opposition Leaders Extend Diwali Greetings to Hindus', *The
     New Indian Express* (4 November 2021).

Index

Abbottabad, 3, 65
Abdullah, Farooq, 2, 7
Abdullah, Sheikh, 27, *see also*
   Indira–Sheikh Accord
Afghanistan, 5, 10, 20–26, 32, 68,
   72, 76, 152, 154, 156, 169,
   179–180
Afghaniyat/Afghans, 21, 32–33, 90,
   105, 119, 122, 130, 167, 169
Agra, 105, 196, 204–205
Ahmad, Shamshad, 197, 245n9
Aiyar, Mani Shankar, 103, 155,
   240n29
Akbar, M.J., 134
All Parties Hurriyat Conference,
   33–34, 179
Ambala, bombing at, 185
American Psychiatric Association,
   42
Anand, Dev, 102
Ansari, Hamid, 1, 7
anti-Sikh riots, 107
Articles 35A and 370 (Indian
   Constitution), abrogation of,
   25–26, 28, 34, 36, 177, 200–
   201, 209, 212, 214, 219, 222
Ashokan empire, 105

Attari flag-lowering ceremony, 86,
   see also Wagah–Attari border
Azad, Ghulam Nabi, 27
Azad Kashmir, 34–35

Babri Masjid, destruction of, 125
Bachchan, Amitabh, 103
backchannels, 203, 206
Baglihar Hydroelectric Power
   Project, 234n33
Bajpai, 115, 241n38
Bajwa, Gen., 80, 144–145, 172,
   204, 242n11
Balan, Vidya, 103
Baluchistan, 63, 137
Bashir, Salman, 156
Basit, Abdul, 244n21
Bharatiya Janata Party (BJP), 2, 27,
   31, 126, 174–175, 228–229
bilateral relationship, 125, 153,
   158–159, 185, 190, 211
Bollywood, 21, 102, 130
Bose, Subhas Chandra, 102, 131,
   239n16
Botham, Ian Terence, 104, 241n32
British, 105
British India, pre-Partition, 90

bullying, 48, 82

CAA–NRC, 229
Carré, John le, 1, 5
Chand, Dhyan, 98, 102
Chander, Krishan, 102, 239
Chaturvedi, Sanjay, 86
Chaudhuri, Nirad C., 102, 239
Chidambaram, 27
China, 23–26, 99, 146–147,
    153–154, 163, 166, 170, 177;
    as 'Iron Brothers,' 25
China–India–Pakistan peace, 25
China–Pakistan Economic Corridor
    (CPEC C), 25
Chishti-order dargahs in Ajmer and
    Delhi, 229
Christians, 123, 125, 132
CIA, 64
Clausewitz, theory of, 220
composite dialogue, 11, 20, 73,
    196–198, 204, 227, 230
confidence-building measures
    (CBMs), 50, 139, 212, 214
conflict resolution, 226
cooperation, 11, 22, 142, 158–
    189
counter-narcotics operations, 228
COVID, 24, 172
cricket, 49, 55, 61, 81, 92, 96–98,
    102, 134, 144, 151, 160–162

Davidson, William, 40–41
Davidsson, 205
defence mechanisms, 38, 42
Desai, Morarji, 103, 240
diplomacy, 5, 40, 43, 86, 124
Director General Military
    Operations (DGMOs), 183
Director of the Intelligence Bureau
    (DIB), 66
Dixit, Madhuri, 103
Doda hydroelectric project, 21

Dosanjh, Balbir Singh, 240
Doval, Ajit, 76, 134, 150–151,
    169, 171, 219, 243n15
Dulat, A.S., 1, 5–6, 37, 40–41,
    44, 73, 78, 84, 87, 140, 144,
    190, 193–194; birth of, 46;
    childhood, 47–48; at college,
    52; family, 45; first job, 58–59;
    intelligence work, 77; linguistic
    background, 88; mentor, 59–
    60; parents, 87–88; professional
    aspirations, 54–55; schooling,
    49–50; skills and instincts,
    63–67, 77–78; as teenager,
    51–52; Punjabi Sikhs, 89
Durani, Muhammad Asad, 2–6,
    8, 13, 15, 18, 20, 33–34,
    48–50, 82, 84, 140–141,
    143, 190, 192, 194; birth of,
    45; at college, 53–54; family
    background, 89; first job of,
    58; games, 61; intelligence,
    76; mentor, 60, 60–61;
    migration, 90; parents of,
    87; peacemaking, 74–75, 78;
    schooling of, 47; skills, 61–62;
    Adolescence, 50–51
Durrani, Osman, 122

Einstein, 41–42, 125
empathy, 74–75, 78
ethnicity, 85, 90, 119, 127

Federally Administered Tribal
    Areas/Baluchistan (FATA), 137
film industry, 103; Indian films,
    101, 165–166
fishermen, 182–183
Flight 814, hijack of, 23
foreign policies, 141–158, 220;
    establishments, 142–158, 187
Franco– German reconciliation,
    227

Freud, Sigmund, 41, 191

Gandhi, Indira, assassination, 107
Gandhi, Mahatma, assassination of, 99, 131
Gavaskar, Sunil, 102, 240n23
Gawkadal massacre, 31
Ghafoor, Asif, Maj. Gen., 3
Gilani, Yousuf Raza, 199
Gilgit-Baltistan, 34–35
Gujral:,I.K., 11, 103, 197, 218; meeting Sharif in Male, 233; sub-regionalization, 172

Hadlee, Richard John, 104, 241n33
Haider, Salman, 74, 197, 245n7
Hayat, Sikandar, 94
Heroes, 101–103, 131
Hindus, 28, 30, 89, 91–95, 100, 103, 123, 125, 131–132, 228, 230
Hindustani, 112–115, 119
Hindutva, 123, 125–127, 131, 160, 212
Hinglaj Mata temple in Balochistan, 228
Ho Chi Minh, 33
Honour Among Spies, Durrani, 17, 47, 193
humanitarian aid, 21–22, 182; to fghanistan, 24
humanitarianism, 169
Hussain, Mushahid, 177, 244n22

identities, 42, 84–87, 91, 97–112, 119–120; large-group, 84–86; national, 95–98, 100, 104, 131, (see also nationalism); religious, 117–139
identity formation: in adolescence and adulthood, 97–101; in childhood, 87–97

Inam-ul-Haq, 175
independence, 84, 102, 158, 210
India–China rivalry, 24
Indian Coast Guard and Pakistan Maritime Security Agency memorandum, 184
Indian National Congress party, 31, 126, 184
Indian Premier League (IPL), 161
India–Pakistan relations, 2, 24, 35, 43, 77, 131, 139, 152, 160, 168, 174
Indira–Sheikh Accord, 27, 235n39
information technology (IT), 172
intelligence, 59–64, 66, 68, 73, 81–82, 110, 192, 199; agencies, 3, 9, 161, 203
Intelligence Bureau (IB), 30, 59, 62–63, 66–68, 71, 98
inter-caste marriages/ intermarriage, 89, 93
International Council of Jurists, Switzerland, 211
international relations, 20, 152, 164, 190, 220
Inter-Services Intelligence of Pakistan/ISI, 1, 6, 62, 66, 69, 134, 141, 156, 201
IPS, 61, 63, 81–83, 98
Iran, 19, 23–25, 76, 154; Islamic Revolutionary Guards Corps, firing into Iraq, 234n32
Islamabad, 21, 29, 118, 134, 171, 196, 214–215, 219; 2004 conference, 198
Islamism, 127

Jadhav, Kulbhushan, 3, 182, 244n23
Jagmohan, 30–31
Jaishankar, S., 114
Jaish [-e-Mohammad], 201

Jammu and Kashmir, 2, 5, 26, 28–29, 35, 204, 208–209, 214, 216, 230

Jammu Kashmir Liberation Front (JKLF), 32

JI [Jamaat-e-Islami], 197

Jinnah, Quaid -e-Azam Mohammed Ali, 90, 99–100, 102

Johnson, Boris, 16

kabaddi matches, 161–162, 218

Kapil Dev Ramlal Nikhanj, 104, 240n32

Kapoor, Raj, 102

Kardar, Abdul Hafeez, 96

Kargil, 149, 157, 196, 198, 203, 205, 214

Kartarpur Corridor, 171, 173, 215, 218–219; and religious tourism, 186

Kashmir, 21, 32, 74, 101, 107, 151, 180, 185; policy, 202, 207; Sinha, on, 29; statehood, 209, see also Articles 35A and 370 (Indian Constitution), abrogation of

The Kashmir Files, 29, 31–32

Kashmiris, 28–29, 31–33, 35–36, 74, 76, 170–171, 176–180, 187, 198–201, 203, 207, 209–213, 217–219; Hindus, 29, 33; Pandits, 29–32, 132, 214, 229

Kashmiriyat, 32, 213

Kashmir Solidarity Day, 158–160

Kashmir: The Vajpayee Years, Dulat, 30, 68

Khaliq, Abdul, 102, 105, 240n26

Khalistan, 107

Khan, Ayub, 51, 53–54

Khan Niazi, Imran Ahmed, 12, 103–104, 136, 144, 148, 151, 160, 171–172, 183, 214–216, 240n30

Khan, Nyla Ali, 2

Khan, Riaz Muhammad, 4, 156, 243n18

Khan, Shahryar, 156, 243n17

Khilona, Urdu monthly, 239n15

Khomeini, 207

Kissinger, Henry, 180, 234n26

Kumar, Ashok, 102

Ladakh (eastern), 24

bin Laden, Osama, 3, 65, 106

Lambah, Satinder 150, 243n14

languages, 60, 88–90, 111–116, 119, 128–129; English, 88, 90, 111–116, 119; Punjabi, 88–90, 97, 104, 108–109, 111–116, 119–120, 128, 138, 244; Nepali, 112

leadership, 67, 106, 142, 202, 206

le Carré, John, 1

Levy, Kenneth, 191

Line of Control [LOC], 35, 175–176, 178, 184–186, 196; ceasefire on, 28, 177

majoritarianism, 125

Manekshaw, Sam Hormusji Framji Jamshedji, FM., 107, 241n35

Manjrekar, Vijay, 98

marriage, 45, 93, 122–123, 138

medical: diplomacy, 182; tourism, 167, 169, 173

Menon, Shivshankar, 15

migration, 87, 94; see also Partition

minorities, 29–30, 51, 125–126, 128, 193, 229; in Kashmir, 30

Mishra, Brajesh, 67

Mishra, Pankaj, 102, 240n22

missiles, 181

Modi, Narendra, 25, 29, 108, 127, 136, 158, 160, 169, 171, 195,

199, 212–213, 215–216: at
Lahore, 241
Montgomery Jail, hand-woven
durrees of, 96
Montville, Joseph, 40–41
Most Favoured Nation (MFN), 175
Mughal-e-Azam, 166
Muharram in Lucknow, 229
Mukherjee, Rani, 103
Mumbai, 21, 161, 164, 184, 196,
205, 243; 26/11 attacks, 4, 20,
160, 184, 204
Musharraf, Pervez, 12, 36, 136,
177, 196–197, 200, 205,
207–208; four-point solution
on J&K 35, 236n45
Muslims, 14, 28, 66, 90, 92,
94–95, 97, 100, 103, 123–126,
131–133; Bakerwals, 29–30; in
Bhopal, 66; Gujjars, 29–30; in
Kashmir, 66; in Pakistan, 229

Narsimha Rao, 208
Nath, Prem, 102
National Conference party, 30
National Democratic Alliance
(NDA), 27
nationalism, 96–97, 104, 138, 213
National Olympics, 96
national security, 141–142
Navlakha, Gautam, 220
Nehru, Jawaharlal, 99, 105
1971 war, 106, 139, 152, 166,
241n35
nuclearization, 196

Odero Lal temple in Sindh, 228
Operation Bluestar, 107
Oslo Dialogue, 73

Pakistan: as 'all-weather' friend
to China, 24; army, 82, 150;
cricket team, 96; Hindus;

identity, 90, 127; Independence
Day, 159; Iran, Russia and
China configuration, 25; Sikhs,
229
Pakistan Movement, 90
Parliament of India, attack on, 184
Partition, 23, 42, 47–48, 66, 85,
92–96, 99, 104–105, 135, 137,
139, 182; communal riots, 94
Partition Horrors Remembrance
Day, 158–160
Pashto, 90, 113
Pashtuns, 32, 92, 109, 138
Patil, Smita, 103
peacemakers, 11, 43–44, 72–74,
79, 126, 129, 137
peacemaking, 5, 39, 42–44, 72–73,
75–78, 82–83, 114–115, 135,
137–139, 171, 173, 190–191,
194, 201–202, 204
peace marchers, 222
People-to-People Diplomacy, 40,
117–139
Persian, 89–90
police officers, 66, 69
political psychology, 220
psychiatrists, 5–6, 37, 40–43, 80,
84, 116, 152, 162, 167, 216,
222–224
psychoanalysts, 5, 43, 191
psychologists, 42, 225
psychology, 5, 37–43, 80–81,
91, 109, 114, 116, 137, 140,
189–190, 230
psychotherapy, 152, 190, 224
Pulwama attack, 18, 26, 118, 163,
204
Punjabiyat/Punjabis, 92, 97,
108–109, 138, 219
Puri, Amrish, 103
Putin, Vladimir, 79

Quad [Quadrilateral Security

Group of Australia, India, Japan and the United States], 26

Rabbani, Raza, 3
Ram, N. 112, 241n36
Ramdas, Laxminarayan, Admrl, 184, 244n24
Rashtriya Swayamsevak Sangh (RSS), 197
RAW, 6, 13, 38, 64, 66–68, 71, 82
Rawalpindi, 44–45
realpolitik, 11, 28, 42, 126, 204
Rehman, Fazlur, 168
religion, 32, 85, 89–91, 119–125, 131–132, 138, 213
religious tourism, 171, 173, 186, 228–230
repatriate prisoners, 182–183
Republican Guard, 64
Riaz, Fahmeeda, 125
Roshan, Hrithik, 102
Roy, Arundhati, 102, 240n21
Russia, 13, 23–25, 154

Saeed, Aisha, 2
Sahay, C.D., 114
Sahni, Balraj, 102
Sayeed, Mufti Mohammad, 31
Sayeed, Rubaiya, kidnapping of, 31
Sharada Peeth temple complex, Neelum Valley, 229
Sharif, Muhammad Nawaz, 3, 114, 136, 149, 151, 156, 172–173, 187–189, 197, 233n37
Sharif, Shahbaz, 151, 201, 214, 216
Shekhar, Chandra, 103, 240n28
Siachen, 170, 214, 230
Sialkot, 44, 83, 91, 105
Sikhs, 30, 86, 91–94, 96, 101, 124–125, 132, 172–173, 229–230

Simla Accord, 227
Singh, Balbir, 102
Singh, Bhagat, 102, 131, 239n17
Singh, Khushwant, 102, 121, 239n20
Singh, Manmohan, 1, 7, 9, 39, 127, 136, 151, 174, 184, 194, 199
Singh, Milkha, 102, 105, 240n25
Singh, Sushant, 2
Singh, Tavleen, 196
Sinha, Aditya, 1, 211
Sinha, Yashwant, 1, 29, 176
Sir Creek, 214, 230
South Asian Association for Regional Cooperation (SAARC), 167; member countries, 228; summit in Islamabad, 245n10
South Asian Free Media Association (SAFMA), 220
spies, 4, 12, 17, 44, 47, 182, 193
Spy Chronicles, 1, 4, 7, 38, 40, 47, 62, 206, 211–212, 221, 223
Srinagar–Muzaffarabad bus route, 229
sub-regionalization, 172, 218, 229
survival of the fittest, 48, 82
Swami, Praveen, 2
Swaraj, Sushma, 167–168, 244n20

Taliban, 20–23, 25, 153
territorial disputes, 42, 137
terrorism, 107–108, 151, 199, 201, 205
Thapar, Karan, 200
Track I, 42–43, 116–118, 222
Track II diplomacy, 40–43, 49, 68, 74, 84, 86, 113–114, 116, 134, 138, 158–159, 221; limits of, 117–139
trade, 170, 180, 182, 186, 199, 214–215

Train to Pakistan, Singh, 102,
    239n20
Tuchman, Barbara, 222
Turkey, 23, 144, 154
Twitter [now X], 167

Ukraine Crisis, 11, 16, 25, 79,
    179–180, 234n26
United Nations Security Council
    (UNSC) resolutions, 210–211,
    219
Urdu, 89–90, 111, 113–115, 119,
    125, 168, 239n18
United States/America, 21–22,
    25–26, 64–65, 76, 145, 169,
    197; 9/11, 177, 179; leaving
    Afghanistan, 22; war in Af–Pak
    region, 106
Uyghurs, 124

Vajpayee, A.B.77, 103, 108,
    136, 144, 146, 149, 168, 177,
    195–196, 198; bus to Lahore,
    136, 172, 194

Varthaman, Abhinandan, 26,
    235n38
violence, 83, 137, 203,
    225–226
visa access, 219
Volkan, Vamik D., 84

Wagah, 85–86, 155
Wagah–Attari border, 85
Washington, 19, 202
weapons of mass destruction
    (WMDs), 64
Wesley Scala, J., 191, 244

Yadav, Laloo [Prasad, 168
Yusufzai, 89–90

Zafar, Imad, 2
Zardari, Bhutto, 147
Zardari, Bilawal Bhutto, 147, 151,
    173, 215, 243n12
zero-sum power considerations,
    42
Zia-ul-Haq, Gen., 123, 241n39

About the Authors

Amarjit Singh Dulat is a former head of the Research and Analysis Wing (R&AW), India's external intelligence agency. After retirement, he was appointed adviser on Kashmir in the Prime Minister's Office and served there from January 2001 to May 2004. During this time, he accumulated a vast reservoir of goodwill with Kashmiris of all shades. As *Jane's Intelligence Digest* put it in 2001, 'Well known for his social skills, Dulat preferred dialogue to clandestine manoeuvres.' In his heyday, Dulat was referred to as 'Mr Kashmir'.

Dulat was born in Sialkot, Punjab, in December 1940. After India's partition, his father Justice Shamsher Singh Dulat relocated his family to Delhi. After schooling in Delhi, Simla and Chandigarh, Dulat joined the Indian Police Service (IPS) in 1965, and then the Intelligence Bureau (IB) in 1969, where he served for almost thirty years. At the IB he headed the Kashmir Group during the turbulent 1990s till he joined and headed the R&AW.

He is the author of *Kashmir: The Vajpayee Years* (2015; co-authored with Aditya Sinha), *The Spy Chronicles: R&AW, ISI and the Illusion of Peace* (2018; co-authored with Lieutenant General Asad Durrani and Aditya Sinha) and *A Life in the Shadows* (2022).

Lieutenant General Asad Durrani is a former director-general of the Inter-Services Intelligence directorate of Pakistan. He is the author of *The Spy Chronicles: R&AW, ISI and the Illusion of Peace* (2018; co-authored with A.S. Dulat and Aditya Sinha) and *Honour Among Spies* (2020).

Neil Krishan Aggarwal is a psychiatrist and social scientist at Columbia University. He does research on and teaches the psychology of cross-cultural conflicts, negotiation and peacemaking. A descendant of post-Partition families, he writes on how Hindus, Muslims and Sikhs view themselves and each other's communities. *Covert* is his fifth book.

HarperCollins *Publishers* India

At HarperCollins India, we believe in telling the best stories and finding the widest readership for our books in every format possible. We started publishing in 1992; a great deal has changed since then, but what has remained constant is the passion with which our authors write their books, the love with which readers receive them, and the sheer joy and excitement that we as publishers feel in being a part of the publishing process.

Over the years, we've had the pleasure of publishing some of the finest writing from the subcontinent and around the world, including several award-winning titles and some of the biggest bestsellers in India's publishing history. But nothing has meant more to us than the fact that millions of people have read the books we published, and that somewhere, a book of ours might have made a difference.

As we look to the future, we go back to that one word— a word which has been a driving force for us all these years.

Read.

 Harper Collins
 4th
 HARPER FICTION
 HARPER NON-FICTION
 HARPER BUSINESS
 HarperCollins *Children's Books*

 HARPER DESIGN
 Harper Sport
 HARPER PERENNIAL
 HARPER VANTAGE
 हार्पर हिन्दी